AF785009

PIPE FITTINGS

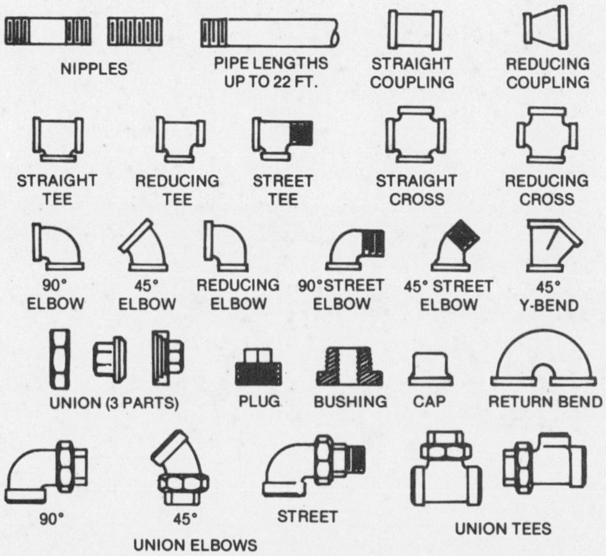

Here are the common steel pipe fittings. Nipples are simply short lengths of pipe threaded on both ends. Reducing fittings join two different sizes of pipe.

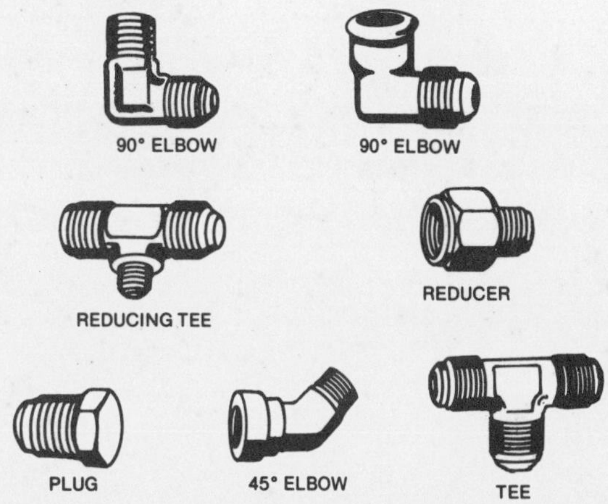

Compression fittings of the flared-tube type are the easiest for the novice to handle when working with copper tubing.

STANDARD STEEL PIPE (All Dimensions in Inches)					
Nominal Size	Outside Diameter	Inside Diameter	Nominal Size	Outside Diameter	Inside Diameter
1/8	0.405	0.269	1	1.315	1.049
1/4	0.540	0.364	1 1/4	1.660	1.380
3/8	0.675	0.493	1 1/2	1.900	1.610
1/2	0.840	0.622	2	2.375	2.067
3/4	1.050	0.824	2 1/2	2.875	2.469

SQUARE MEASURE

144 sq in = 1 sq ft
9 sq ft = 1 sq yd
272.25 sq ft = 1 sq rod
160 sq rods = 1 acre

VOLUME MEASURE

1728 cu in = 1 cu ft
27 cu ft = 1 cu yd

MEASURES OF CAPACITY

1 cup = 8 fl oz
2 cups = 1 pint
2 pints = 1 quart
4 quarts = 1 gallon
2 gallons = 1 peck
4 pecks = 1 bushel

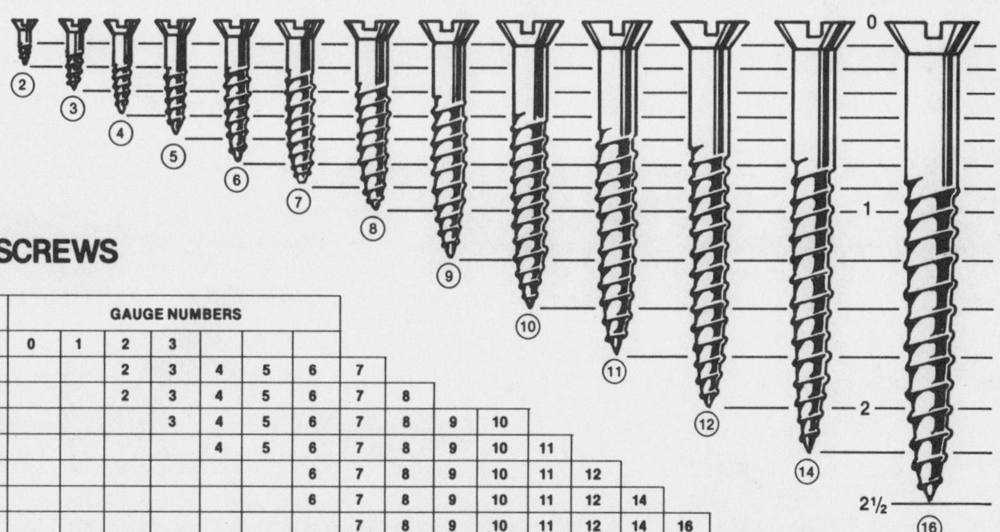

WOOD SCREWS

LENGTH	GAUGE NUMBERS																
1/4 INCH	0	1	2	3													
3/8 INCH			2	3	4	5	6	7									
1/2 INCH			2	3	4	5	6	7	8								
5/8 INCH				3	4	5	6	7	8	9	10						
3/4 INCH					4	5	6	7	8	9	10	11					
7/8 INCH							6	7	8	9	10	11	12				
1 INCH							6	7	8	9	10	11	12	14			
1 1/4 INCH								7	8	9	10	11	12	14	16		
1 1/2 INCH							6	7	8	9	10	11	12	14	16	18	
1 3/4 INCH									8	9	10	11	12	14	16	18	20
2 INCH									8	9	10	11	12	14	16	18	20
2 1/4 INCH										9	10	11	12	14	16	18	20
2 1/2 INCH													12	14	16	18	20
2 3/4 INCH														14	16	18	20
3 INCH															16	18	20
3 1/2 INCH																18	20	24
4 INCH																18	20	24

WHEN YOU BUY SCREWS, SPECIFY (1) LENGTH, (2) GAUGE NUMBER, (3) TYPE OF HEAD—FLAT, ROUND, OR OVAL, (4) MATERIAL—STEEL, BRASS, BRONZE, ETC., (5) FINISH—BRIGHT, STEEL BLUED, CADMIUM, NICKEL, OR CHROMIUM PLATED.

YOU'll ENJOY YOUR RV days much more if you're a savvy RV pilot. On page 2404 you'll find some special handling—and equipment—tips that may help avoid trouble.

In this volume . . .

SANDING ALWAYS has been the most tedious shop job, but it's much easier now, thanks to new belt and pad sanders, and modern abrasives. Learn all about sanding on page 2503.

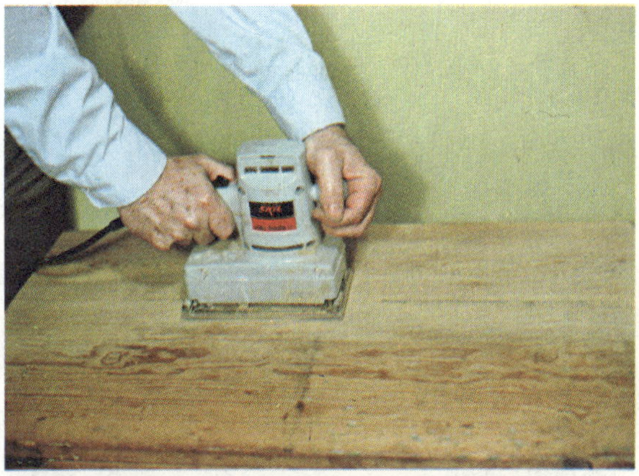

THAT HOUSE at the top of the opposite page was remodeled into the beautiful lakeside home shown just below. The other pictures on these pages show some of the stunning alterations that were made inside the home. You too can update an older home with dramatic changes that will make it more beautiful, more comfortable, and increase its value. See the galaxy of ideas on pages 2416 through 2441.

THIS EASY-TO-BUILD wall doubles the use of a bedroom, and minimizes the disputes when it's shared by two children. The freestanding wall clearly draws the line between the youngsters. You needn't be a master carpenter to build it. It consists of a simple 2x4 framework covered with plasterboard or plywood paneling. See the details on page 2464.

Popular Mechanics

do-it-yourself encyclopedia

in 20 volumes

a complete how-to guide for the homeowner, the hobbyist—
and anyone who enjoys working with mind and hands!

All about:

home maintenance
home-improvement projects
wall paneling
burglary and fire protection
furniture projects
finishing and refinishing furniture
outdoor living
home remodeling
solutions to home problems
challenging woodworking projects
hobbies and handicrafts
model making
weekend projects
workshop shortcuts and techniques
hand-tool skills
power-tool know-how
shop-made tools
car repairs
car maintenance
appliance repair
boating
hunting
fishing
camping
photography projects
radio, TV and electronics know-how
clever hints and tips
projects just for fun

volume 16

ISBN 0-87851-081-8
Library of Congress Catalog Number 77 84920

© 1982 THE HEARST CORPORATION

All rights reserved. No part of this book may be reproduced or used in any form or by any means—graphic, electronic, or mechanical, including photocopying, recording, taping or information storage and retrieval systems—without written permission of the publishers.

The Hearst Corporation cannot assume responsibility for proper application of techniques, implementations or proper and safe functioning of any of the manufactured or reader-built items, products or projects resulting in whole or in part from all or any part of any plans, prints, projects or instructional materials published in this volume.

The Hearst Corporation cannot assume responsibility for the continuing availability of any special parts listed in articles in this volume.

MANUFACTURED IN THE UNITED STATES OF AMERICA

contents

VOLUME 16

How to be a savvy RV pilot

By V. LEE OERTLE

All it takes is one close call or an accident to make you realize that there are some special tricks to driving a recreational vehicle or pulling a trailer. It is important to make sure that everything is securely fastened and you are driving with confidence but defensively

ANTISWAY CONTROLLER should be installed to keep rig from straddling the white line as at left, above. Trailer towers should always stay in the right lane except to pass. Whipping back and forth, and sway, are danger signs.

SUDDEN STOPS can be a part of any vacation, and stopping distance is much longer with a large heavy rig. Brakes and tires must be kept in top shape, all loose gear must be secured and children kept out of aisles.

TIE-DOWNS were forgotten by the driver who borrowed this pickup camper. A fierce gust of wind actually blew the camper right out of the truck cargo box. Remember your camper also requires separate insurance.

■ THE DAY of my accident I should have noticed the clues ahead of time. Summer heat had leached oil up through the blacktop pavement and patches of it made purple splotches against the ribbon of highway. Then the Utah sky ripped open with rain and the oil began to drift over the crown of the road. The bus ahead of me slowed down yet spray from its jumbo tires opaqued my windshield with an oily film.

Then, with no warning, the back end of my pickup camper skated around and I found myself traveling backward! The driver behind me stabbed his brakes, started to skid, and I knew we were all going off the highway. Later I learned my big flotation tires had hydroplaned up onto the layer of water and oil. My truck slid sideways down the sloping shoulder as I tightened my seat belt. Then the rear wheels struck a rock and we rolled until we came to rest upside down in two feet of ditch water. I opened the belt release, fell onto the cab roof, and forced my door open to wade away unhurt in the knee-deep muck. Through my shock I heard the truck engine running wide open though upside down, and I stumbled back to shut it off as other drivers stopped above to offer help. The cab was badly damaged but the camper body holding up the truck was only dented and not crushed. The accident, however, has made me give a lot of thought to factors affecting RV safety:

While under way in any kind of recreational vehicle, make a habit of stowing away securely all loose gear in you camper. Heavy tools should be stored in a special bin; not in the cab or passenger compartment. Passengers should remain seated and preferably safety belted.

Pickup camper owners should pay more attention to tie-downs. A strong wind can blow the camper out of the cargo box. Vibration can loosen turnbuckles, so they should be regularly tightened. A camper body that pulls out during an accident may then be struck by a following car.

Travel trailer accidents can result when a big trailer towed by too small a car starts to sway. Other causes include too much speed and cheap

TRAILER CARGO on a flatbed trailer must be secured as well. Without chain binders at all four corners, the racer could plunge forward during an emergency stop, and crash through the camper.

MIRRORS at the left and right are particularly needed by the RV driver as faster cars continually pass him. Use a windshield scraper when mud and snow collect if the mirror is too far out for easy cleaning.

STABILIZER JACKS should be checked regularly. If your tent-trailer jacks are left in a down position by mistake, they could catch in a chuckhole or on railroad tracks and tear the trailer away from the car.

SEE ALSO
Blizzards, driving . . . Campers . . . Trailers, tent . . . Vacation homes

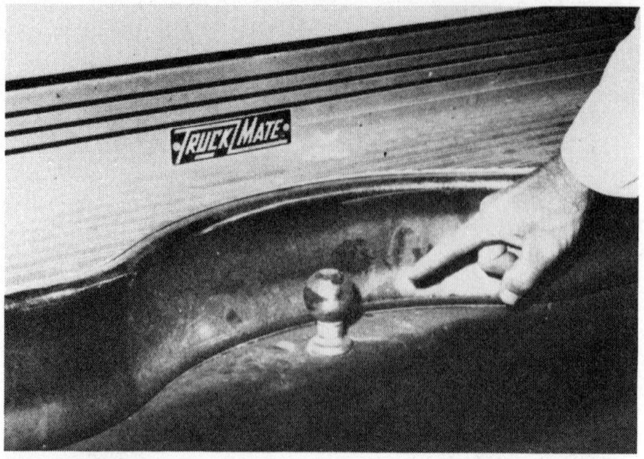

BUMPERS of most cars and trucks will flex too much and are not usually designed to take the many stresses of towing unless they are specially braced as shown here. Stiffeners should run back to the frame rails if you are towing large trailers.

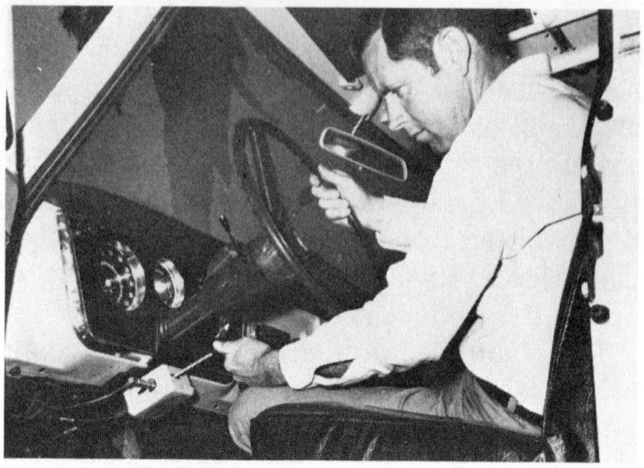

ELECTRIC BRAKES for the trailer you are towing should be adjusted on a regular schedule before there is any chance of an emergency stop. Set them so that they come on just ahead of the car brakes to prevent any possibility the trailer might jacknife.

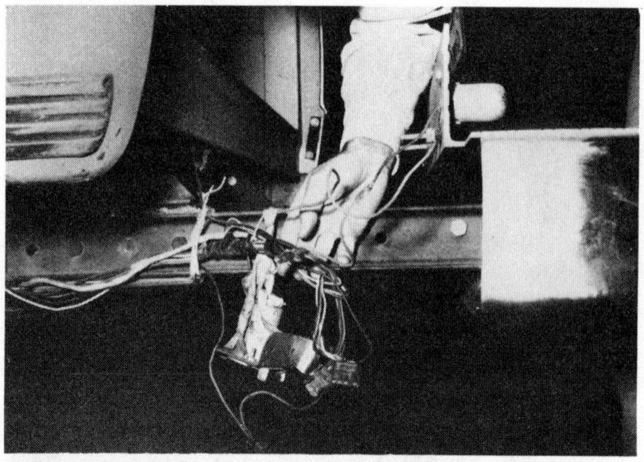

THIS ELECTRICIAN'S nightmare of wires is typical of using too many trailer hookups. This might happen if you use boat, horse and travel trailers interchangeably. In this situation the couplers could drag on the pavement and cause a fire. Keep all connections neat.

THIS PICKUP camper hit a carport roof and crumpled the corner of the cab. Fortunately it did not twist or buckle the frame. The accident revealed the basic strength of this somewhat fragile-looking rig. The window glass didn't even break.

ROLLED OVER three times by the author, this camper body shows surprising strength. It is made with foam-sandwich construction. As described in the article, the truck landed upside down but only the cab was badly damaged after skidding off the road on a rainy day.

FRONT-BUMPER load, like the trail-bike shown in this photo, can cause a serious accident if it falls in front of RV. For safety's sake, a rear bumper mounting is much better. But be sure the unit is set in a special carrying rack and double-strapped as well.

bumper hitches. Use equalizing hitches and anti-sway bars.

Motor homes should allow extra stopping distance, avoid tailgating and save brakes by using lower gears.

Tires must be the right size and with good tread of the same pattern at each end of an axle. Slow down during heavy rains.

Strap down boats carried on camper tops, bicycles and trail bikes on bumpers.

A TOWED VEHICLE should be given special care in hooking up. Use a strong safety chain plus proper brake and light couplers. The hitch should be strong enough so that it can take the strains of a heavy load. The extension bumper shown in this photo had too much flex.

BUILT-IN jack legs must be hinged and strapped securely in place to prevent dropping and dragging the camper off the truck body while it is in motion. Sidewall brackets, floor bolts and turnbuckles can all be combined to hold the camper in the truck box.

REAR LIGHT check is important in daytime as well as at night. It is one of many safety checks you should make before any trip. Be sure to examine your brake stoplights and turn indicators regularly and always carry spare bulbs for them.

Should an accident happen, make sure all passengers are out of the RV, shut off the motor and propane supply, take pictures, record witnesses and light warning flares away from possible fumes.

EXTRA-WIDE RIMS must be used when you switch to superwide tires. Without this precaution you are inviting an accident. The rim shown fits 10-16.5 Super-Single that provides the truck with the wheel strength to match the tire weight capacity.

SHUT OFF the propane tanks before starting a trip as a safety precaution. This simple step could help prevent a fire in the event of an accident in which the LP gas lines are ruptured. Prechill your LP refrigerator and start it again at the campground.

TURNBUCKLE hold-downs have a way of vibrating loose, especially on a rough road. Check them at every gas stop. Don't try to tighten them by applying leverage with a long-handled tool as it might break them. Snug turnbuckles tight with your hand.

How to winterize your camper

By V. LEE OERTLE

ON MANY travel trailers utilizing a full underbelly, the only place stabilizer jacks should be set is under the words "Jack Pad," stenciled on the coach. These words indicate the location of the frame channels.

■ IN ONE WINTER your recreation vehicle can be ruined if you're not careful. That's right—improper winter storage can give your RV a down-at-the-heels look before spring.

The first important decision you must make is where to store your rig. This can make all the difference.

Above all, don't park it under a tree. Falling limbs can puncture the roof. Bird droppings can stain the exterior. Tree sap can be the devil to remove.

Avoid locations with heavy pedestrian or vehicle traffic, such as gateways, pathways, busy parking lots. The less the traffic, the less the damage to your RV. Also, watch out for spots where gates can swing open and strike the coach. In a storm, a wildly-swinging gate can severely damage the aluminum skin. It's easily punctured but hard to repair.

The best parking-storage locations are in wind-protected spots, or under a carport or roof of some kind. Many owners prefer to cover their coaches with a tarpaulin. Aluminum does not rust but eventually it begins to pit and corrode. Once the finish is dulled by weather, it takes a cleaning with acid to bring back the gloss.

SEE ALSO

Campers . . . Camping . . . Trailers, tent . . . Vacation homes . . . Winterizing, autos

stabilizing the vehicle

Next, stabilize your RV properly. If the coach can be parked on a paved surface, that's best. Otherwise, set wood blocks underneath the stabilizer jacks. All four corners of the coach should be stabilized so that wind-action won't rock it about. *Caution!* Some travel trailers have locations plainly labeled jack pads. Use stabilizer jacks *only* at those points. On any trailer, place stabilizer jacks under main frame members. *Never* place jacks under outboard struts or wooden channels.

Now, pay attention to your tires. Much misinformation surrounds the proper storage of tires. Latest research indicates that wherever industrial air pollution (smog) is a problem, tires should be elevated off the ground and deflated to 10 p.s.i. *Reason:* Deflating tires allows outer pores to close up. Inflating tires stretches the rubber and makes it more susceptible to damage. But remember, don't deflate tires that are carrying a heavy load. The best protection is to block up the axles with wood or concrete piers, deflate tires to 10 p.s.i., and cover tires with plywood or metal panels as protection against sunlight. This last step is extremely important in desert and Gulf Coast states, less critical in northern regions. Strong sunlight deteriorates tires rapidly.

Surest protection for tires during the winter is indoor storage. If you don't plan to use your vehicle during the winter months, jack up the chassis and remove the tires, deflate them and store them in a shaded, well-ventilated area.

With the RV anchored, you can tackle the interior. Coach interiors collect stale odors during idle storage. Causes can be traced to such things as leftover fish bait, a forgotten cheese

VACUUM ALL interior screens before storage. Dust on screens collects moisture which encourages rust. Also vacuum the cabinets, closets and drawers.

DRAIN, FLUSH and cleanse water tank so that all stale water tastes are removed. Keep the tank lid tightly closed during storage to keep out dust.

sandwich in a hunting jacket, or a spilled puddle of gasoline under a leaking portable generator. Look throughout the coach for leftover foods and beverages, opening all drawers, cabinets, storage bins, closets, and appliances. Something innocent as a cabbage leaf is potent when trapped in the airtight interior. With meticulous care remove soiled handkerchiefs, hunting boots and all dirty clothing. This will eliminate the source of many stale or sour odors.

Get those stains, too. Don't leave that streak of tomato juice on the dinette seat. Remove that tar stain from the floor tiles by the front door. Food stains on the table, cushions or bedding will be three times harder to remove after winter storage.

Remember not to leave metal objects in the sink or lying on the drainboard; even stainless steel can leave trace stains due to condensation of moisture inside a tightly closed coach. Vacuum all screens and the interior of all cabinets, closets and bins. Clean and wax the floor and all appliances. When you're sure that the interior is clean and fresh-smelling, then—and only then—start buttoning it up.

Now, shut off the LP-gas supply *at the tank.* On a trailer, that will be on the front frame. Twist the shutoff handle *clockwise* until it has seated firmly.

Enter the coach and be sure all appliance controls are set to the off position. Remove range burners and vacuum dust from the orifices. Replace burners and close the range cover to block dust. If the range lacks a cover, wrap burners in aluminum foil to prevent rusting.

Next, work on the plumbing. Because it can freeze, the plumbing system is particularly vulnerable. To prevent ice damage or bad taste next spring, follow these instructions:

1. Drain the water heater.
2. Drain the water tank and flush it for at least 20 minutes with clean water. Close the drain valve. Add half a box of baking soda and five gallons of water and let it stand overnight. Then drain the tank and flush it one last time. This action neutralizes unpleasant odors or bad taste.
3. Drain the sanitary holding tank, preferably at a service station outlet. Flush it thoroughly. Tighten the valve, and add a small amount of deodorant chemical to the tank. Where neces-

SIMPLE TOUCH-UP with spray paint over rust spots on the frame will prevent worse damage during storage.

sary, use air pressure to rid the sink trap, shower trap and internal plumbing lines of water. If overlooked, as frequently happens, these areas may freeze and break. Flush the toilet several times to rid lines of water.

4. Use a cup and sponge to drain the last bit out of the toilet commode. One coach manufacturer reports this item tops the list of frost-damaged hardware.

5. Place a cupful of antifreeze in each of the drain traps: shower, sink, tub, toilet and commode.

Just to make *sure* that all the water is out of the lines, raise the lift jack on the front of the trailer all the way, then lower it all the way down. This tilts the frame enough to drain stubborn pockets of water. On truck mounts and motor homes, you can accomplish the same thing by parking on a severe angle for a few minutes with all drains open.

Place aluminum foil between glass and screens to keep the sun from fading interior fabrics on cushions, gaucho beds and mattress covers. It's best to remove all bedding and blankets from the coach and store them in your home. But if you must leave bedding in the coach, cover it with plastic *loosely* laid over the fabric. This precaution will prevent wet spots and mildew stains in the event of a leak or draft which may let rain enter the coach.

One common mistake beginners make is to cork up the coach like a wine bottle. Don't do it! Proper *ventilation* is necessary even in the coldest climates. Condensation will become a problem in a closed, cold coach. Roof vents should be tightly closed, but one window or sidevent can be left open about one-half inch on the wind-protected side of the coach. Take the extra precaution of taping a plastic cover underneath the vent window inside the coach. In a severe climate where prolonged subfreezing temperatures are the rule it may be necessary to close vents and windows securely. In this case, the coach should be opened every time a brief sunny period comes along.

Now, observe the following tips for specific types of recreational vehicles:

- *Travel trailers*. Spray a light oil onto the spring leaves. Lube zerc fittings on spring-shackles. Pull a plastic bag over the front coupler handle and tie it down (keeps coupler from rusting). Clean and repack wheel bearings on the chassis.
- *Pickup camper coaches*. If the coach will not be used during winter months, remove it from the truck with loader jacks. (You can rent loader jacks from many equipment yards or local coach dealers.) Loosen hold-down bolts or turnbuckles. Set coach down on wood blocks, *never* directly on ground. While the coach is off the truck, inspect its exposed underbelly for signs of splitting or swelling. Coat exposed areas with heavy mastic or weather-sealing paint recommended by local coach dealers. (Some sealers become sticky in hot weather.)
- *Motor homes*. All self-propelled recreational

SEVERE FLAT-SPOTTING and rusted hub caps may result when you leave tires on trailer during the winter.

Winterizing Special Gear

Some recreational vehicles are equipped with air compressor-type water-pressure systems. Turn the air compressor switch to OFF. Disconnect inlet and outlet hoses from pump and *rotate the pump manually* to expel water trapped inside.

Remove the 12-volt storage battery from the coach. Get it recharged to peak strength, then replace it. Do *not* reconnect battery cables to terminals. Spray a little anticorrosion coating onto the terminals and cable-heads. In extremely cold climates store the storage battery where it cannot freeze.

Don't forget the *water purifier!* They're popular these days. Remove the cover plate and make sure all water is out of it. (In the spring, replace the inexpensive filter cartridge with a new unit.)

Load-equalizer hitches should be removed and stored inside the storage bin or in your garage. The spring bars should get a light coat of spray paint. Bearing-ends of hitchspring bars should be lightly coated with bearing-grease and wrapped in foil.

Clamp-on side-view mirrors on the towing vehicle can be removed and stored for the winter.

If you have a portable electric power generator, it should be winterized. Drain the fuel tank. Drain and change the oil. Clean and replace the air-filter. If the unit is bolted inside the coach, just keep it covered. Otherwise, remove the generator and store it inside your garage. Set it on wood blocks, not on the bare floor. Wrap the generator with a plastic bag but do it loosely to provide for ventilation.

vehicles should be given a complete chassis-lube before storage. Engine maintenance should include oil change, oil-filter change, air-filter cleaning or replacing, and so on. Any service performed on your family car should also be performed on the motor home or van camper. Follow the same advice on tires: block up, deflate. If vehicle might be used occasionally during the winter, do *not* deflate tires, but rotate them at least once or twice each month to avoid flat-spotting.

• *Tent-trailers*. Clean fabric tops thoroughly *before storage*. Do not fold down a wet top. Dry it out first. Remove stains from fabric sidewalls or tops immediately. Keep the unit locked.

Despite all these precautions it's a mistake to ignore the recreational vehicle during the winter. At least once a week, walk around it and make a quick visual inspection. After every storm, enter the coach and look for signs of leakage or puncture-damage to roof. Don't let anyone lean objects such as bicycles, chairs or garden tools against the coach during the winter. In time, such treatment will dimple or dent the aluminum.

Using these winter-storage tips will save you time, money and trouble when you hit the road in the spring.

DEFLATE THE tires and store them indoors. Locate the jack under the frame rail, not an outboard strut.

REMOVE GENERATOR and service gas engine to avoid leaks which may cause unpleasant odors and stains.

With the price of recreational vehicles on the rise, you may not want to trade in or buy a new RV. If not, here's how to update the one you have

By V. LEE OERTLE

ADD BUILT-IN JACKS to your camper; then you can unload the coach anywhere.

Smart ways to improve your recreational vehicle

LET'S SUPPOSE you have had your camper, trailer, van or motor home a couple of years and it's still in great shape. Maybe you don't want to trade, but you've got the itch to do something to improve it. Perhaps you have already purchased about every available option, including a portable generator and an airconditioner. What then?

Cheer up! Here are 15 ways to spruce up any recreational vehicle to increase convenience, extend its free range, sharpen performance, and in general make it a better traveling vacation home.

• *Bigger tires.* The first step should be to examine the rubber. Check the tire size and rating. Have your RV dealer tell you what is the widest tire your particular model can handle. For example, hundreds of thousands of pickups are still being sold with 7.50x16 tires, or with the smallest flotation units in size 8.00x16.5. Take a giant step toward improved stability by switching to the 9.50x16.5 or 10x16.5 supersingle, duplex-type tires. You'll need new wheels, of course, to go with them. Make sure you buy brand-name drop-center wheels for supersingle tires. Cheap imitations on the market sell for as low as *one-third* the price of specially-made flotation tire wheels. Cheap wheels negate the value of big tires; they're dangerous.

SEE ALSO
Campers . . . Camping . . . Vacation homes

Many motor home owners can use the larger 12x16.5 tires. Wide tires increase traction, improve flotation and make a great difference in highway stability.

• *More water.* Most standard water tanks range from 15 to 20 gallons, occasionally to 30 gallons. An average family uses 5 to 8 gallons of water daily while vacationing, including water for drinking, cooking, bathing and sanitary flushing. Figure it out. At 5 gallons per day, a 20-gallon tank would last just four days. (If you think I'm overestimating, run your own survey.) Increase your range away from water supplies the easy way. Install an *extra* water tank under a bed, or inside a closet or storage bin. Place it on the floor and near the axle to minimize the effect of extra weight. I put a 50-gallon tank in my own trailer last year, and more than doubled my free time afield.

• *Larger holding tank.* Your sanitary system is pretty well locked into the limits of the holding tank capacity. Fifty gallons of water cannot be held in a 22-gallon holding tank. Since space under the coach frame is limited, replacement of the existing tank is best. Holding tanks up to 50 gallons in size are available.

• *Another butane-propane bottle.* Though many persons refer to LP-gas containers as "tanks," the trade calls them *bottles.* One 5-gallon gas bottle will hold enough fuel to fire a three-burner range and a gas lamp for about five to six weeks of three-meals-a-day usage. But when the same 5-gallon bottle is used to fire a gas refrigerator, space heater and water heater con-

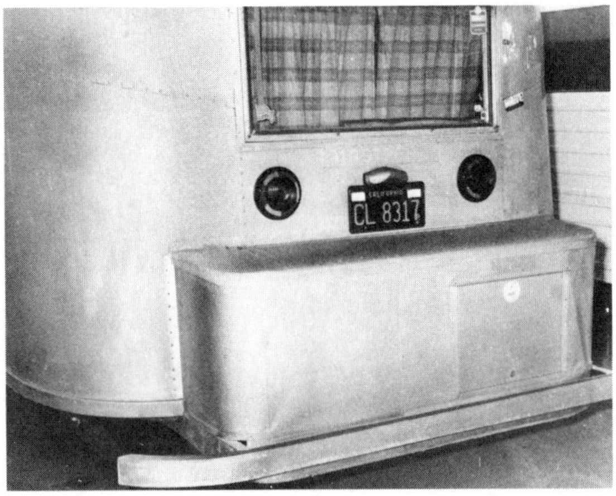

EXTEND YOUR REAR BUMPER and add a trunk that will provide you with space for lots of spare gear.

sumption will zoom to five or six *days* per 5-gallon bottle. What a difference! There are a couple of practical alternatives. You can replace the existing 5-gallon bottle with a 7-gallon size. (Most storage bins have a little extra bottle size.) Or add an *extra* 5-gallon or 7-gallon gas bottle and double your fuel range afield. It's comforting to know your fuel capacity can outlast a five-day snowstorm.

• *Better heating.* Thousands of standard coaches without space heaters have been sold. Suffer no longer. You can get a small space heater that fits into unused closet or floor space, is modestly priced and very efficient. You can even get one for your tent trailer. My Apache Mesa had one, complete with a vent-plate sewn into the fabric wall.

• *Instant water heater.* Did you know you can obtain a flash heater for your coach water system? For somewhere around a hundred bucks, you can find one that lets you wash in warm water, or run a cupful for coffee or tea just by turning a tap. It's instantly ready. This compact unit hangs on the wall like a decorator item. If you're an inveterate hot-drink camper, here's how to eliminate midnight pumping, firing up the range, or running a hot-water heater all night just to have a little hot water on cold mornings.

• *Added storage space.* If your coach seemed a bit overstuffed on your last vacation, you need more storage space. You can cut through *the outside wall* into a closet or under the bed area with a sabre saw. Ready-made bin-doors complete with piano hinge are available at ridiculously low prices. See your coach repair shop or local trailer dealer. An outside-access storage bin is extremely handy for muddy boots, wet clothing, fishing creels, upland game and other items that would be unpleasant inside the coach.

BUY A HOLLOW BUMPER for your motor home or trailer in which to store easy-to-reach sewer hoses.

INSULATE WATER LINES and holding tank with foam or fiberglass to avoid freezing during winter camping.

REPLACE THE MANUAL water pump in an older coach with a modern 12-volt electric pump in a few hours.

INSTALL A NEW sway-control device; load-equalizer hitch or trailer dolly alone can't eliminate sway.

SWITCH the exhaust pipe from single to a twin system to increase performance and reduce the heat load.

BE SURE wheels can take big tires before you switch to them. The wheel shown is for a 12 x 16.5 tire.

A FOLDING TRAILER DOLLY tilts out of the way for travel but provides good support at the site.

SUPERWIDE TIRES double the foot print and provide improved stability, flotation and more traction.

Even in the limited enclosure of a camper coach, you can box-in those wall-to-ceiling corners and add extra wall shelves very easily. Do the same in the cab-over bed section. Wherever you find unused wall space, add a shelf. On motor homes and trailers you can add a backwall trunk. Simply build a wood or metal framework, attach it to the rear wall and cover it with matching metal. A friend of mine built a lightweight metal frame, attached it to the back trailer wall and covered it with prepainted aluminum in one day. The next morning, he sealed the edges and installed a ready-made bin door picked up from a local trailer supply.

• *Built-in camper jacks.* If you own a pickup camper, you'll increase the convenience of your equipment if you install a set of built-in loading jacks. With them, you can remove the coach from the camper, save considerable fuel, and free the truck for other duty. Sometimes it's desirable to unload the coach at a campground to free the pickup for hunting and fishing side trips.

• *Eliminate swaying.* A load-equalizer doesn't automatically stop fishtailing. An equalizer hitch is designed to distribute heavy tongue loads to car and trailer areas better able to handle it. To eliminate swaying you need a sway-control device. This consists of a sliding arm restrained by friction-pads. Tension on the pads is adjustable to provide a dampening action at the exact level you need. For light loads, all you need is light tension to prevent feedback and whipping. There is also a sway control that operates hydraulically. Test a sway-control device with your load-equalizer to learn the difference.

• *Check trailer attitude*. Hitch up your trailer with a normal vacation load and full water tank, and park it on a level pad. Step back 50 feet and drop down on one knee. Study the trailer. Are the trailer and car frames riding level-horizontal? A trailer tongue high or low in front will not tow smoothly. It'll whip and sway easily, bottom over chuckholes and drag its tail in the street. If tongue is high, reduce tension on hitch spring bars. If it's low, increase tension. It may be necessary to move the hitch-head up or down, or to increase or reduce length of the hitch-ball shank to attain that level ride.

• *Pressurize the water system*. Does your older model have a hand-pumped water supply? Install a modestly-priced 12-volt water pump. Then your coach water system will operate at the turn of a faucet. Battery drain is low, convenience of the tap-ready water supply is great. Among other kinds of pressure systems are compact air compressors. I prefer the simple 12-volt pump—you needn't worry whether your old water lines and tank are air-tight.

• *Replace thin mattresses!* In the early days of coach-building, many 2-inch mattresses were provided for standard models. Even today, you'll find a few in over-head bunks, though most are 4 inches thick. Most any RV dealer can obtain a 5 or 6-inch mattress on order. Thicker mattresses provide both extra warmth and comfort.

• *Add an overhead bunk*—maybe two of them, to handle the extra guests your kids chronically invite along. Simple hangerbrackets screw to the wall for pipe-support hammocks. Or install sliding-type bunks which pull out for sleeping, push back to the wall to eliminate overhead restrictions.

• *Get heavy-duty shocks*. Years of road-testing recreational vehicles convinced me that standard shock absorbers on a motor home, pickup, or sedan rarely are any good after 10,000 miles. On some models, shocks succumbed at 5000 miles. In any case, heavy-duty shock absorbers will greatly improve performance, stability and tracking ability. They prevent wheel-hop; help keep your vehicle in a straight line. They minimize tire wear, too, and keep them in balance longer. On some test models, the difference in general stability after switching to heavy-duty shocks was positively amazing.

• *Replace chemical toilet* with a new recirculating model with greater capacity *without* adding a holding tank. A space about 2 by 2 feet is enough for the recirculating toilet.

REPLACE the thin mattresses that came with your RV with 5 or 6-inch foam slabs and cover them yourself.

SABRE-SAW an opening, add flanges and a bin door from a trailer supply to make a storage box.

DOUBLE YOUR LP-GAS SUPPLY by adding a second gas bottle and installing a switch-over valve connection.

Dramatic changes you can make yourself

By HARRY WICKS

■ THE DRAB-LOOKING HOUSE on the narrow lot in the photo below was originally built to serve as a lakeside summer home.

When new home prices and mortgage money started to spiral out of sight, the owners, Mr. and Mrs. Roger Wothe of Wayzata, Minn., abandoned their search for a new home. They decided they could get more house for the money remodeling their weekend home.

The house was full of problems, almost too many to solve. The living area was inadequate for the owners and their two growing boys. And the narrow parcel of ground ruled out any expansion into the side yards. Combined, the two levels had a scant 960 sq. ft. of living space. A complete front-to-rear remodeling changed the picture.

Roger Wothe, who heads up Environments, Inc., a firm that specializes in store interiors and fixtures, designed and implemented the changes himself. Before he ever lifted a hammer, he spent one year in the planning and drawing stages.

AS SHOWN in these before and after photos, the house underwent a dramatic transformation. You might not even suspect it was the same house.

THESE PICTURES of the kitchen and dining area show the pass-through connecting the two. Also shown are the contemporary-styled cabinets. These have been equipped with invisible latches for a more modern look.

"The floor plan was opened to all kinds of possibilities," he said, "but things started to happen when I made the decision to move the stairs outside."

The first step was to build a new circular staircase in a round "tower." What had been a small deck in front of the living room was then enclosed to double its size. Twelve feet were added to the rear of the house and interior partitions were reshuffled.

With remodeling completed, the chalet-style boasts an impressive 1900 sq. ft. of living space laid out for a lot of living. It is chock-full of dramatic and sensible ideas. Some features can be duplicated easily; others require professional know-how. All are handsomely designed and installed with care. Whether you are a do-it-yourselfer or prefer to hire others to make renovations, you're almost certain to spot some ideas that seem made to order for your house.

As shown on the previous page, the dramatic change is obvious in the "after" shot of the completed remodeling. The tower which houses the circular staircase blends well with the chalet styling, and by breaking the severe slope of the roofline adds interest and pleasing balance. It creates the impression that the whole house is wider than the original building when in fact it is not. The tower windows are insulated units manufactured by Viracon, Inc.: they're designed to be heat-absorbing and glare-reducing.

Wothe wisely made an asset of that huge expanse of exposed roof by covering it with attractive, handsplit cedar shakes. A wood preservative was applied and the shingles were left to age naturally.

The existing roof line was continued over front and rear additions to integrate the design.

The new roof was planned with energy conservation in mind, too; A 6-ft. overhang was added to the length of the house on both sides to shield it from the summer sun, which would tax the airconditioning system. But the design admits warming rays from the lower-angled winter sun to assist the heating plant.

The rough-sawn cedar siding enhances the natural beauty of the house's lakeside site. The siding was finished with Olympic's No. 714 stain and the trim with Olympic's Coffee stain.

SEE ALSO

**Additions, house . . . Attic dormers . . .
Basement remodeling . . . Family rooms . . .
Garage remodeling . . . House additions . . .
Kitchens . . . Remodeling, exterior**

THE NEW LIVING ROOM features beamed ceilings and lots of glass for an open look.

Rather than hide the exterior doors with storm or screen doors, Wothe installed Taylor insulated steel doors (which eliminate the need for either). Door exteriors were painted with epoxy enamel and the interiors were covered with a Formica wood-grain pattern matching the interior oak trim.

The remodeled and enlarged kitchen has a false A-ceiling. Space created between it and the old ceiling is used to route wiring, pipes and ductwork. Gone is the bothersome stairway that had cramped the old kitchen. In the expanded area now appears an appliance and cabinet layout that would please the fussiest of chefs. The kitchen is flooded with light; eight Lightolier recessed-can fixtures installed in the ceiling are angled to provide even, shadowless lighting.

The 6x6-in. ceiling beams are also false. Hollow and fashioned of red oak, they—like all interior trim—are finished with Pratt & Lambert's Oriental Walnut oil stain. To minimize daily upkeep, kitchen walls are treated with Jumbo Weave (by Fashon), a fabric wall covering that resists bumps, bangs and scrubbing. For underfoot comfort, the Wothes finished the floor with Dimensions, a Polyester III commercial carpeting by Viking.

If there is a single attention-getter in the kitchen it is the functional pass-through connecting kitchen and dining room. What used to be a doorway was closed at the bottom and neatly framed with trim. The countertop was built to create a 12-ft.-long ledge (not visible in the photo) on the dining room side for buffet-style entertaining.

Another reason for the opening was to allow better use from the dining-room area. Perched on stools, the Wothe youngsters use that side of the counter for breakfast, lunch and snacks. The dining room wall seen opposite the pass-through is clad with ½-in. plywood (instead of plaster or plasterboard) and covered with Fashon Jumbo Weave. The owners periodically change picture groupings—this wall lets them drive nails wherever they want without the need for patch jobs.

The living room was doubled in size when the additions were completed. The two walls facing the lake were opened up to let in the view—but not the heat. Fixed sash here are also of Viracon,

A SKYLIGHT above the shower is used to bring natural light into the bathroom as shown at left.

THE TWO WINDOWS that used to flank the fireplace have been closed and replaced with a slit window at the right.

THE VANITY shown below was built by the owner to complement the matching drapes, ceilings and walls.

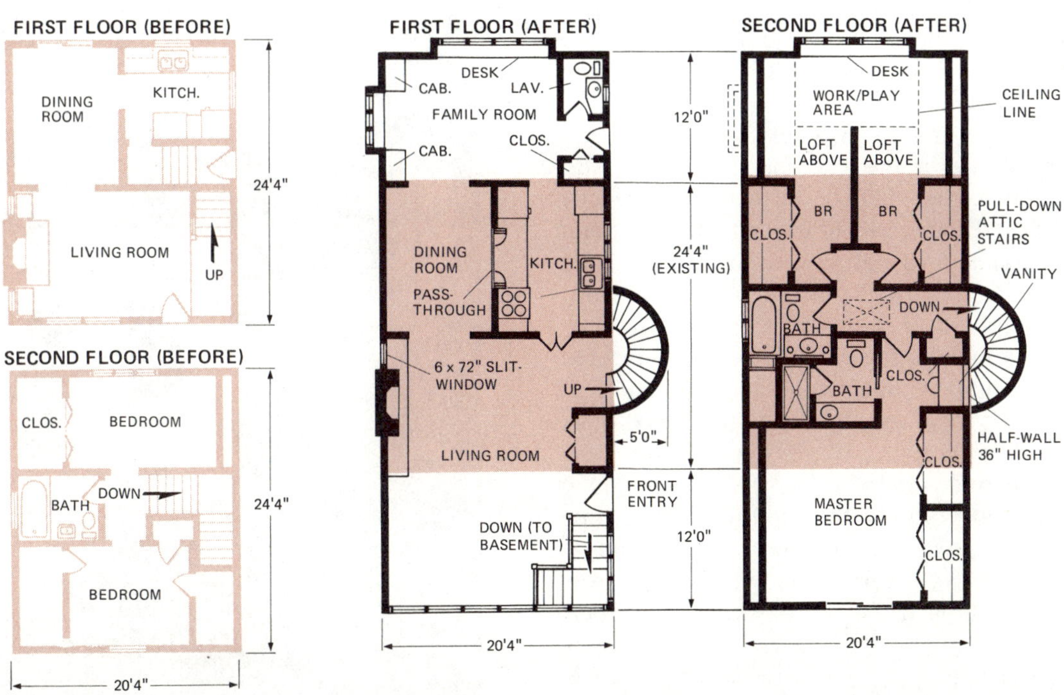

THE LILLIPUTIAN SIZE of the lot that this home occupies is appreciated when you know that the fence in the foreground separates the Wothe property from a neighbor's. The railing on the second level (false balcony) de-emphasizes the tall look and repeats the balcony detail on the house front. Generous use of wood decking creates an illusion of a larger house and lot. The view of the house from a distance shows how railroad-tie walls blend with the styling.

while all operable windows are Andersen Thermopane. The owner made the frames.

The pair of "useless" fixed windows flanking the fireplace in the original living room were closed in, and a 6x72-in. slit window was installed behind the mantel. Note that this window is the only opening on that sidewall. It creates a dramatic focal point as light streams in over the heavy mantel. The fireplace was enlarged and a massive, rough-hewn mantel added.

The shower in the bath added off the master bedroom has a skylight because this was the only way natural light could be brought into the room. The ceramic-tiled stall shower has a door that's framed in bronze metal to match the vanity mirror frame.

A new look for the old bathroom was created by using drapery that matches the walls and ceiling. The pattern shown is a cotton fabric from Design Group II.

The active pattern on the walls, ceiling and drapery underscored the need for a handsome vanity design that would hold its own. Built by the owner, its luxurious sculptured look was achieved through the use of standard lumberyard moldings.

For structural reasons, the stair tower is erected on a concrete slab. Such a construction provides a solid base for anchoring circular stairs. Treads are cantilevered from the wall, thus eliminating the need for a post. Because of this, the handrail runs around the inside perimeter of the treads—rather than the outside—which is typical of factory-built circular stairs.

THE CIRCULAR STAIRS were precut in the shop, then assembled and welded at the job site.

You can get a new home—without moving

By HARRY WICKS

SKETCH shows original porch that was enlarged to 16 by 30 feet to yield a family room and larger kitchen.

TODAY, ADDING TO or remodeling your home, rather than searching for a newer, larger house, is often the wiser choice for a homeowner. Depending upon size and selection of finishing materials, it is almost certain to be the less expensive approach.

Money isn't the only factor. Most of us like where we live, and if you have youngsters in

SEE ALSO
Family rooms . . . Garage remodeling . . . House additions . . . Kitchens . . . Measurements . . . Remodeling, exterior . . . Remodeling ideas

school, a family shift will require more than a few adjustments.

Since the property that this Minneapolis family owned would permit them to build the room they needed, their decision was to stay put and add on. They also increased their living area by adding a lighted patio. And, since the original house was due for a reroofing, the entire house was covered with hand-split cedar shakes.

The vaulted ceiling is simply ½-in.-thick plasterboard over 2x6 collar beams. To finish, the plasterboard was heavily textured with paint and the joints covered with decorative oak beams.

For general use, the lighting concealed behind the wood soffit close to the ceiling gives sufficient illumination. It consists of fluorescent strips which reflect off the painted ceiling. For decorative appeal, oak dentil molding was used around the room where walls and ceiling meet.

The original heating plant was capable of handling the new room; thus, it was not necessary to install new heating equipment. But the builder did relocate the thermostat, placing it in the new room. The single thermostat handles the entire house adequately from this location.

a new home, continued

CAREFULLY planned addition has bypassing doors located to give the best view of the outdoors. The fireplace is built of kasota stone and has an oak mantel.

continued

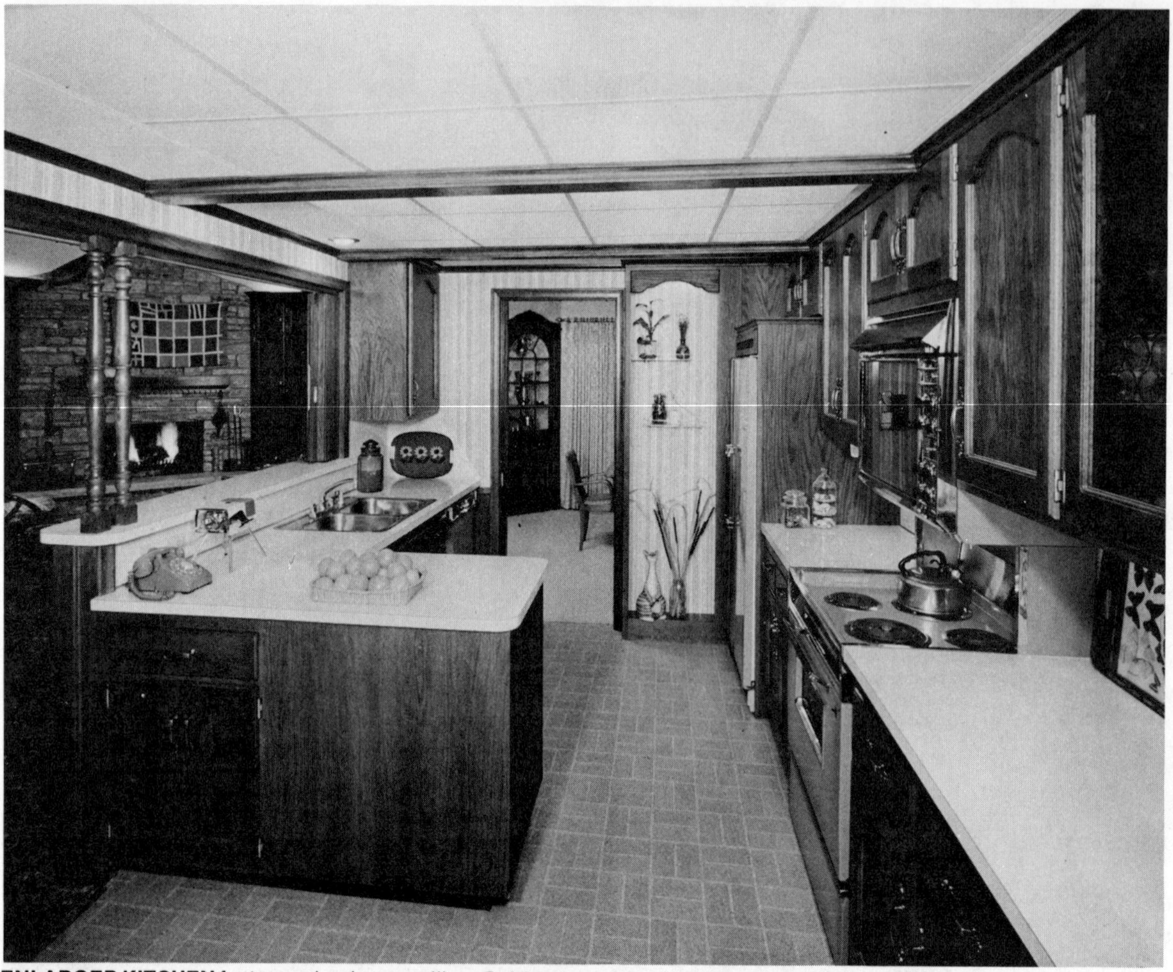

ENLARGED KITCHEN features a luminous ceiling. Oak beams were added for a visual tie-in with the new room. The cabinets are also of oak with a suede finish, white laminate was used on the countertop.

Desiring overall, even lighting, rather than one or two ceiling fixtures, the homeowner chose a luminous ceiling for the kitchen. Even here, the owner decided to "customize." The plastic, which comes in 2x4-ft. sheets, was halved to create 2x2-ft. sections. Installation was standard using the metal grid system. For visual tie-in with the family room, simulated beams were spaced at intervals across the ceiling.

The kitchen cabinets, custom-made, are also of oak. As seen in the photos and floor plan, strategically placed accordion doors can be kept open for general everyday use or closed when desired. They were placed at the peninsula counter so that area can be left open.

The brick-patterned vinyl flooring was picked up from the old kitchen and relaid.

To make the step platform by the sliding doors, slate was simply embedded in concrete. The concrete patio has a smooth steel-trowel finish and raked lines radiating from the platform. The outdoor lighting was solved by simply setting a plastic globe on steel pipe, which, of course, is erected in a footing.

What makes this addition particularly attractive is continuity of design, both indoors and out. It is obvious that the homeowner and builder worked closely together on the project and it shows in the finished product. The new hip roof ties in perfectly with the existing house roofline. And that is important. A poorly or hastily conceived addition will almost always result in a structure that has a tacked-on look. This is something to avoid if you want to add to, rather than detract from, the value of your home.

It might even pay to have an architect look at your home and make suggestions so that you will avoid this common pitfall.

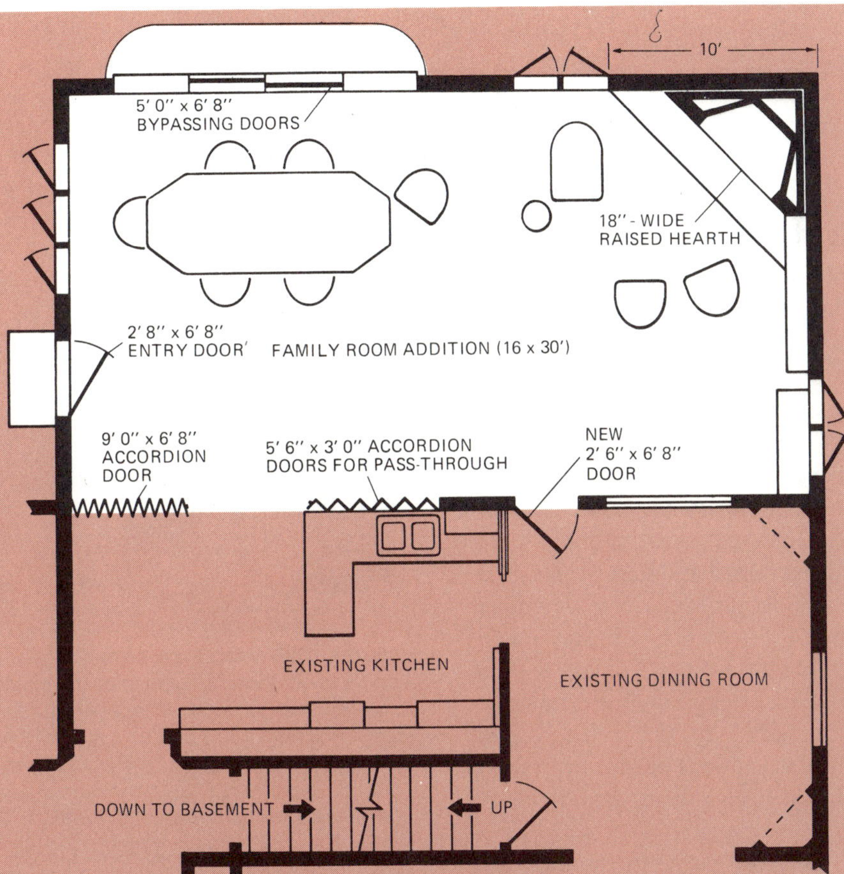

ACCORDION DOORS are used when it is desirable to hide kitchen from view. The floor plan shows how careful planning insured that this addition would integrate with the existing home.

Facelifting—cheapest way to get a 'new' home

Instead of simply repainting your home, take a look at some of these ideas to give your house a striking new look. With imagination on your part, your old home can become a new one

IF YOUR HOME is due for repainting, step back and take a long, hard look at it, then decide whether a paint job alone will give you the look you really want. Chances are the house, as well as its shrubbery, can stand some "pruning." Ornate but useless gingerbread and hardware can be removed, for example. In some cases removal of an "improvement" (something a former owner made that you probably wouldn't have) will restore the house to its original architectural concept—resulting in aesthetic improvement. And older homes will nearly always benefit by grading and landscaping that brings them visually closer to the ground.

Several such low-cost ways to update your home are described here. While your particular house may not be shown here, you'll find many ideas that will work for you.

SEE ALSO
Garage remodeling . . . Landscaping . . . Railings . . . Retaining walls . . . Steps . . . Windows

CHARM AND VALUE are added to this tract-type single-level dwelling, typical of the most economical homes to be built today. The simple design lends itself to easy, inexpensive improvement. Note how the colonial touches—windows, shutters, plants, and lamps—add charm. The garage extension lengthens and adds to the convenience and value of the home.

RESTORE true character to a roomy, two-story frame home with little more than careful selection of color and the removal of some "improvements" that violated the building's original character. Here, removing a wrought-iron rail and adding carriage-house-style fascia restores the balance and importance of the first floor.

CHANGE FOR THE BETTER here amounts principally to relocation of the porch steps for better access to and from the driveway. Moving them eliminates the need for a front walk that divides the house down the middle. The clean, unbroken lines of the new porch give the facade better proportions and the house an improved overall appearance. Removing the overgrown bushes and replacing them with the low-profile plantings lets the new front show to advantage. If the upkeep of a porch that is glass enclosed doesn't pay off in well used living space, consider a change that will simplify the maintenance and improve the general looks.

A CHANGE IN GRADE can make the major difference. The good features of this house are all but lost in its height. To bring it down to earth, a retaining wall is added parallel to the sidewalk. The yard is then filled and landscaped to conceal the foundation. A colonial-style entry, new windows (note the special treatment of bathroom window above the entry), plus the addition of dormers, shutters and coordinated coach lights adds up to a rather ambitious remodeling job. But it all combines to reveal the house's true potential. If your home has a roofed niche, as shown at the top, it can be left as is or enclosed (sketch at right) for additional space.

SLIDING GLASS DOORS provide a quick way to enclose a porch. You need to frame the opening, but you eliminate insulation, sheathing, siding, wallboard, taping and painting. The Andersen doors shown are double-glazed.

How to add sliding doors and windows

■ ROOMS that have ample windows usually seem bigger and more pleasant than underlighted, closed-in rooms. Adding a new window or expanding an existing one is not a hard job. Start early on a fair day and you'll be done before supper.

For a more ambitious project (and a lot more light), try opening a room by installing sliding glass doors. More framing is required, but you can still plan it for a one-day job.

Modern windows and sliding glass doors come ready to install. Some, like the Andersen Perma-Shield windows we used, have a flashing flange built into each unit. Nail it to the sheathing, cover it with siding and the exterior is finished—the wood, wrapped in vinyl, needs no painting.

SEE ALSO
**Additions, house . . . Attic dormers . . .
Burglar proofing . . . House additions . . . Patios . . .
Security, home . . . Sliding glass doors . . .
Storm doors and windows . . . Windows**

plan the opening

You already have at least one window in the room. Your wall is clean, solid and freshly painted. So you'd be crazy to cut a big hole in it, right? Wrong. Just make sure you cut the hole in the right place.

■ Stay away from electrical outlets. Rewiring will add time and trouble to the project.

■ Don't box yourself into a corner; stay away from the extra corner studs and leave room for trim.

■ Try for an opening 1½ in. in from an existing stud. Add a jack stud and eliminate inside patching on one side.

■ In general, select a unit that matches the style of those already on your house. Matching the sill height and grille pattern will make the window

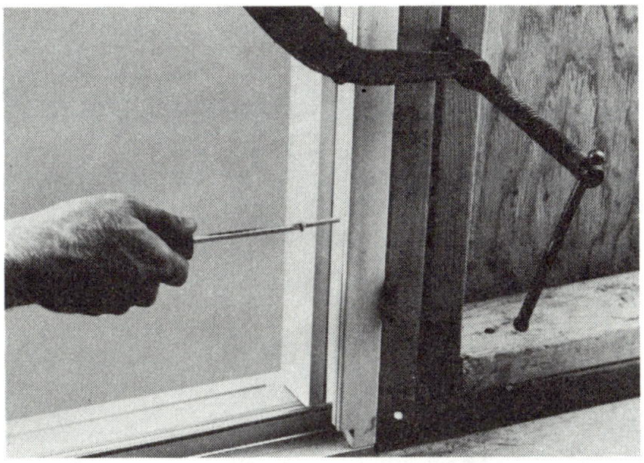

C-CLAMPS will draw the Perma Shield vinyl flashing against the sheathing. Shim between the frame and stud for a vertical alignment.

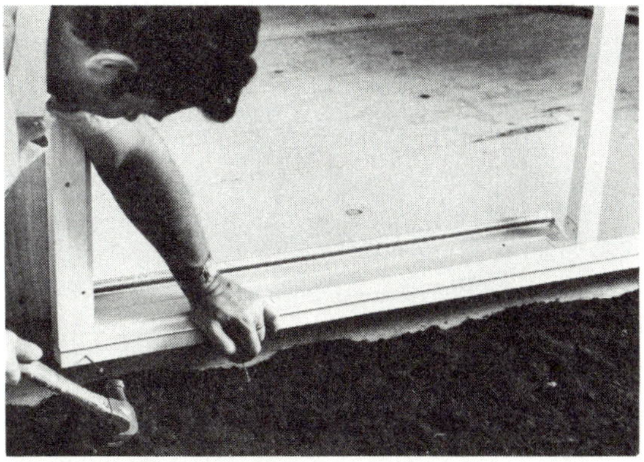

TREATED SILL SUPPORT is attached beneath the overhanging metal sill with 10d casing nails. You can also glue this joint for added strength.

STATIONARY door panel is installed first. Predrilled holes for fastening the brackets assure proper alignment of the panels with the frame.

METAL BRACKETS are screwed to the door and frame at the head and the sill. These brackets serve to lock the stationary panel in place.

FOLLOW ROUGH-OPENING dimensions supplied with your unit for framing. The weight load from a second story or roof rafters is transferred to the double studs at each end.

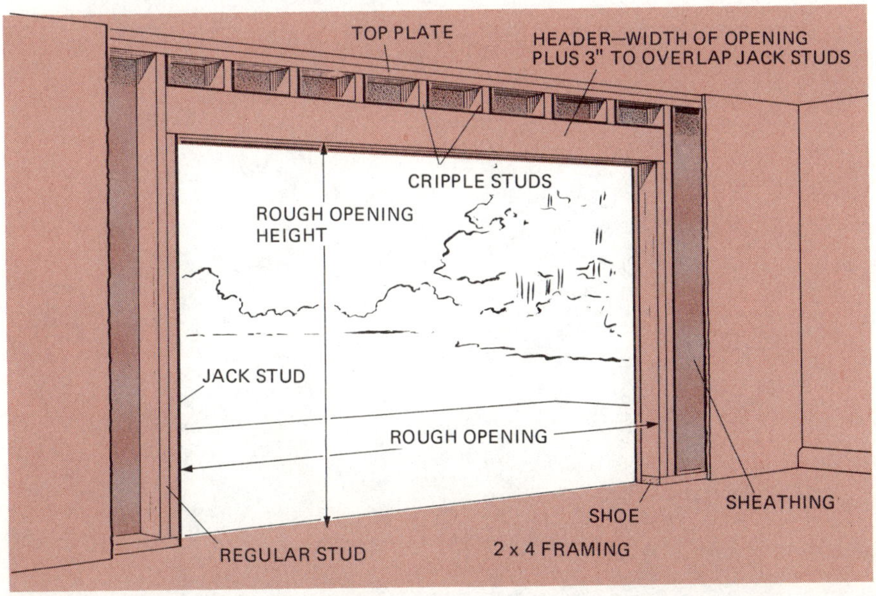

ADJUSTABLE ROLLERS on the operating door ride on a rib in the sill. A vinyl thermal barrier runs the length of the sill to provide insulation.

A HEAD STOP screwed to the head jamb completes the installation of the track for the doors. Rollers can be adjusted to the proper height.

THE FINISH CASING is installed by nailing through sheathing into the studs with 10d casing nails.

WINDOWS do eventually wear out. Rotting sills or a warped sash may be beyond repair.

REMOVE THE WINDOW. Add filler studs and sill to fit the new unit. The siding stays intact.

ADD SHEATHING over the new framing. Cover with tar paper and then lift the window into place.

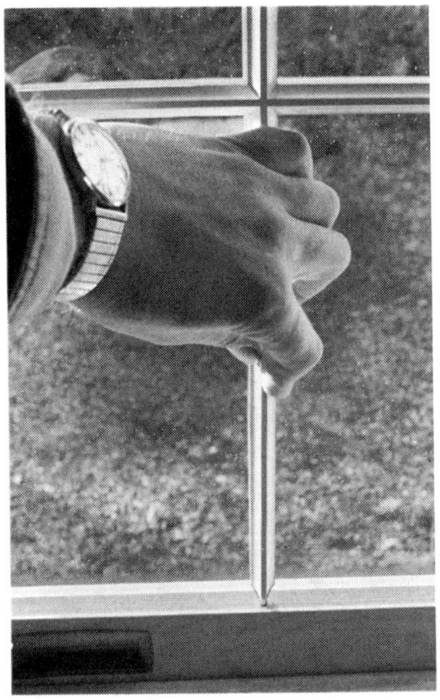

TO REMODEL WITH A NEW WINDOW, follow these steps: First, pick a window in the style you want that's slightly smaller than the existing one. This way you add to the frame and leave the siding intact. Second, add filler studs, sill, sheathing and tarpaper. Third, install the new window, caulk and replace exterior siding. Fourth, add insulation and wallboard to the interior; tape, paint and add grille clips if desired.

look as if it grew there. This holds true for sliding glass doors.

headers and sills

Any time you remove a stud you weaken the wall. Where the location of your window or door is not adjustable, you may even have to remove a critical load-bearing support.

Weight carried by the studs you take out must be transferred to double studs at each side of the opening with a header. On a moderate-sized window, two 2x4s spiked together will do. Nail header between the side studs; support each end with a jack stud. The space between these jack studs is the rough-opening width. Play it safe and increase the dimension required for your unit by ¼ in. This will give you room to shim for perfect alignment.

The header over a sliding glass door must be stronger to carry the weight of a second story wall and roof rafters. *Tip:* overbuild rather than skimp on material. In many new development houses cracks appear in the wall around openings. Insufficient headers above and beams below are often the cause.

To be safe, use double 2x6s for a 5-ft. slider, 2x8s for a 6-ft. unit, 2x10s for anything bigger. On three-panel sliders, use 2x12s. If weight from above causes your header to deflect (the engineering term for sag), your doors won't glide smoothly.

RIGID FLASHING flange is part of the window and is nailed through sheathing into studs. Siding removed from around the opening is recut and replaced.

REMOVE INTERIOR trim carefully. When adding a new window or replacing an old one, fill in with insulation and patch the interior wall before trimming.

Great remodeling ideas

Whether you're planning a new home or fixing up an old one, here is a collection of ideas to spark your imagination. Some should be perfect for your home. All are easy do-it-yourself projects

WHEN A DEEP BAY presents a drapery problem, a clever departure from common louvered shutters is to fit the window with four equal-size frames and cover them with matching drapery material. Colorful panels tie in beautifully with companion drapes. Hinged to fold like bifold doors, they fold back wide when full daylight is desired. The frames can be made from molding obtainable at your lumber yard. Just add hinges and knobs.

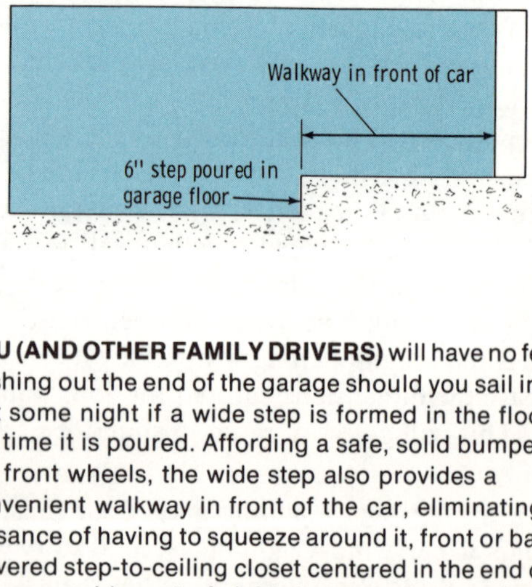

YOU (AND OTHER FAMILY DRIVERS) will have no fear of pushing out the end of the garage should you sail in too fast some night if a wide step is formed in the floor at the time it is poured. Affording a safe, solid bumper for the front wheels, the wide step also provides a convenient walkway in front of the car, eliminating the nuisance of having to squeeze around it, front or back. A louvered step-to-ceiling closet centered in the end of the garage provides out-of-sight storage for tools, paints and kid's toys.

SEE ALSO

Bathrooms . . . Closets . . . Doors . . . Entryways . . . Garage remodeling . . . Magazine holders . . . Moldings . . . Room dividers . . . Storage walls . . . Windows

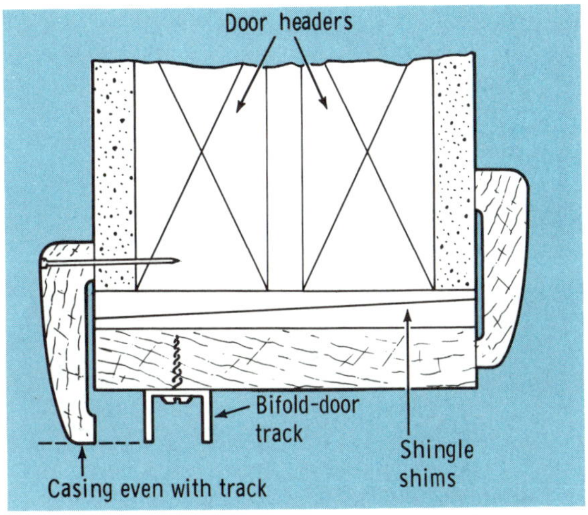

REQUIRING NO MORE WORK than applying a casing around any door, this stunt for concealing the track of bifold doors is one that's applicable to both new construction and remodeling. As the sketch shows, it's simply a case of applying the top casing so it's even with the bottom edge of the track. Corners of the trim are mitered in the normal way but the side members are shortened. Nailing is limited to the edge of the casing. If you wish, a thin shim can be inserted in the cavity in the back of the top casing to also permit nailing into the frame header.

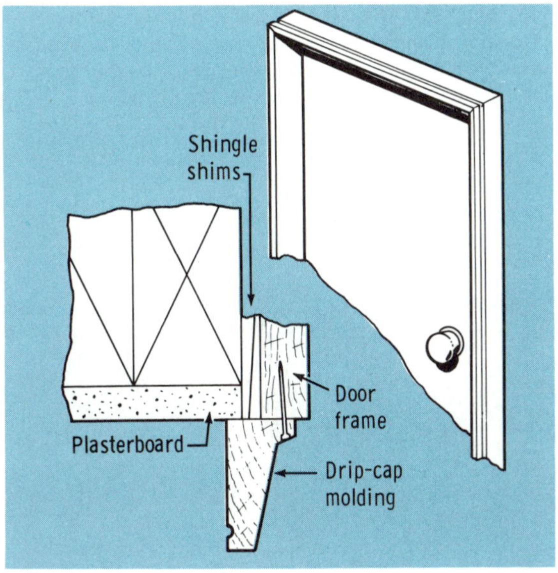

NO REASON why you always have to use customary flat casing around doors and windows. You can create a most interesting picture-frame effect by framing the door with common drip-cap molding. Decorative in itself, the molding produces a pleasing shadow effect, when mitered at the corners and applied taper-side in. The sketch shows how the molding is set back ¼ in. from the edge of the door frame and nailed on edge through its lip. Molding thickness will usually cover the gap between the frame and the wall. The idea is most practical when molding is applied to one side of the door, opposite the door's swing.

A HIGHLY FUNCTIONAL BENCH for a modern entryway is this "masonry" one which offers storage for boots and other rain gear. Basically, it's a plywood box fitted with doors and covered with simulated sheet stone such as DecroWall. A slab of cored latex rubber, fitted with a tailored cover, provides a comfortable cushion.

Fir plywood, ¾ in. thick, is used for the rough box which has a top but no back or bottom. A brace across the back at the bottom helps to reinforce the end. Typical cupboard-type lip doors are made to lap a frame in the opening and the edges of the stone. The stone treatment goes perfectly with a simulated slate-tile floor, such as the vinyl asbestos surface shown.

TALL PANELS OF COLORFUL FIBERGLASS provide interesting "stained-glass" windows in this paneled wall facing an unattractive view. Designer Gregory D. Ivy found the windows blended with the vertical paneling, gave a colorful glow to the formal atmosphere of the dining room, and solved the view problem perfectly.

Actually, the fiberglass windows look so attractive you might consider using them even when you aren't trying to cover an undesirable view.

The 8-in.-wide rough openings (12 in. apart) were framed with 1⅛ x 6½-in. members to project ¼ in. beyond the interior and exterior paneling. A rabbet for the fiberglass was formed with ⅜ x 1-in. strips placed 3 in. in from the inside edge. A second strip was used to hold the glass in place. As shown above, the windows are as attractive from the outside as the inside.

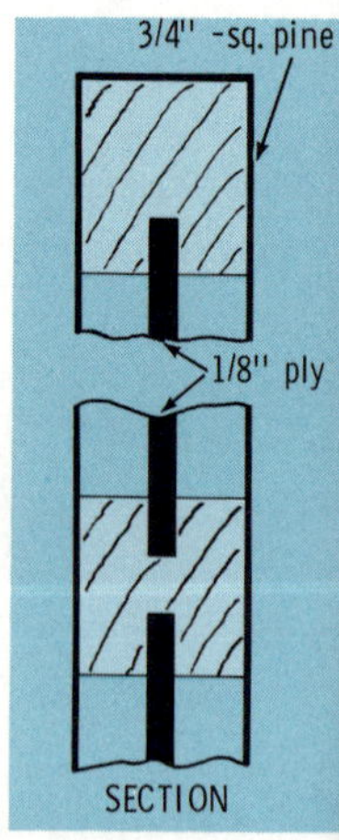

THE GRACEFUL CHARM of a leaf-pattern grille can add a classic look to an austere foyer which features a plain glass panel. This one consists of five ready-cut wood scrolls grouped in a single mitered frame and held in the recessed window with four screws. The detail shows how the ¾-in.-sq. frame members are grooved down the middle to fit over the edges of the scroll-cut panels and form a frame.

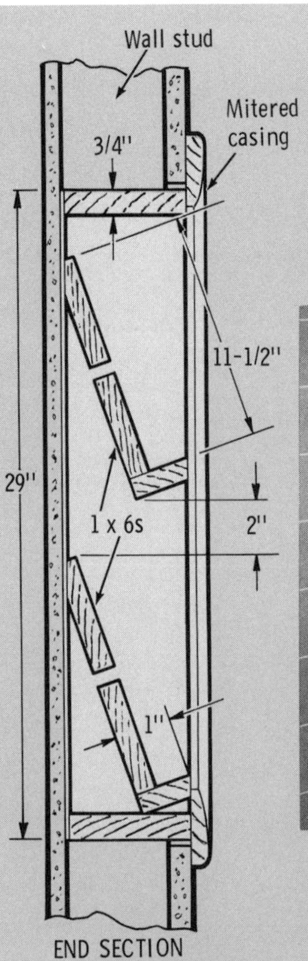

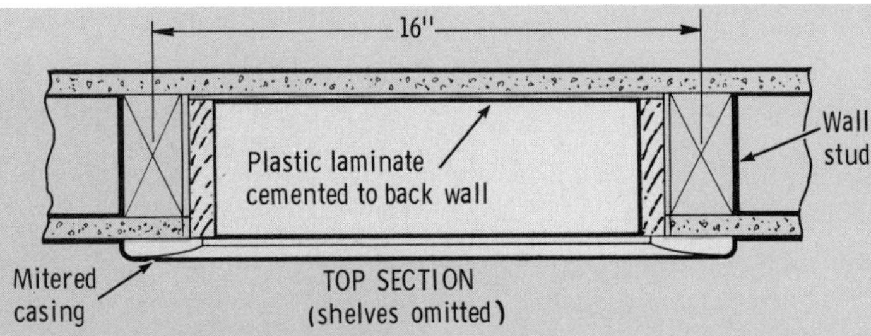

IF YOU ARE ONE who likes to read and soak in the tub, a built-in rack for magazines makes a practical improvement for the bathroom. This one takes no space since it fits flush in the wall. Cut the opening in the wall first. If it's ceramic tile, it will be a bit harder than if plasterboard, although you don't have to do too neat a job since the rack's frame laps any rough edges. The rack is made without a back to gain full depth. The inside wall is painted or covered with plastic laminate before the rack is set in place.

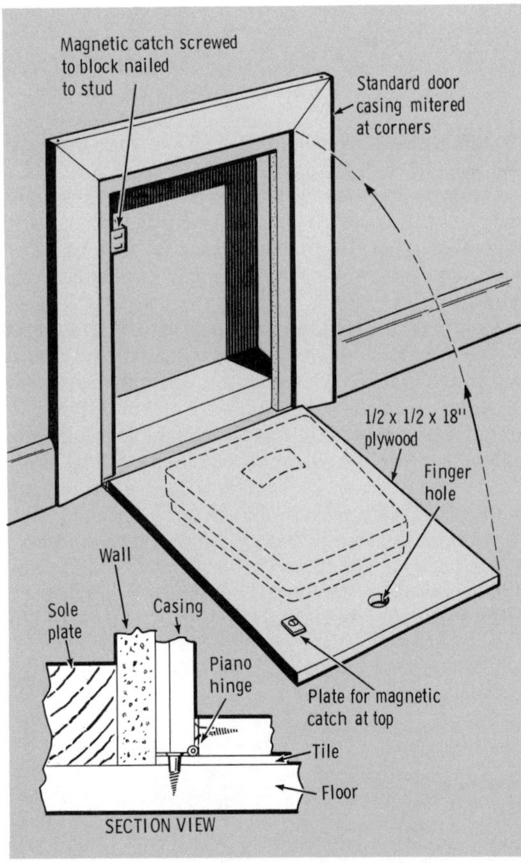

PARDON THE PUN, but a bathroom scale can get underfoot when standing around waiting for that once-a-day weigh-in. However, you can make a scale disappear in the wall and yet be Johnny-on-the-spot by attaching it to a swing-up door. First, pick a spot between two studs and cut a hole that's ½ in. smaller on three sides than the door. Then hinge the door to the floor so it swings flat against the wall and laps the opening. Finally, the baseboard is cut back for a mitered casing which frames the door. A magnetic catch holds the door shut, and a finger hole lets you give a tug to open it. How you attach the scale to the plywood door depends upon the type of scale. Some have holes in the bottom which are adaptable, or the bottom can be drilled for small bolts. Both door and casing can be painted to match the baseboard.

IF YOUR BEDROOM is your only haven when Suzie or Johnny invites the gang over for Saturday night, you won't feel so marooned with a get-away-from-it-all spot like this. Likewise, when the adults take over downstairs for an evening of bridge, it will serve the kids as a comfortable out-of-the-way place to read, watch TV or do homework.

It's a great idea for putting a spare bedroom to good use, the main feature being a divider wall which earns its keep and then some. A his-and-hers affair, it's split down the center to provide a dressing table and mirror on one side and kneehole desk and shelves on the other. The big full-length mirror lets everyone look his best. It starts out as a T-shape wall with a 10-in. soffit. Desk and vanity are built-in against a dividing wall.

The dimensions are not critical and will have to be adjusted to your floor plan. The version shown here was painted white with dark stripes around the drawers, mirror, etc. to provide contrast. Again, you can finish it to suit your decor.

We illuminated our version with standing floor lamps and lamps placed on the desk, but you could also place fluorescent bulbs in the top.

MAYBE YOU DON'T KNOW what it means to be able to store table linens without creases, but your wife does. And she'll think you're the greatest guy ever if you surprise her with a built-in buffet cabinet like this one. It takes only 11 in. in depth and hides behind sliding doors which masquerade as wall paneling. Camouflaged by a picture, the unit looks like an unbroken wall when the doors are closed.

Actually it's two cabinets in one, one side having adjustable shelves for china and crystal, plus two drawers for silverware; the other having rows of 1-in. poles for hanging 52-in.-wide table linens. With no creases or folds, the linens can be used immediately without a second pressing.

If you have plastered walls, you'd still create a second wall 11 in. out from the existing wall, frame a 10-ft. opening, then set the premade cabinet in it and add trim around three sides. The silverware drawers measure 10x22x9 in. and swing out for full access. Dowel pins in the front corners of the drawers pass through fixed shelves, above and below. Clearance is left at the sides so the drawers will swing in and out without binding.

The best place to locate the cabinet is in the dining room near the table so that the silver, linens, china, and crystal will be at hand when you are entertaining. Whichever wall you choose, you will want to panel the wall to match the cabinet if it's not already paneled.

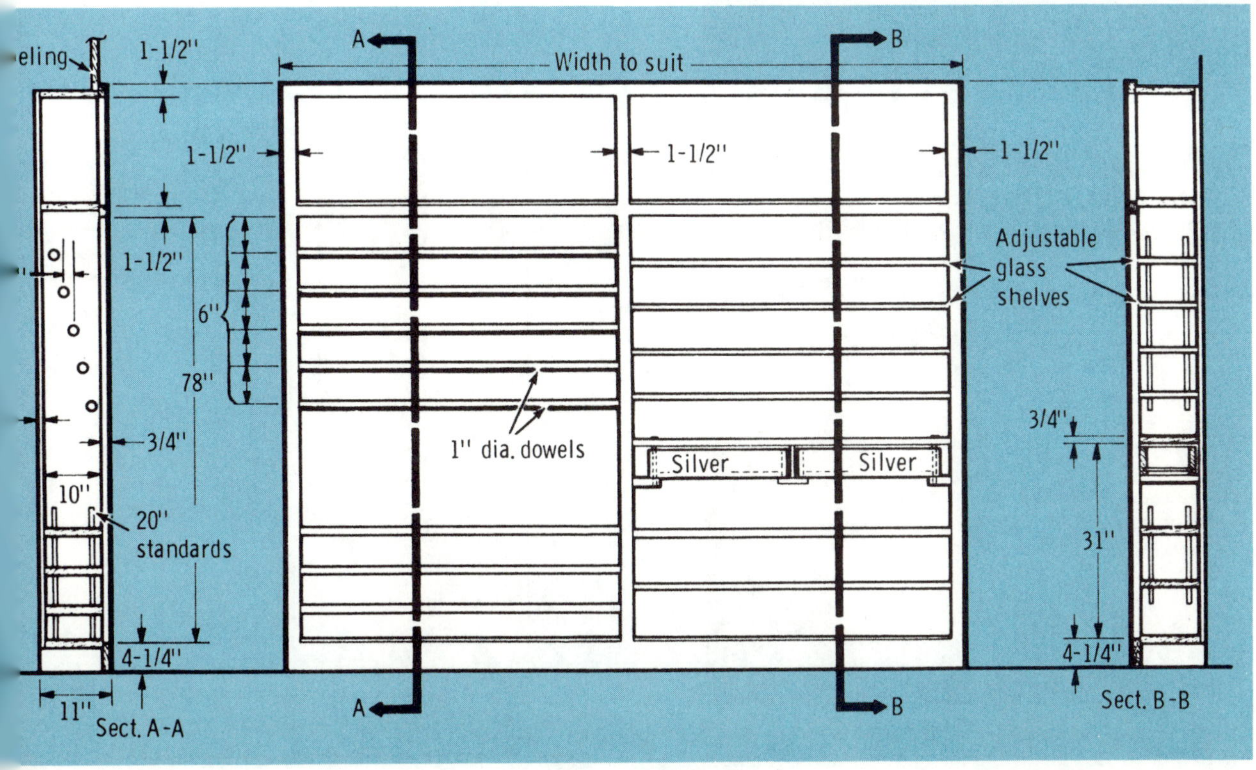

OUT OF SIGHT but not out of mind, there's an extra bed waiting for that unexpected overnight guest.

A SWING-UP PANEL, actually the bed's leg, is opened first and locked at a 90° angle by table-leaf brackets.

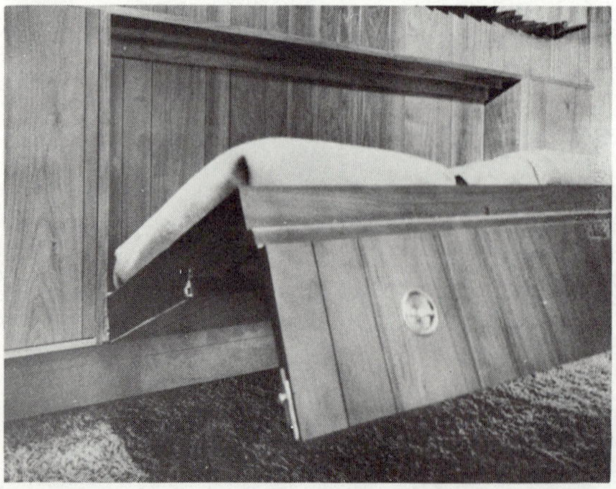

THE BED can be swung down when the bolts at the sides are unlocked. Seatbelts hold the mattress and bedding.

HOW ARE YOU FIXED for an extra bed? Could you put up an unexpected guest for the night? This bed is stored out of sight for just such emergency use. It swings down like a Murphy bed and up again.

As you see in the photos at the left, the bed pivots flush in a shallow cabinet that's only 12 in. deep and which extends wall to wall. Flanking bedding-and-storage cabinets at each end of the bed add to its overall convenience. The resulting ledge across the top provides a welcome shelf area for books, bric-a-brac, toys and pictures.

The tray-like bed frame holds a standard 6-in.-thick foam-rubber mattress. This along with a double sheet, bedspread, blanket and pillow is strapped in place with regular car seatbelts to fold intact.

The original unit was installed in a small dressing room off a master bedroom paneled with prefinished plywood. The paneling shows through the open back when the bed is down and provides a finished look. Matching paneling was used on cabinet doors and underside of the bed to give the unit a built-in appearance.

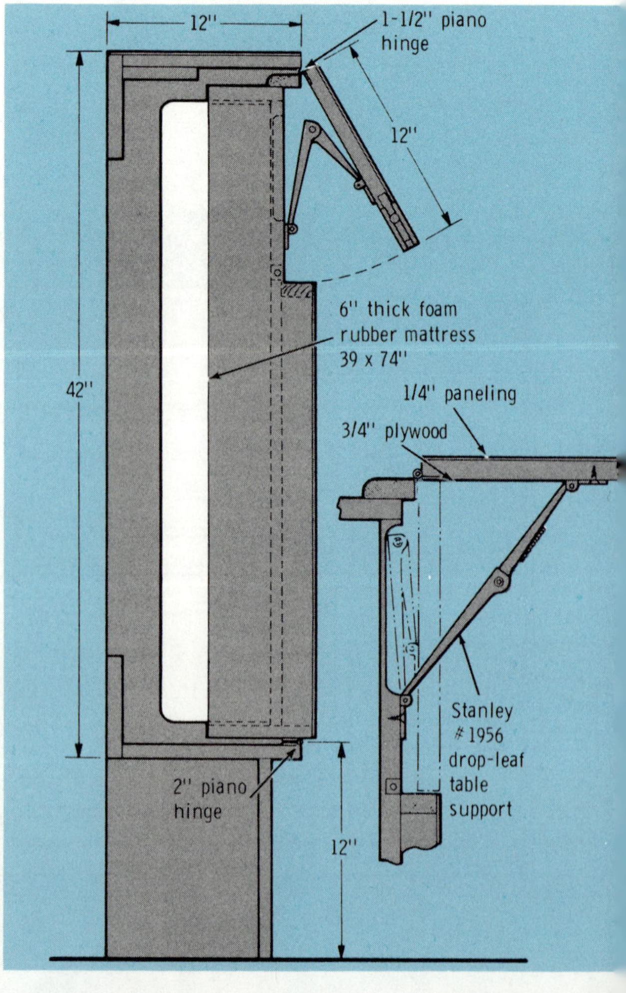

Basically, the unit consists of three cabinets, all more or less built in place and supported by a single shelf board 12 in. off the floor. Top and bottom cleats, screwed securely to wall studs, hold all units firmly to the walls and floor.

In the drawing, note how the bed's hinged "leg" folds flush in a recess extending across the top. Clearance for the spring-loaded drop-leaf table supports which hold the leg at 90°, is provided by routing wells in the bottom bed board. King-size piano hinges are used to hinge the leg as well as the bed. Sliding flush bolts lock the bed shut. Room for a bolt at each end of the leg is provided by making the latter an inch or so shorter than the bed. The mattress sits on a piece of ¾-in. particle board.

Finish the unit to match the walls. All exposed edges should be covered with wood tape to match the panelling. The cabinet doors on each end are held closed by hidden magnetic touch locks.

Now when Aunt Ethyl drops in unannounced, you're ready. Just push the surrounding furniture out of the way and fold her bed down from the wall!

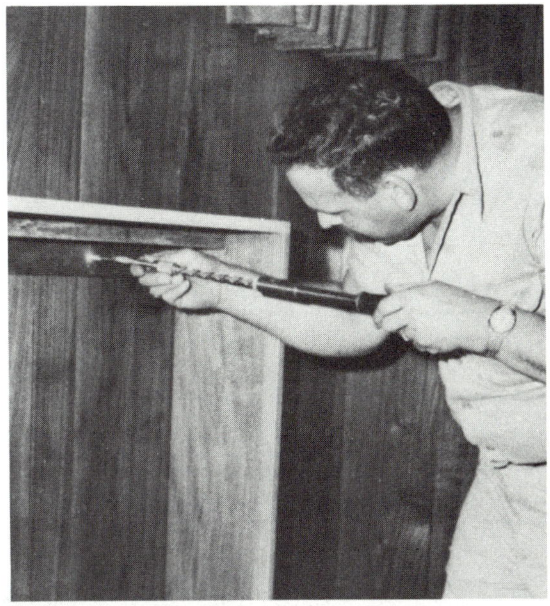

THE BED CABINET PROPER is anchored to wall and studs by driving screws through top and bottom cleats.

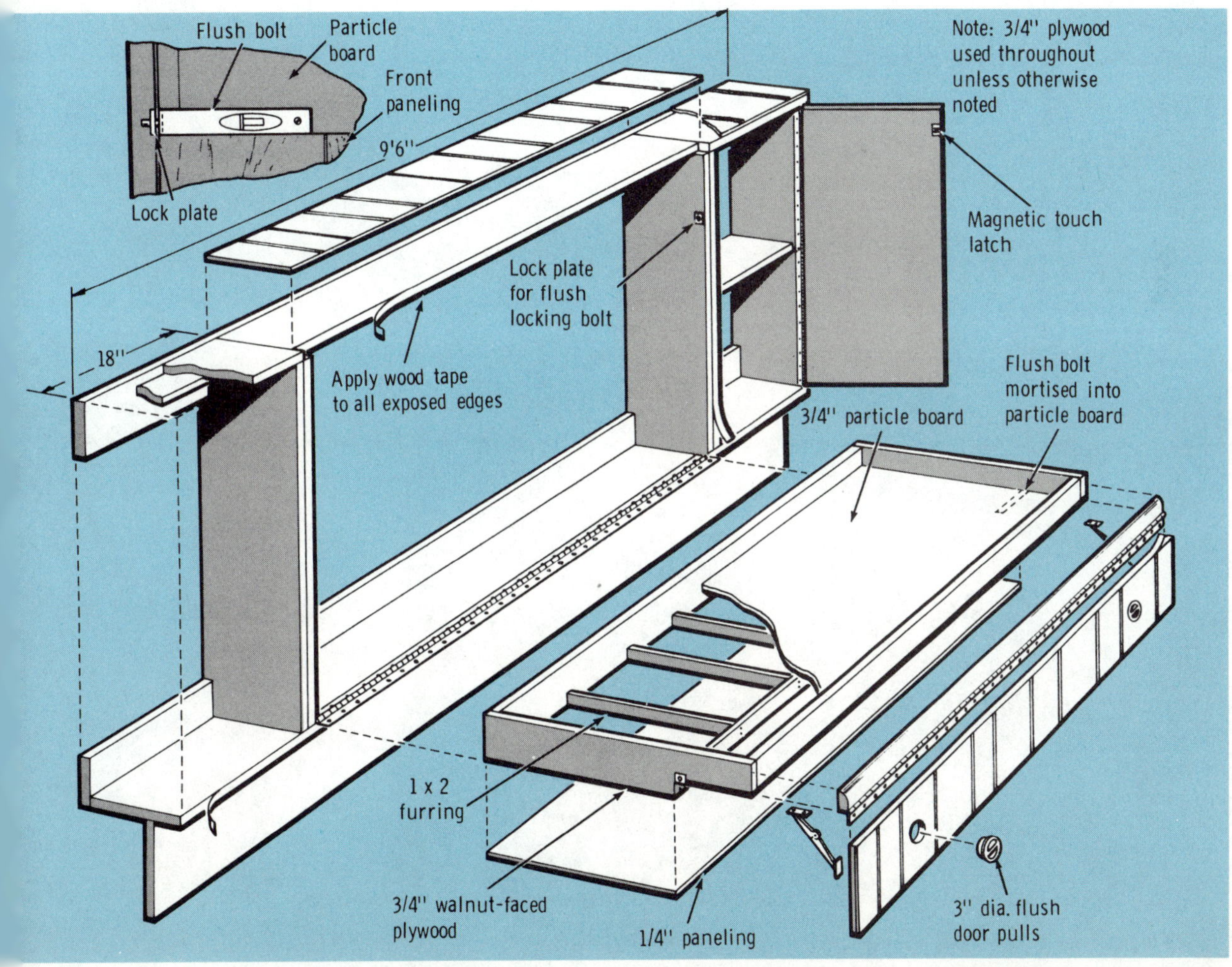

How to repair a fiberglass boat

By MORTON J. SCHULTZ

You can save yourself big money by repairing your fiberglass boat yourself. Here's how to go about making each of the five basic patches

SEE ALSO

Boat storage . . . Boat testing . . . Boat trailers . . . Canoes . . . Kayaks . . . Pontoon boats . . . Sailboats

NO MATTER WHAT ITS SIZE, if your boat is made of fiberglass you can save yourself a bundle of money by repairing it yourself.

Not long ago, for example, a yard wanted to charge a friend $74 to patch a couple of gouges in his 42-foot ketch. When we got through doing the job ourselves, it cost $5 for materials and it looked great.

As long as you know how to match the repair procedure to the damage, repairing a fiberglass hull is easy. But a lot of people fall flat on their

transoms, for too many believe one repair will suffice for all types of damage.

There's another misbelief we should clear up now. Through-the-hull fractures seldom occur with fiberglass boats. Fiberglass is a high-strength material with superior resistance to impact. Only a direct collision will cause a punctured hull.

Even if a hull is fractured, you stand a good chance of being able to fix it yourself if the puncture isn't spread over a wide area. A good book on fiberglass boats in general that deals with repairing infrequent through-the-hull fractures is *Fiberglass Boats* by Boughton Cobb, Jr. He's manager of the Fiberglass Industrial Materials Division, Owens-Corning. The book can be ordered for $3 from Yachting Publishing Co., 50 W. 44th Street, New York, N.Y. 10036.

Our concern here is how to fix damages that occur frequently. This surface distress can be divided into five classes: gouges, scratches, crazed cracks, wrinkles and loss of gloss.

Most fiberglass boats are made of two layers of material bonded together by chemical action. The outside layer is a colored gel coat, a special resin material containing concentrated color that provides a smooth, finished surface. The layer beneath the gel coat is a polyester resin which adheres to and is reinforced by laminations of fiberglass mat, cloth or woven roving.

Gel coat and polyester resin are cured by a catalyst that allows them to form a hard, strong mass. The only one of the five categories of surface damage which destroys this mass is a gouge, and that's a good place to start.

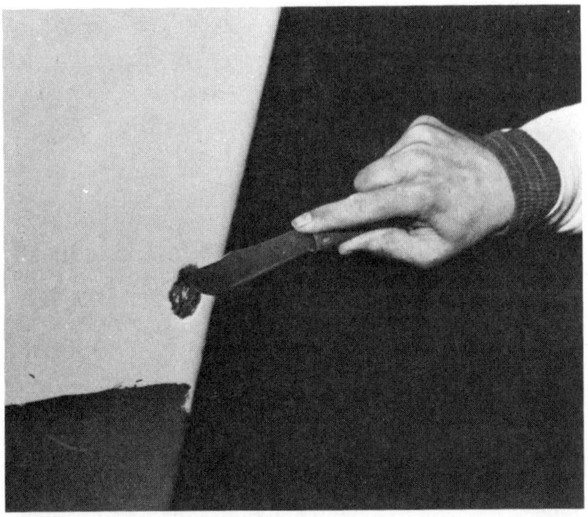

REPAIR PUTTY must have a firm seat on which to hold, so scrape away all loose, distressed material.

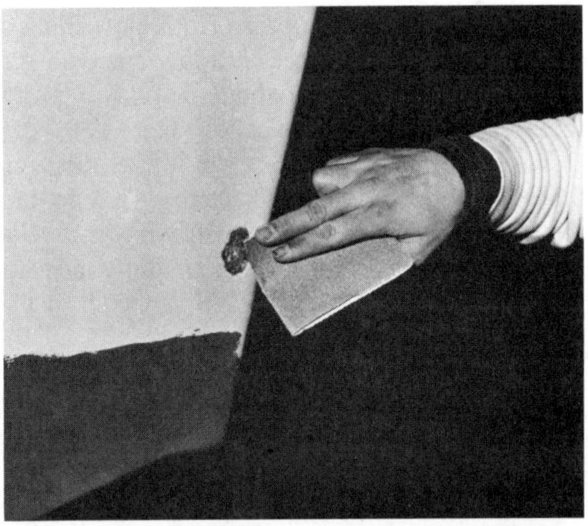

THE GOUGE is then sanded with 100-grit sandpaper to remove dirt and provide a roughened surface for putty.

MIX CATALYST and plastic repair putty on a clean piece of scrap prior to application of the putty.

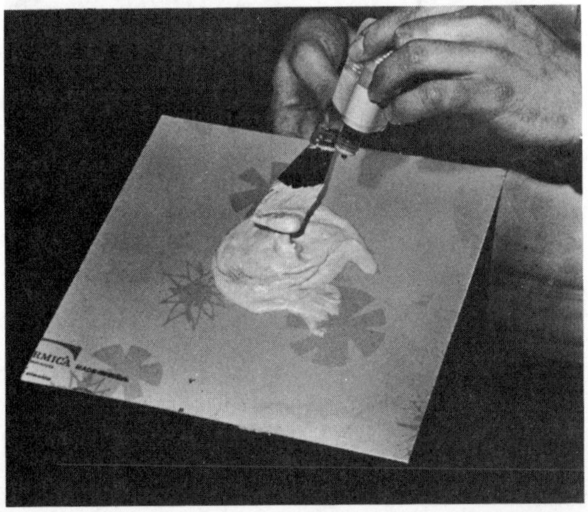

OVERFILL THE GOUGE about ¼ inch. Press the putty firmly into place to squeeze out all of the air.

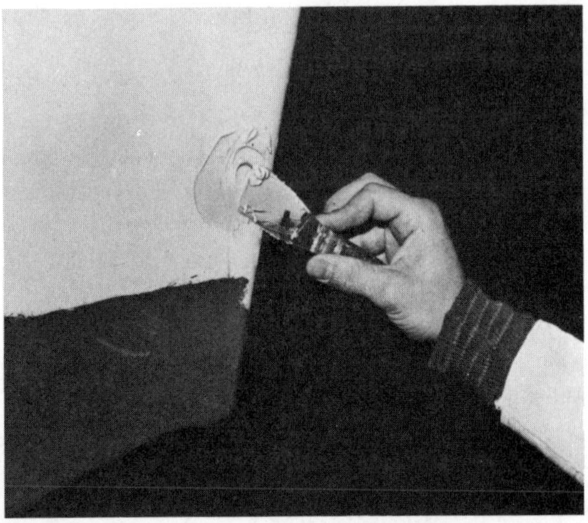

Repairing gouges. Once the gel coat-polyester resin formulation is gouged, the damaged material has to be cleaned out to reveal the fiberglass. Rout it out with a putty knife or similar tool.

Clean and rough up the fiberglass with a piece of 100-grit sandpaper to assure that the repair putty will have a good base. Then swab the whole area with a cloth that has been saturated in acetone or lacquer thinner to clean away dirt and grime. The area to be repaired must be clean!

Buy fiberglass plastic repair putty at a boat store—polyester is the most suitable. Mix this thoroughly with the catalyst as instructed on the can and apply very firmly. Press the putty in hard to force out air, and build it up about ¼-inch above the surface. Now cover the repair with a piece of cellophane. Press it into place with a single-edge razor blade or rubber squeegee. Cellophane protects the patch from air while it's curing. Hold the squeegee at a low angle so it's almost flat. Don't worry about the excess putty that oozes out around the cellophane.

Mask off the damaged area in preparation for finishing. When the putty becomes hard to the touch, remove the cellophane and sand with 220-grit sandpaper to remove excess putty and to surface the patch. Use a vibrator sander if available. If not, use a sanding block.

wet-sand to remove scratches

Wash away sanding dust with water, then hand-sand the area with *wet* 400-grit sandpaper to remove scratches left by the coarser paper, and repeat using 600-grit paper.

Wash the area again, and buff to remove remaining scratches and to restore gloss. If you have a power buffer, hold it at a 45° angle and use a lightly abrasive rubbing compound, such as Mirro Glaze No. 1. If you buff by hand, use a slightly harsher grit compound, such as DuPont No. 7 or No. 101S.

To complete the repair, apply the gel coat finish; ideally, the same used by the boat manufacturer so the color matches. Request the company to tell you where to get it. This material can be brush-applied if you have no spray equipment, but a spray finish is neatest and should be used if possible.

Removing scratches. A scratch caused by sideswiping the slip is a most common problem for fiberglass boat owners. To get rid of this, first wash down the area with acetone or lacquer thinner to remove grease and grit that can cause additional scratches during the repair.

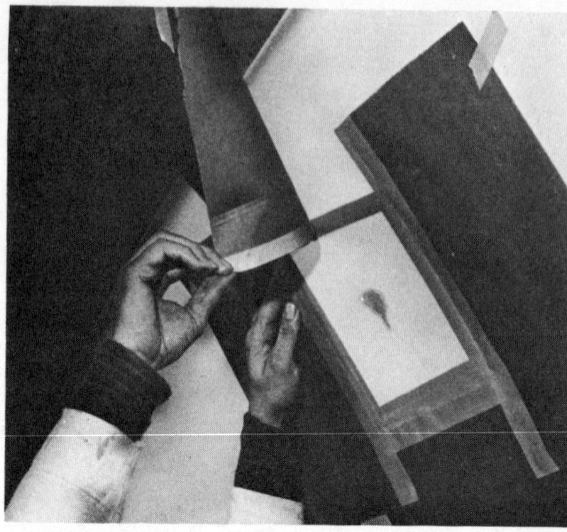

MASKING can be done before or after sanding the patch. It's necessary to avoid affecting adjacent areas, especially if the gel coat is applied by spray.

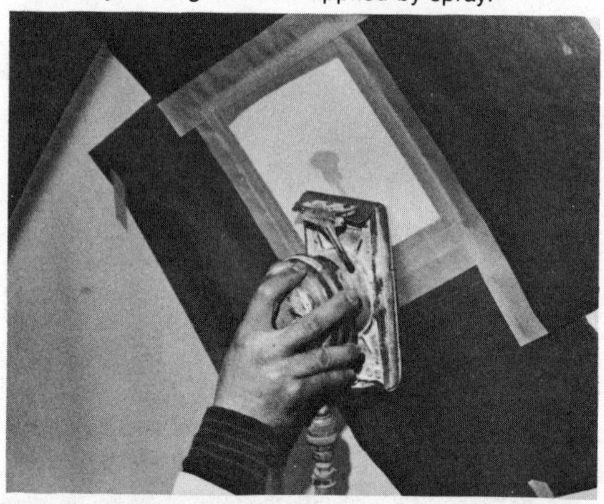

IF YOU HAVE a vibrating sander, use it. Start with 220-grit paper, washing the sanded area frequently with water as you work to keep the repair zone free of dust.

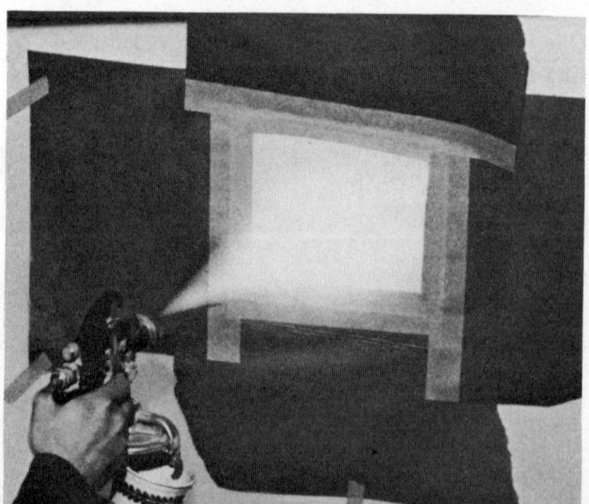

SPRAY FOR best results. All you need is the spray head and compressed air. You can use a paper cup for a dispenser as demonstrated above.

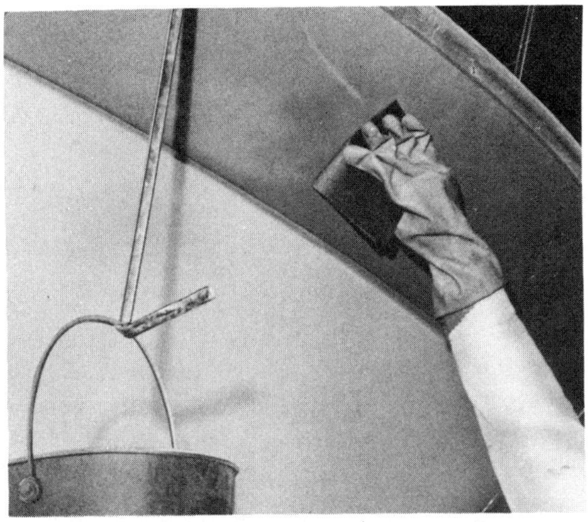

KEEP SANDPAPER WET while removing scratches. That's what the bucket's for. Keep your eye on the scratch and stop sanding as soon as it disappears.

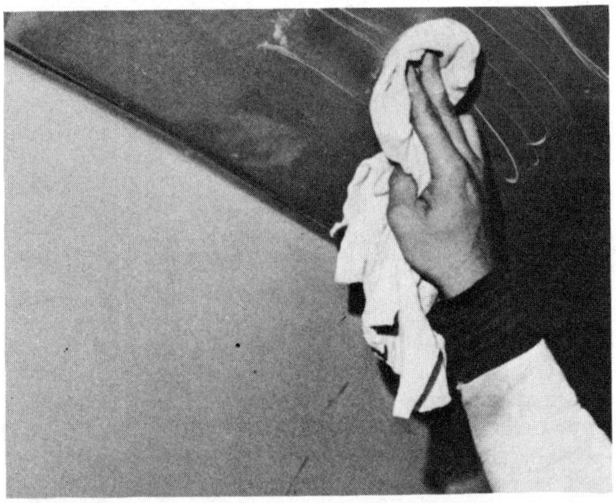

AFTER THE SCRATCH is out, buff the area by hand to finish the repair. A soft cloth and a heck of a lot of elbow grease should wrap up the job for you.

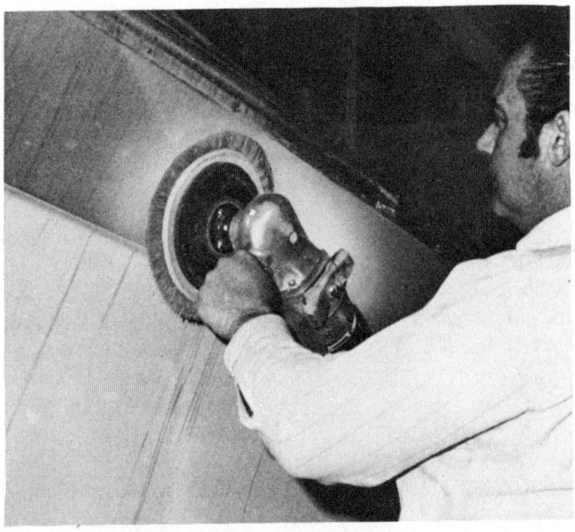

TO ELIMINATE the above step, you can buff the entire boat to restore gloss to all dull surfaces. An electric buffer is the ticket for this task.

Now, sand the scratch with wet 400-grit sandpaper. Keep a light hand on the paper and a keen eye on the scratch so you can stop sanding as soon as the scratch disappears. If you go crazy with the paper you could sand right through the gel and have a bigger headache.

Complete the repair by buffing as described above.

Handling crazed cracks. Crazed cracks in the gel coat often look like a spider web. To remove them, block-sand the area with 100-grit sandpaper.

All crazings must be removed. If not, what's left will spread after the boat has been returned to use and you'll be back where you started.

As you sand, try not to make ripples and indentations in the gel coat. If you're lucky and none appear, you can spray or brush on the gel coat after sanding is completed. However, rippling the gel coat is often hard to avoid when you sand crazed cracks. Thus you'll have to apply plastic repair putty over the area, then sand, buff and finish as described for gouges.

Getting rid of wrinkles. An owner may find gel coat wrinkles over his new boat, a result of sloppy manufacture. Wrinkles look like the "hilly" region of a topographic map.

With a putty knife, scrape off as much wrinkled area as you can. Remove the rest with 100-grit sandpaper. Sand until smooth, and follow by swabbing thoroughly with acetone or lacquer thinner.

use a squeegee

Mix a quantity of fiberglass plastic repair putty and apply smoothly with a rubber squeegee. Cover the area with cellophane as explained above until the putty cures. Sand the spot again with (in order) 220, 400 and 600-grit paper to remove excess putty and smooth the spot. Then apply the gel coat. This treatment should render any wrinkles or other imperfections invisible.

Restoring gloss. You may want to do this after repair work. However, since it takes very little time for the results you get, you may wish to make it a periodic job.

Wash down the boat with acetone or lacquer thinner to remove loose grit and grime. Using a compound with the grit of Mirro Glaze No. 1, buff the craft with polisher at a 45° angle. Apply minimum pressure to corners and edges. This will help to save the gel coat.

To complete the job, use a fresh polishing pad lightly held flat against the surface, and buff to restore the boat's lost gloss.

How to build retaining walls

■ THOUGH A SLOPED piece of ground is often attractive, just as frequently it is a homeowner's headache. Water and wind erosion can raise havoc with the land and, though seeding may solve the problem, it creates another: The resulting growth is hard to maintain. In most cases, a retaining wall—if properly built—is the answer.

One important point to keep in mind: Water trapped behind a retaining wall will cause damage by freezing. Thus, you will need good drainage, such as that provided by laying perforated drain tiles alongside the base of the inside wall as shown. Though drain tiles are desirable behind a dry (stone or tie) wall, they are a *must* behind masonry walls. Tiles should be pitched about 1/4 in. per lineal foot and lead to a dry well (or should be elbowed out through the earth at the end of the wall). You should also cover the tiles with at least 1 ft. of coarse gravel. Any moisture will then flow along the asphalted wall and be picked up by the tiles.

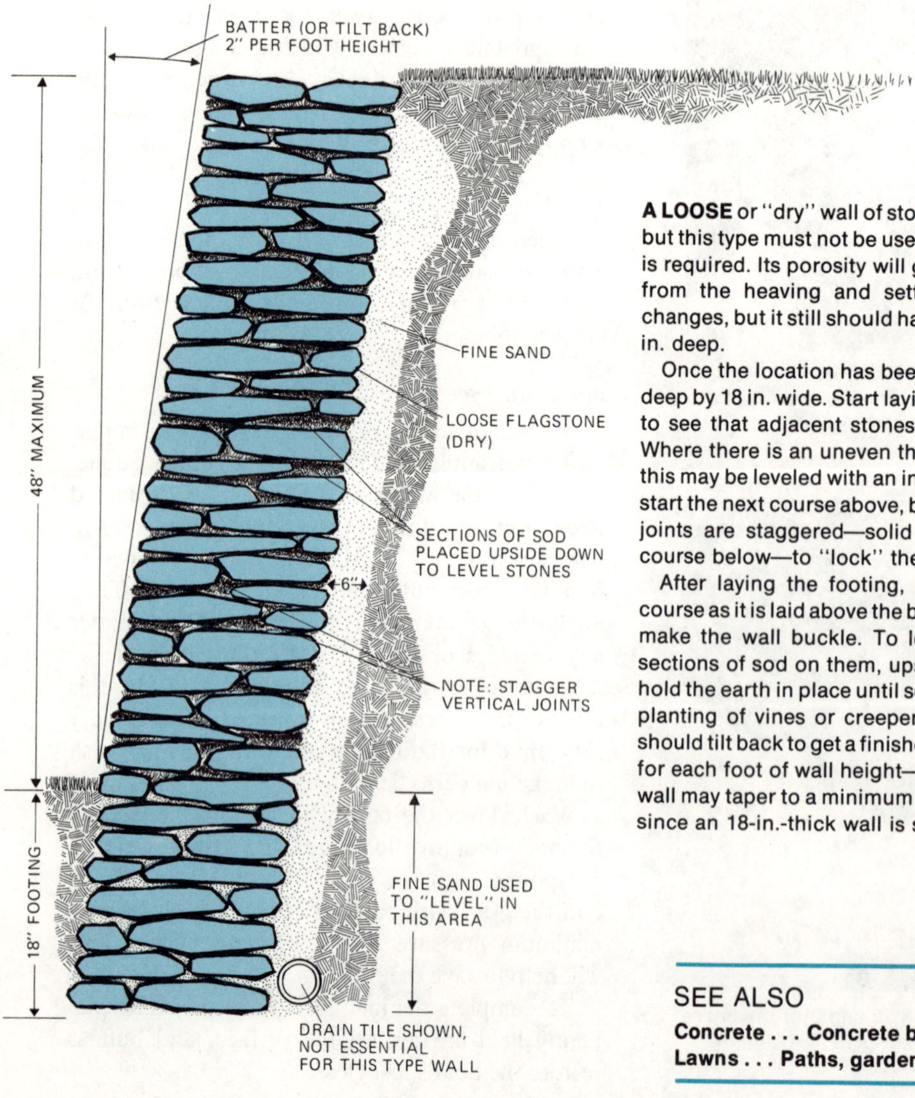

A LOOSE or "dry" wall of stone or flagstone is easiest to build, but this type must not be used when a height of more than 4 ft. is required. Its porosity will give such a wall some protection from the heaving and settling that's caused by weather changes, but it still should have a dry footing (sand) at least 18 in. deep.

Once the location has been determined, dig a trench 18 in. deep by 18 in. wide. Start laying the stone in place, taking care to see that adjacent stones are nearly the same thickness. Where there is an uneven thickness of stones in the footing, this may be leveled with an inch or two of fine sand. When you start the next course above, be sure to place the stones so that joints are staggered—solid stone above each joint in the course below—to "lock" the wall together.

After laying the footing, backfill and tamp behind each course as it is laid above the base grade; backfilling later could make the wall buckle. To level stones above grade, place sections of sod on them, upside down. Roots of the sod will hold the earth in place until settling is complete, also facilitate planting of vines or creepers in the finished wall. The wall should tilt back to get a finished face batter (rake) of about 2 in. for each foot of wall height—about 8 in. for a 4-ft. wall. A dry wall may taper to a minimum thickness of 12 in. at the top, but since an 18-in.-thick wall is stronger, it's recommended.

SEE ALSO

Concrete . . . Concrete blocks . . . Landscaping . . . Lawns . . . Paths, garden . . . Patios

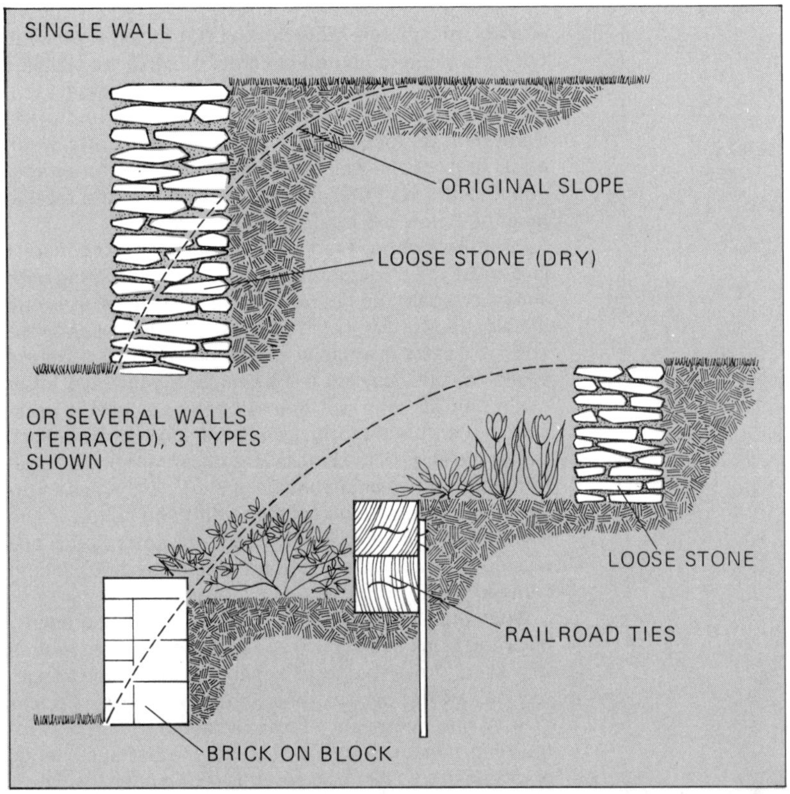

THE HIGHER THE WALL, the more complicated and more difficult it will be to construct it. Especially for a greater drop, you may want to consider the alternative of "stepping" or terracing the slope with two or more smaller walls. These may be of different types, as shown in the drawing at left, or all the same.

To avoid the nuisance of having to mow grass on the steps, ornamental planting is suggested. Height of the walls and depth of the terraces will, of course, depend on the original slope of the land, and you must have enough horizontal space to step a given height or you will have to build a higher wall. As a rule of thumb, the depth of each terrace must be at least equal to the height of the wall below it; otherwise, the condition will be the same as that of a single wall that has been built too high and not strong enough.

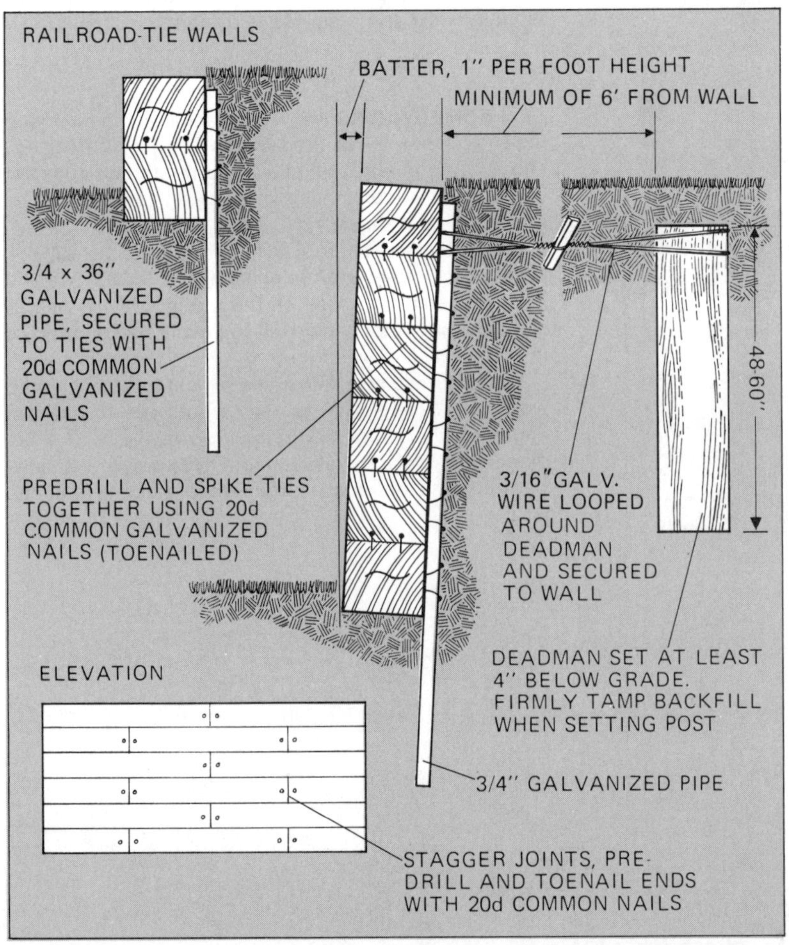

A RETAINING WALL made of used railroad ties is nearly as easy to erect as a dry stone wall. While the footing required is not as deep, hauling and placing ties—weighing about 210 lbs. each—will require help. Ties up to three tiers high can be stacked, if joints are staggered, with only a leveled trench 6 in. deep for a footing. A section of ¾-in. galvanized pipe, driven at least 18 in. into the earth and clinched to the ties with 20d galvanized common nails, will hold them.

Walls higher than three tiers should employ "deadmen" in addition to pipe support. A deadman is a device driven into the ground away from the wall (usually about 6 ft. back) and tied to it to help it resist outward earth pressure. A section of tie in a post hole is ideal as its width will keep it from cutting into the soil. You can also use galvanized pipe of at least 1½-in. diameter driven into the earth. Either type deadman is fastened to the tie-pipe on the wall with several turns of 3/16-in. galvanized tie-wire, tightened like a tourniquet.

For construction of retaining walls greater than 4 ft. high, see page 2567.

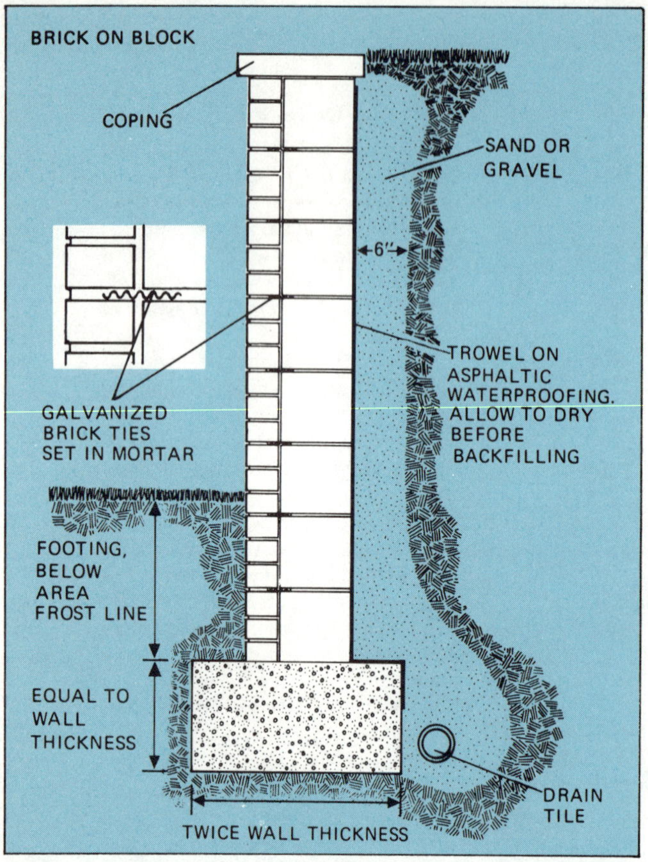

A WALL of concrete block with a brick facing is easier to build than one of poured concrete but, like the walls on the preceding pages, it should be no higher than 4 ft. It can be built in three stages—footing, block and brick. Determine its location and dig the footing of a width equal to twice the wall thickness at its base and a depth equal to the wall thickness. The bottom of the footing must be below the frost line in your area.

Pour the footing; a rented mixer or ready-mix concrete is a must for this operation. Level top of footing with shovel or board; do not trowel. The next day, start laying the blocks. Mortar mix is 1 part cement, about 1 part lime and 4 to 6 parts fine mason's sand. Commercial mixes are available, but cost more than making your own. After mixing mortar with just enough water to make it workable, butter footing for a distance of about three blocks. Butter the ends of the blocks and set them in place. Level by tapping with a board and hammer; trowel excess mortar off joints. Continue for the length and height of the wall. For maximum strength, insert galvanized brick ties spaced 3 ft. apart into mortar to hold the brick facing (veneer).

When the block backup is complete, lay brick similarly, inserting brick ties in corresponding joints. Dress joints with ⅜-in. dowel before they set. For best appearance, you may want to have a professional lay the brick. Coping or a cap is necessary to keep water out and prevent freezing damage. This may be of stone or flagstone, or brick laid in a soldier course, ends facing outward. Block should be coated on the earth side with a thick layer of asphaltic mix, and drain tile set before backfilling.

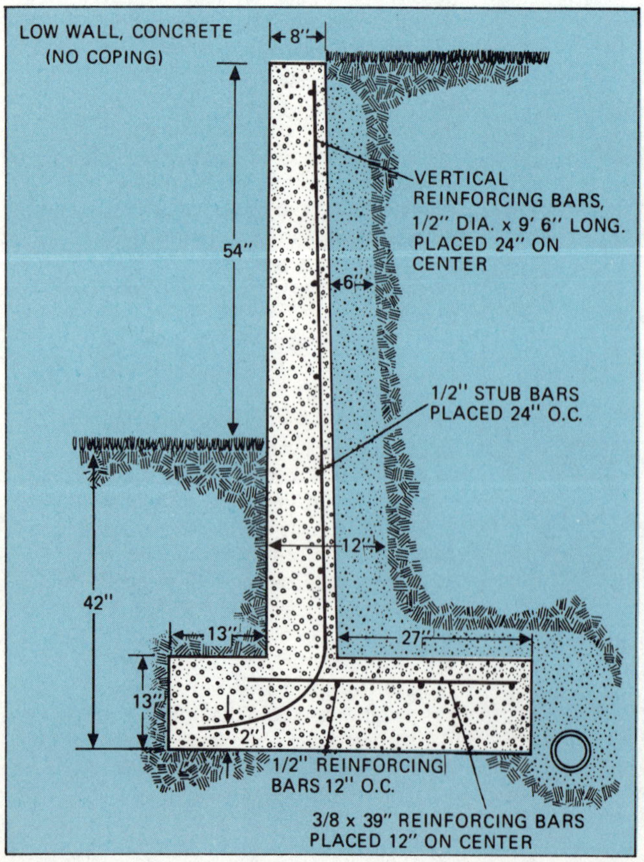

FEW HOMEOWNERS will want to take on the engineering and other work required for this type of wall. But if you should be contemplating having a reinforced concrete wall built, an understanding of the design principles is an important consideration.

The footing used here is an integral part of the wall and is tied to it by steel reinforcing bars. The "head" (weight) of earth behind the wall on the footing determines its size. If a contractor should tell you that a wall of this type is "no problem," watch out.

If a reinforced concrete wall is a must for you, it will be worth the $75 to $100 fee you would pay to have an engineer check your contractor's drawings. The engineer's fee will generally turn out to be only a very small portion of the total cost of a reinforced concrete retaining wall.

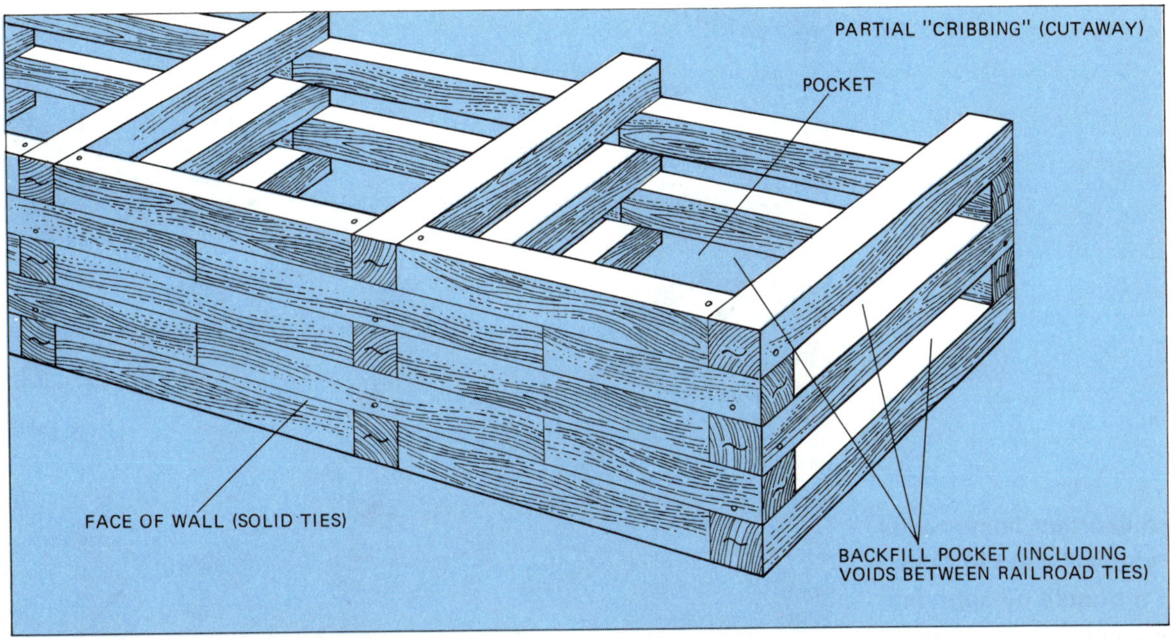

IF YOU NEED a retaining wall higher than 4 ft. and want to build it yourself, the method to use is called "cribbing" railroad ties. The job will be a lot of work, and you should allow plenty of time for it, but the result will be a self-draining wall of great thickness and strength. Essentially the construction of a series of boxes, cribbing requires cutting, predrilling and spiking of ties, as well as the moving of a large amount of earth. *Caution:* Railroad ties are "pressure-treated"—creosoted clear through the wood—so be sure to wear goggles while cutting them (using a two-man saw or portable circular saw with coarse-set or rip blade). Face of the wall is solid, with joints staggered. Holes are predrilled and ties spiked together by toenailing with 20d galvanized common nails. Then the pocket is backfilled. Earth in the pocket acts structurally as part of wall; voids between ties allow for drainage through sides, reducing pressure on face of the wall.

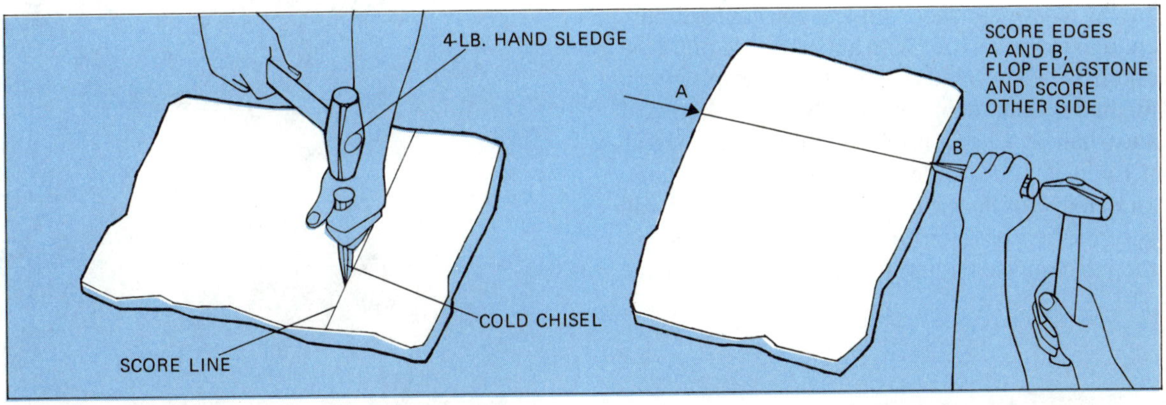

WHEN YOU HAVE to cut a piece of flagstone or fieldstone to get a straight edge to lay, use a cold chisel and hammer or mall (hand sledge). First score a guideline on both flat sides of the stone, then nick the edges about ⅛ in. deep to join the score marks on the flat surfaces. Then lay the stone on the ground to nick the scoring on the flat sides, also to a depth of ⅛ in. When the scoring has been deepened on all four sides, continue tapping, but now with harder blows. Go all the way around, working from the middle of each side outward toward the edges, until the stone breaks along the score.

Done correctly, this entire operation should take about five minutes. Object of the scoring is to make the break occur where you want it; otherwise, efforts with hammer and chisel are almost bound to result in a fractured, useless stone.

If you are like this homeowner, you will want to save yourself a bundle by applying your own shingles all the way up to the ridge. You may have all the tools you need right in your own toolbox

Be your own roofer and save half the cost

■ THE WORST ASPECT of shingling a roof is having to work *up there*. But, if you are fortunate enough to have a roof with a reasonable pitch—a ranch or Cape Cod home, for example—you might consider taking on the job and pocketing at least half of what a professional would charge.

Even if you decide to call in a pro, a good knowledge of how a roof should be applied will put you in a position to make sure that you get the job you are paying for. It's okay to put the

SCAFFOLD HANGERS are necessary for safety. You'll need at least two pairs to work your way up the roof safely. They are attached by driving in 8d common nails after locating the bracket so that shingling can continue. To move the bracket to a new position, it is simply tapped up and the nails that held it are driven home. Use at least a 2x6 plank.

SEE ALSO
Gutters and downspouts . . . House additions . . . Ladders . . . Scaffolding . . . Sheathing . . . Siding

new roof over the old, but if there are already two layers of shingles up there, the roof should be stripped and the job started from scratch. On a new roof, use 1¼-in. galvanized nails. If installing a second layer over asphalt shingles, up the size to 1¾-in. galvanized nails. You'll need that extra length to assure good holding power.

About asphalt shingles: The square-butt shingle measures 12x36 in., has three tabs and is normally laid with 5 in. exposed to the weather. There are 27 strips in a bundle and three bundles make up a square (100 sq. ft.). Store the bundles of shingles flat or the strips are likely to curl as the bundles are opened for use.

repairing old roof

Begin by checking the old roof, nailing down any loose shingles and replacing any that are damaged. If warped or rotten boards (sheathing) are present, usually under bumps or bulges, remove the shingles, replace the boards and weave in replacement shingles.

Start the reroofing by laying the valleys in first. Measure for length and cut the roll roofing. Roll the pieces up and place a roll at each valley. (Your local code might require the use of metal flashing instead of roll roofing.) Width of flashing to use in a valley is determined by roof pitch. The usual is 12 in. wide for slopes of 7 in. in 12 and over; 18 in. wide for 4 in. in 12 to 7 in. in 12 slopes and 24 in. for slopes less than 4 in. in 12.

After applying 15-lb. felt with staples, the starter course can go down. It can be either wood or asphalt shingles (applied upside down) as in the drawing. In any event, the starter course should be applied so it projects at least ½ in. over the eaves. This will prevent water from running back up under the shingles. A ½-in. shingle projection should also be used at the rake (gable) ends.

The shingles are applied on up to the ridge and once all shingles are in place, they can be trimmed at the valleys. Measure at least 2 in. either side of the valley center at the top and 3 or 4 in. both sides at the bottom (eaves). Drive a nail at each of these four spots, attach a chalkline and snap to determine where shingles should be cut.

Use a piece of ⅜-in. plywood *under* the shingles along the valley. Place the carpenter's square along the chalkline on top of the shingles and cut with your utility knife. Remove cutaway pieces, finish nailing the trimmed shingles and apply roof cement to the edges.

Capping at the ridge can be done with a 12-in.-wide strip of roll roofing. But it is more com-

ROOFING TOOLS (top) are few, may now be in your toolbox: square, chalkline, 50-ft. tape, hammer, utility knife and putty knife. Materials (center) are shingles, roof cement and roll roofing. The correct way to walk on a pitched roof (shown directly above) is with weight concentrated on the edge of feet toward the down side. Rubber-soled shoes are essential.

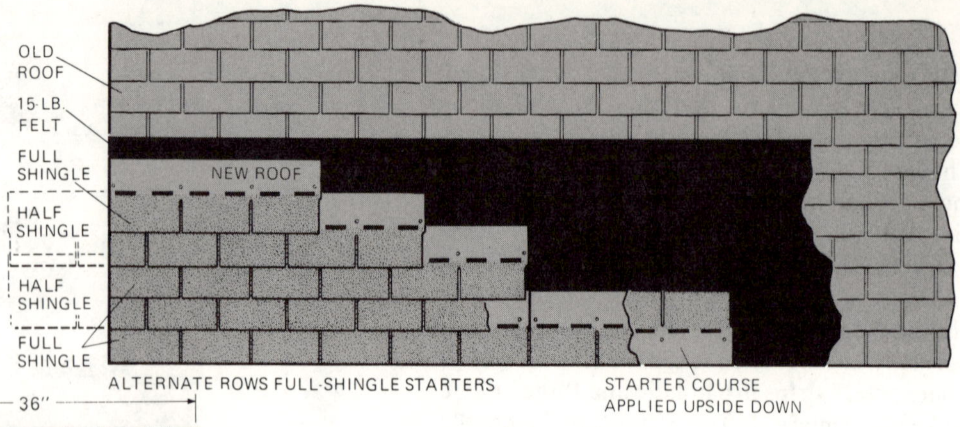

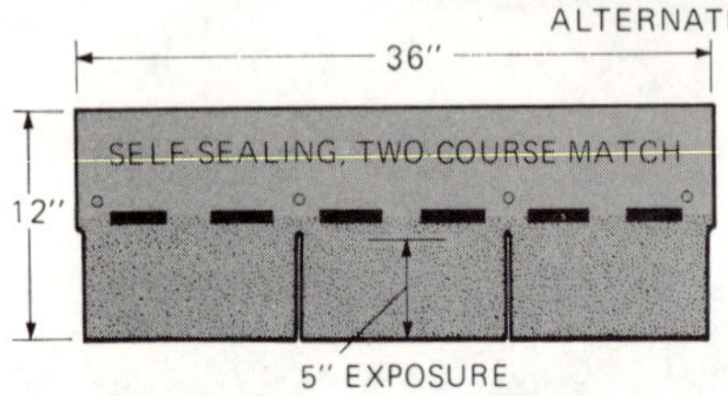

TAB SHINGLES are always applied so that the full tab is centered over a slot below. If length of the roof requires a narrow piece to finish the first course, start the second row with a piece of the same width. Then continue alternating narrow pieces in each succeeding row all the way to the ridge of the roof.

VALLEY TREATMENT

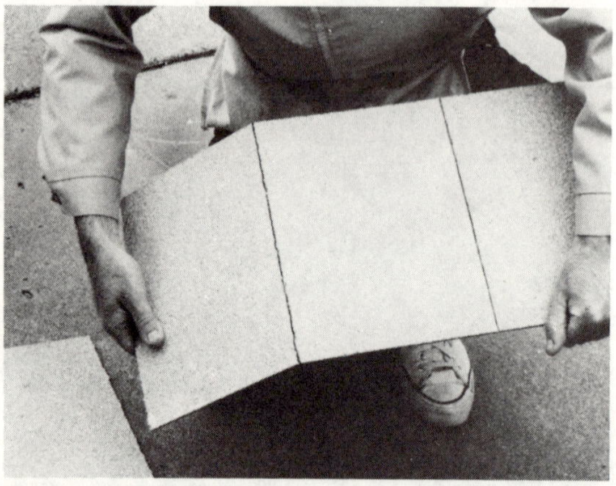

TO CUT an asphalt shingle, score a line with your utility knife, then bend and snap off the piece.

A TYPICAL open valley goes quickly if you use a chalkline to determine the exact angle cutoffs on shingles.

OPEN VALLEY is flashed with 38-in.-wide roll roofing before you move up the roof with the shingle courses. (Note: Some building codes require the use of metal flashing; see text). Width of the valley between courses should increase from top to the bottom. Minimum open width at the top is 4 in. between courses.

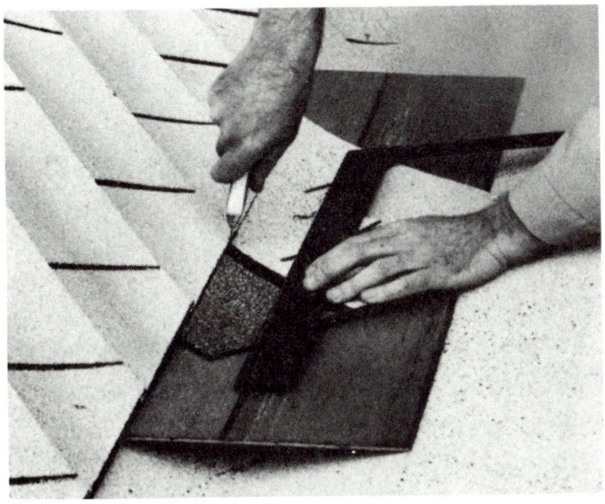

VALLEY SHINGLES are trimmed at one time using a straight-edge on the chalkline and a utility knife.

mon to use full shingles cut into thirds. These are then applied as shown in the photos. Notice that the final ridge shingle receives four nails. Make certain you seal the exposed nailheads with roof cement.

Notice that the shingles shown have adhesive patches above the tabs. These are a sealer-type shingle that will withstand greater wind and rain forces than non-sealer-type shingles. This built-in advantage makes them well worth the few extra dollars of cost.

Words of caution. For maximum traction, use rubber-soled shoes or sneakers when roofing. And don't walk on the edges of the shingles because you are apt to crack them. Instead, place your feet squarely on shingle centers.

WATERPROOFING A STACK

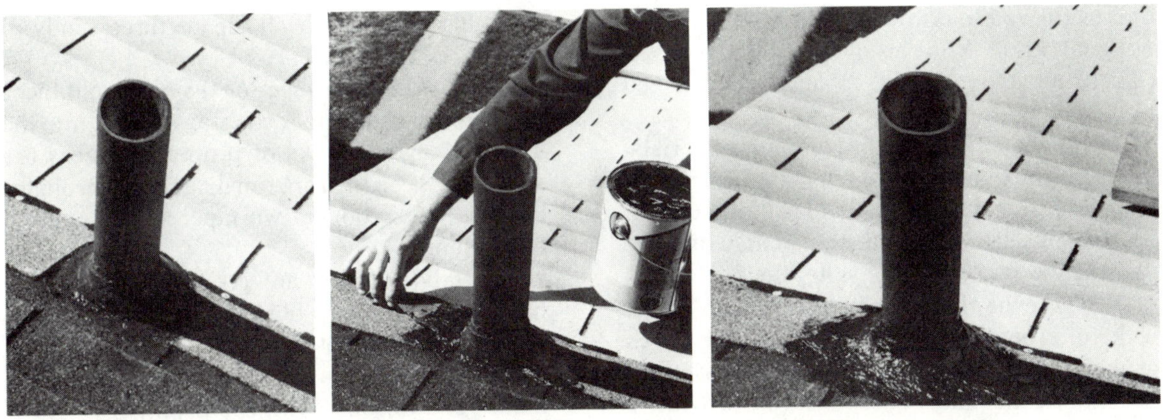

PLASTIC ROOF cement is used to seal the joint around stack in roof. Cement is applied with a putty knife (a wood shingle will also work fine) after shingles are trimmed for a neat job. If desired, paint the cement to match.

RIDGE TREATMENT

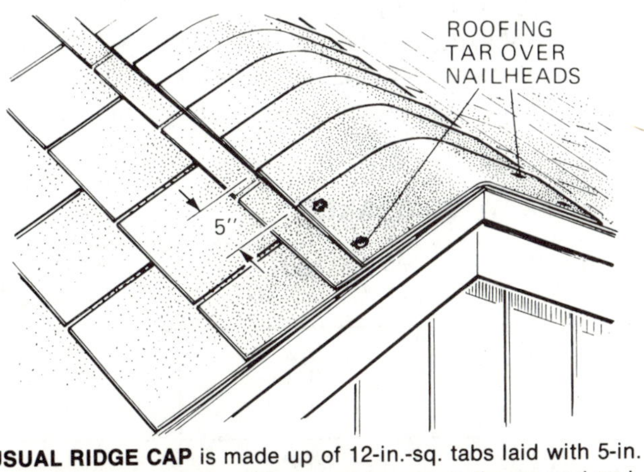

USUAL RIDGE CAP is made up of 12-in.-sq. tabs laid with 5-in. exposure to the weather. These can be cut on the ground and carried up by the armful. Each tab is applied with two nails—except for the last shingle. Here, four nails are used and the exposed heads are then waterproofed with dabs of cement.

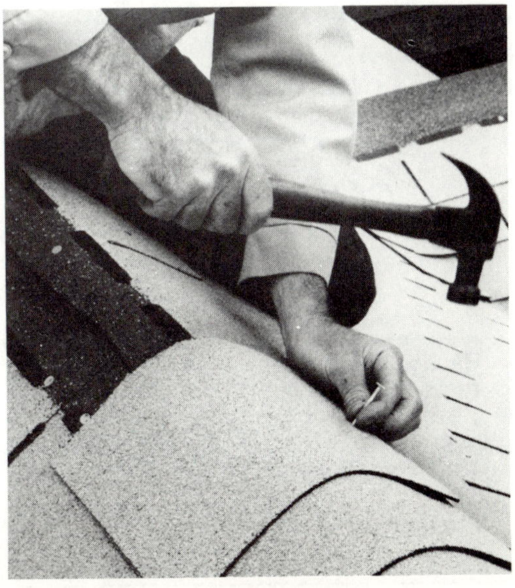

Reroof with wood shakes and shingles

By WAYNE C. LECKEY

Whether you want to switch to the distinctive look of hand split shakes or desire simply to re-cover the wood shingles that are already on your roof, either job is relatively easy if you know what you're doing. Here's how to do the job right

MANY HOMEOWNERS still prefer the rustic, colonial beauty of a wood-shingle roof in preference to asphalt, and if your home has such a roof which needs reshingling with either red-cedar shakes or shingles, a little know-how is all it takes for you to do the job yourself with professional results. You can end up saving yourself a lot of money and have a handsome finished product.

Called the aristocrat of roofing materials, handsplit cedar shakes make a luxurious roof of unsurpassed durability that will actually outlast the house itself. Shakes may be applied directly over the old roof if it's not slate, tile or "asbestos." Where the old roof is to remain, 6-in. strips of the old roofing are removed along the eaves and gables, and replaced with 1x6 boards before the shakes are laid. These boards provide a strong base at the perimeter, concealing the old roof from view.

Over-roofing, of course, has a number of advantages. It gives extra insulation. You don't have to worry about sudden rains while applying the shingles, and there's a lot less litter to pick up from the lawn and shrubs. But where you might be fixing up an old dilapidated house with a beyond-saving shingle roof, you have no recourse but to strip the roof and start from scratch. You have a choice of three kinds of shakes.

- *Handsplit and resawn shakes* have split faces and sawn backs. After cedar logs are cut into the desired length, blanks of proper thickness are split, and these then are run diagonally through a band-saw to produce two tapered shakes from each blank.
- *Tapersplit shakes* are produced entirely by hand, using a sharp-bladed knife called a froe and a wooden mallet. A natural shinglelike taper, from butt to tip, is achieved by reversing the block, end for end, with each split.
- *Straightsplit or barn shakes* are made in the same manner as taper-split shakes, except that the splitting is done from one end of the block only. This produces shakes which are the same thickness throughout.

SEE ALSO

Gutters and downspouts . . . House additions . . . Ladders . . . Scaffolding . . . Sheathing . . . Siding

applying shakes

Shakes can be applied over open or solid sheathing, although in areas where wind-driven snow is encountered, solid sheathing is recom-

MAXIMUM EXPOSURE FOR WOOD SHAKES

TYPE	THICKNESS	LENGTH	DOUBLE COVERAGE	TRIPLE COVERAGE
Handsplit and resawn shakes	½ to ¾″ ½ to ¾″ ¾ to 1¼″	18″ 24″ 32″	8½″ 10″ 13″	5½″ 7½″ 10″
Tapersplit shakes	½ to ⅝″	24″	10″	7½″
Straightsplit shakes	⅜″ ⅜″	18″ 24″		5½″ 7½″

TRY TO drive nails flush with shingle's surface but not so hard that the nailheads will crush the wood.

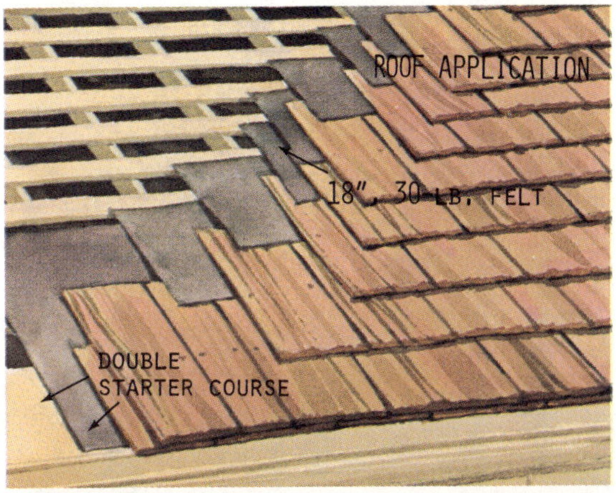

mended. For good drainage, the pitch (slope) of your roof should not be less than one-sixth, or 4-in-12 (4 in. vertical rise for each 12-in. horizontal run). The correct weather exposure is important too, and the chart gives the maximum exposure for standard 18, 24 and 32-in. shakes, in double and triple coverages. Note that the ⅜ x 24-in. shakes should be applied at 7½-in. exposure when the roof pitch is less than 8-in-12.

To begin, a 36-in.-wide strip of 30-lb. roofing felt is laid over the sheathing boards at the eave line. The starter course of shakes is doubled, the bottom course being 15 or 18-in. shakes ex-

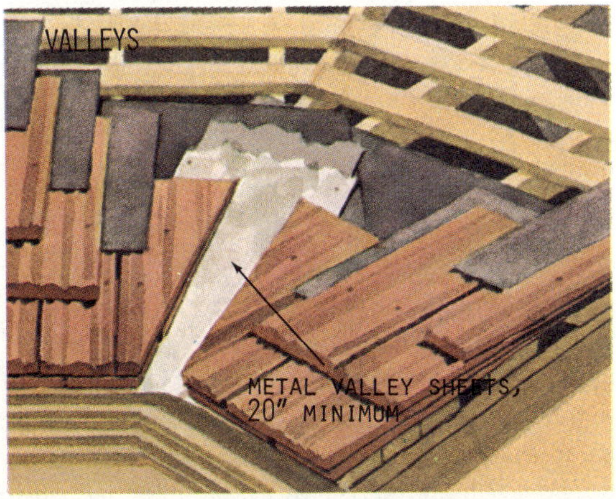

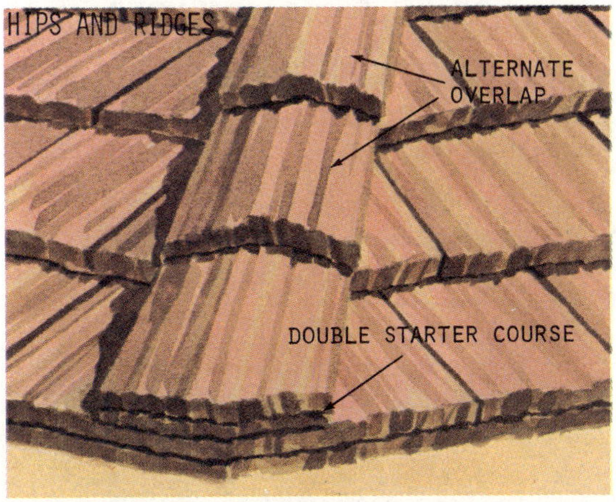

pressly made for the purpose. Wood shakes should extend 1 to 1½ in. out over the eave and rake to form a drip. After each course is completed, an 18-in.-wide strip of felt is placed over the top portion of the shakes. Here the bottom edge of the felt is kept above the shake butts a distance equal to twice the weather exposure. For example, if 24-in. shakes are being laid at a 10-in. exposure, the felt should be positioned 20 in. above the shake butts. The strip will then cover the top 4 in. of the shakes and extend 14 in. onto the sheathing. The individual shakes should be spaced ¼ to ⅜ in. to allow for possible expansion, and the joint offset at least 1½ in. in adjacent courses.

Fasten each shake with just two nails and use only rust-resistant nails (hot-dipped zinc or aluminum) driven 1 in. from each edge and 1 or 2 in. above the butt line of the course to follow. A 2-in. (6-penny) nail normally is adequate, but longer nails should be used when shake thickness dictates. Drive the nails until the heads meet the shake surface but *no further*; nails have less holding power when the heads are driven into the shake.

MAXIMUM EXPOSURE FOR WOOD SHINGLES

ROOF SLOPE	SHINGLE LENGTHS		
	16″	18″	24″
5 in 12 or steeper	5″	5½″	7½″
4 in 12	4½″	5″	6¾″
3 in 12	3¾″	4¼″	5¾″

NAIL SIZES RECOMMENDED

SIZE	LENGTH	GAUGE	HEAD	SHINGLES
3d*	1-¼″	14-½	7/32″	16 & 18″
4d*	1-½″	14	7/32″	24″
5d**	1-¾″	14	7/32″	
6d**	2″	13	7/32″	

*3d and 4d nails used for new construction
**5d and 6d nails used for reroofing

For the final course at the ridge line, uniform shakes are selected. A strip of roofing felt, at least 8 in. wide, is applied over the crown of all hips and ridges and shakes approximately 6-in. wide are sorted out to cover them. Two straightedges are tacked to the roof, 5 in. each side of the center line of the hip.

The bottom course of hip shakes is doubled and the butts are trimmed to align with the starting courses at the eaves. The first hip shake is nailed in place with one edge resting against the guide strip. Then the portion projecting over the center of the hip is cut back on a bevel. The shake on the opposite side is then applied and its projecting edge is cut back to fit. Shakes in following courses are applied alternately in reverse order. Weather exposure of the hip shakes should be the same as that for the roof shakes.

All valleys should be underlaid with 30-lb. roofing felt applied over the sheathing. The metal valley sheets should be at least 20 in. wide. Edges of the shakes are cut to run parallel up the valleys, approximately 5 in. apart. Base and chimney flashing units are laid with each shake course and counterflashed.

An adjustable exposure gauge on the edge of a shingler's hatchet speeds application in making it easy to measure correct exposure and run the courses straight.

applying red-cedar shingles

Red-cedar shingles are applied in much the same manner as shakes. Where they are to be applied over an old roof of wood or asphalt shin-

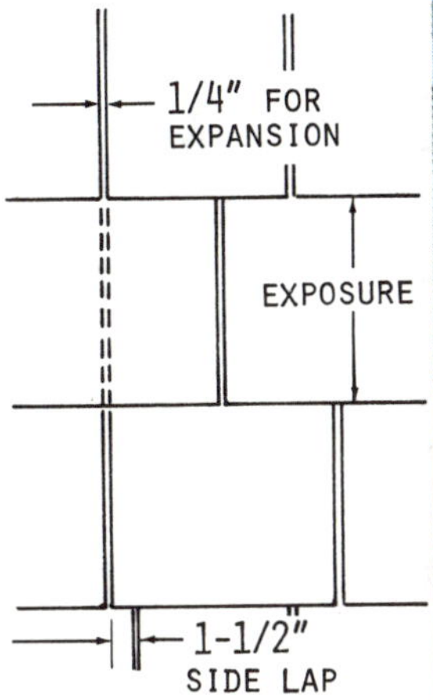

SPACING and location of shingle joints is important to allow for expansion and guarantee a nonleaking job.

ONLY TWO NAILS are used per shingle and are placed so they are ¾ in. above butts of following course.

gles, roof preparation is the same along the eaves and gables. In addition, a strip of lumber is laid in each valley to separate the old metal valley from the new, and the old ridge shingles are replaced with strips of beveled cedar siding, thin edge downward.

Normally, cedar shingles are applied in straight single courses, using a straightedge to keep the rows straight and true. On roof slopes of 5-in-12 and steeper, standard exposures are: 5 in. for 16-in. shingles, 5½ in. for 18-in. shingles and 7½ in. for 24 in. shingles. If the roof pitch is less than 3-in-12, cedar shingles are not recommended.

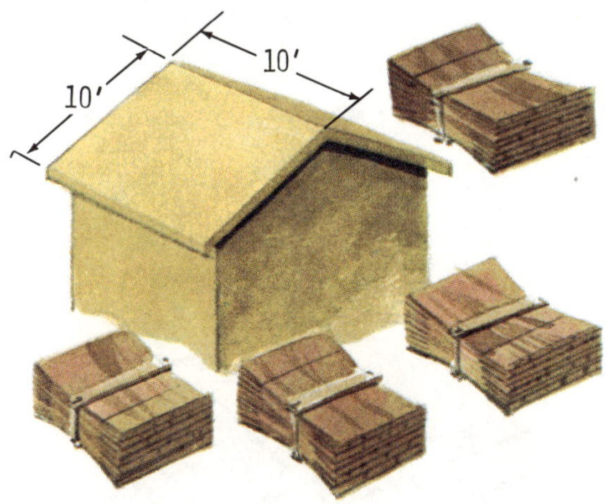

TO ESTIMATE the number of shingles need for your roof, four bundles, which are called a "square," will normally cover 100 square feet of roof area.

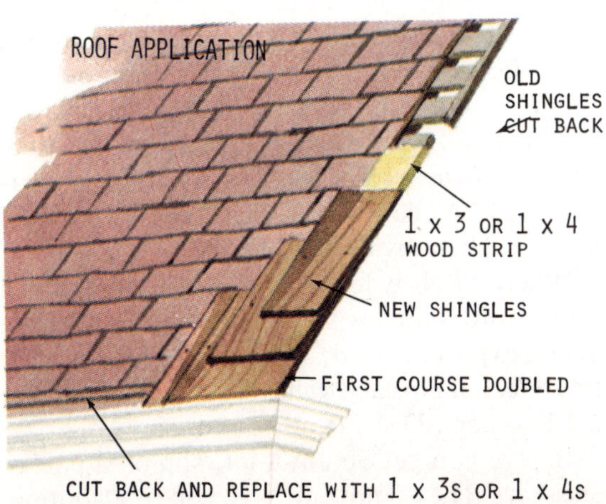

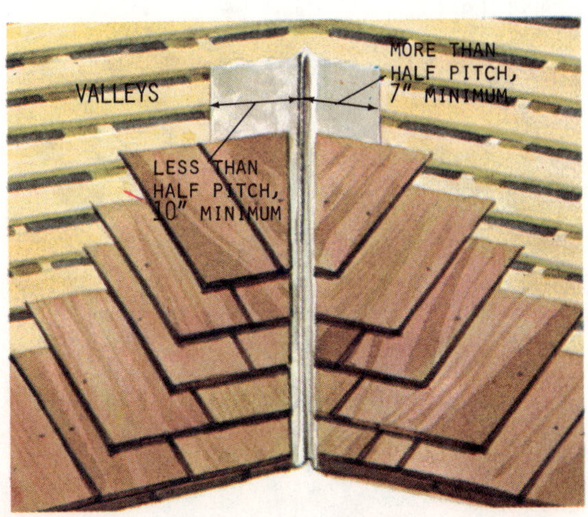

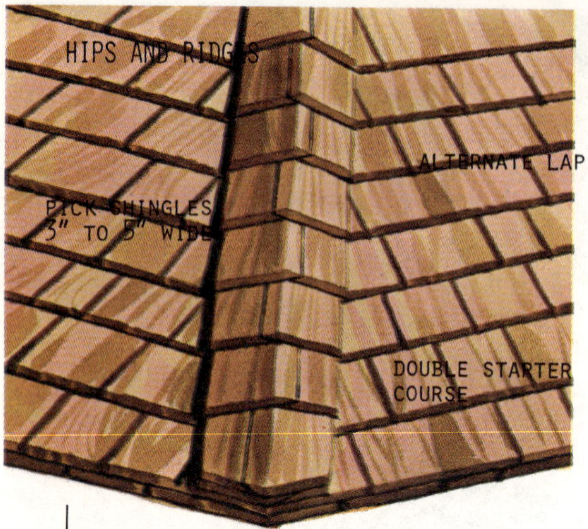

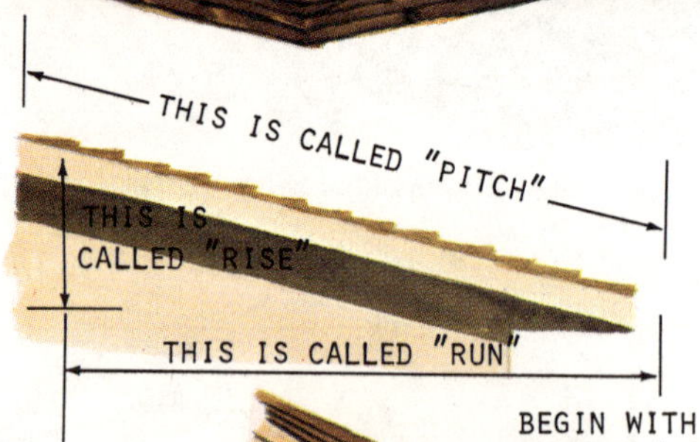

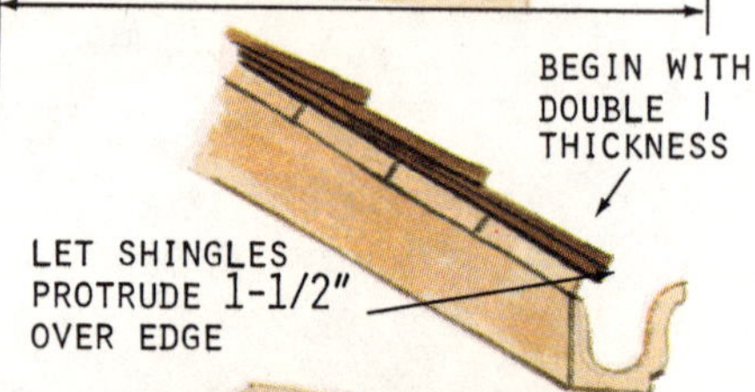

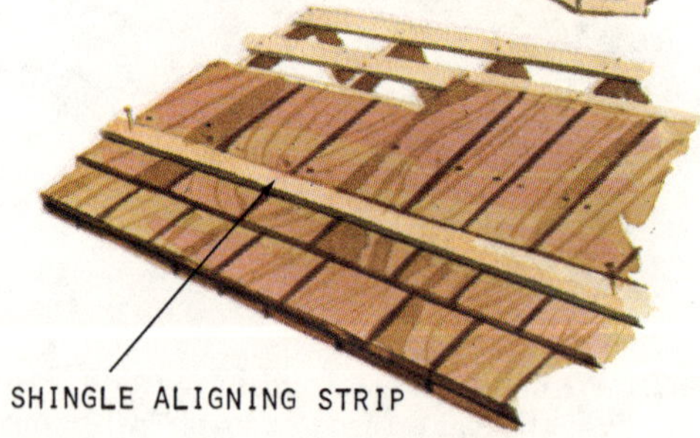

RECOMMENDED PLYWOOD SHEATHING APPLICATION

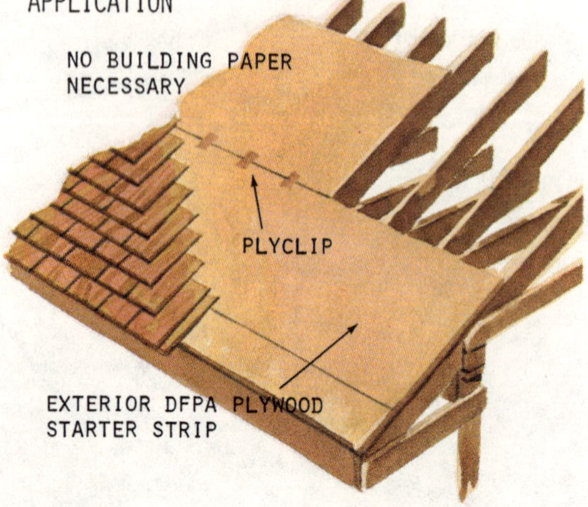

Like shakes, cedar shingles are doubled along the eaves, and the butts of the first course are laid so they hang over the edge 1½ in. to insure proper rain spillage in the gutters.

Space the shingles ¼ in. apart and never have two joints in line if separated by only one course of shingles. Leave a side-lap of 1½ in. between joints in successive courses. Use only two nails per shingle, ¾ in. in from each edge, and locate them so the next course will cover the nails by at least ¾ in. The chart specifies the right size of nail to use. As with shakes, the use of rust-resistant nails is most important. Drive the nails flush, but not so hard the nailheads crush the wood.

Hips and ridges are capped with factory-assembled units lapped to provide the same exposure as in the roof proper.

estimating squares

A "square" of shingles consists of four bundles, so called because they normally will cover 100 square feet of roof area.

To estimate the number of squares you'll have to order for your roof, first determine the square-foot ground area of your house (include eave and cornice overhang). Increase this total square-foot area by 8½ percent if the roof pitch is 5 in 12, 12 percent if it's 6 in 12 or 20 percent if 8 in 12. Then divide total by 100.

Where pitch is less than 5 in 12, allow for a third more shingles to compensate for the reduced exposure. And, add a square for each 100 lineal feet of hips and valleys. As for nails, figure 2½ lbs. per 100 sq. ft. of roof area.

Before you get on any roof, slip on a pair of sneakers. They'll not only give you good footing, but they'll keep from marking up your new roof.

Beautiful walls that serve a purpose

AS YOUR FAMILY GROWS, so does the accumulation of personal possessions. It becomes increasingly clear that the more square feet of living space in your home you can utilize efficiently, the greater your family comfort will be. A logical, and frequently the most economical, place to turn to for desperately needed storage space is a wall. The three wall ideas shown here, in addition to satisfying particular family storage needs, have something else in common: Each is well-designed and adds to the looks and the value of the home.

The long see-through wall shown above is framed to give a deck (or counter) at a height of approximately 36 in. The deck and post enclosures are of nominal 1-in. clear pine. The cabinet on the living room side was paneled; on the opposite side narrow pine shelves were installed to hold a collection of knickknacks.

Above the deck, large dowels (closet poles) were installed to give the illusion of greater room height and size. Thus, several advantages were gained by converting a flat, run-of-the-mill wall into a customized "room divider."

SEE ALSO
Bookcases . . . Cabinet furniture . . .
Family rooms . . . Hi-fi centers . . .
Modular furniture . . . Remodeling ideas . . .
Storage ideas . . . Storage walls . . . Study centers

The unit shown at the bottom of this page was designed by a pro. The homeowners required a built-in that could be used for stereo equipment and a convenient closet for their children to store boots, mittens and so forth. Additionally, they wanted it placed near the front entrance to create an entry way.

The cabinet is 27 in. wide, 39 in. high and 42 in. long. In turn, it is topped by a double-deck set of 18 hand-turned balusters (nine per row). The folding doors on the living-room side are trimmed with factory-made moldings for a decorator touch and fitted with friction catches for easy access. The interior shelves are removable; thus, should storage needs ever change, there is a built-in flexibility to meet them.

The children's side of the cabinet, by the front door, is fitted with sliding doors for quick use. Inside, there is an accordion-type wood hanger with peg hooks for small-fry clothes plus the storage for boots and the like. To match the existing decor in the room, the entire cabinet-divider unit was painted a Wedgwood blue shade.

The third unit shown was designed expressly to handle the storage needs in a playroom next to a kitchen. It's a built-in along a wall, 15 feet long, that has been divided into five equal sections. Each of the five youngsters in the family, from toddler to teen-ager, has his own personal storage area.

Horizontal members are spaced so as to create 13 sections (plus a pass-through to the kitchen for snack serving.). Six of the sections are fitted with doors to protect the older children's more valuable games and possessions from the little ones' inquisitive hands. The remaining lower sections are fitted with 18-in. adjustable shelves.

ENTRY WALL viewed below from both sides, provides storage area for stereo components, closet for children's wardrobe and attractive foyer at the front door. It was designed by Top Recker, A.I.D.

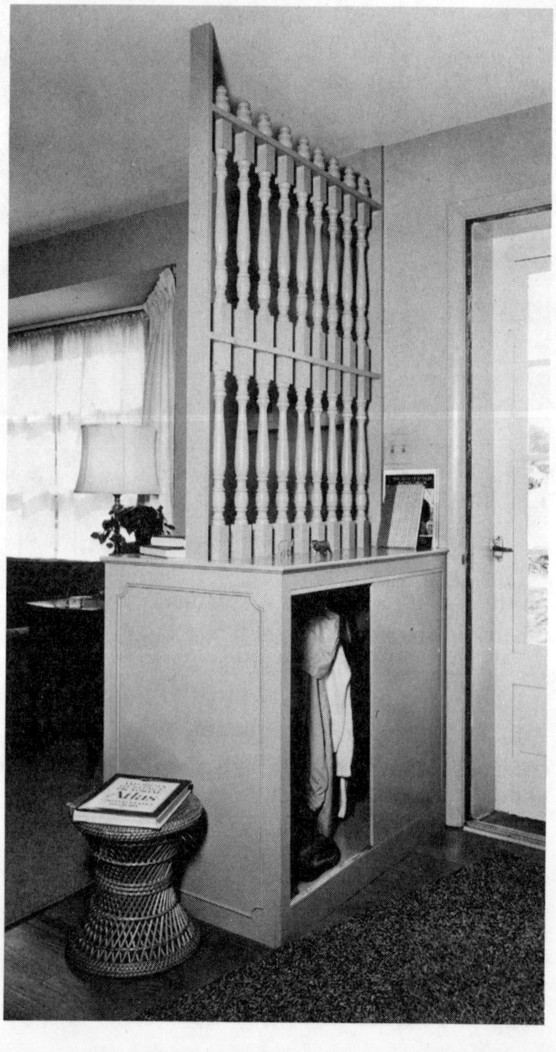

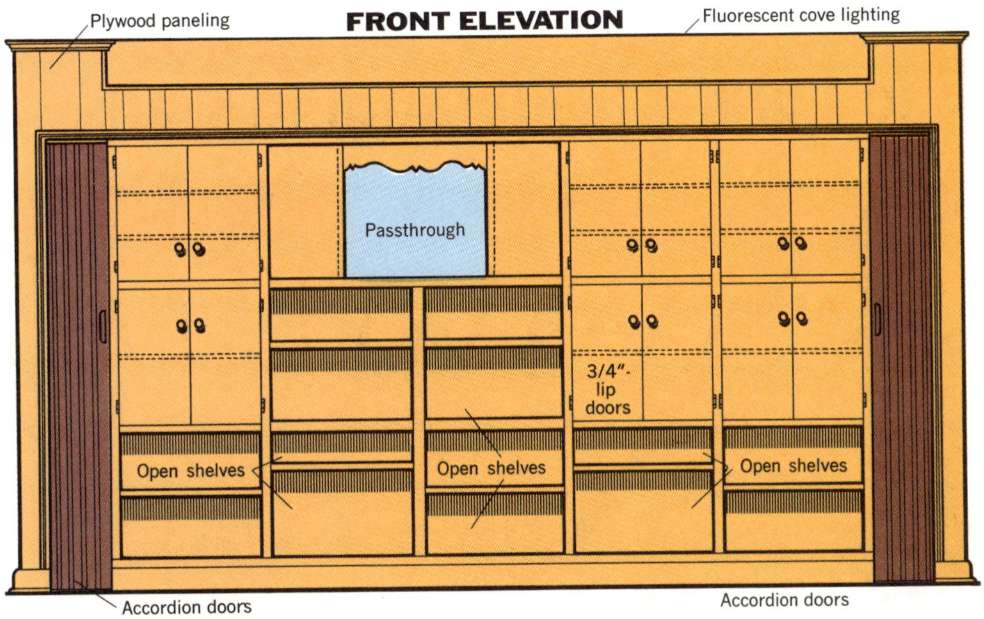

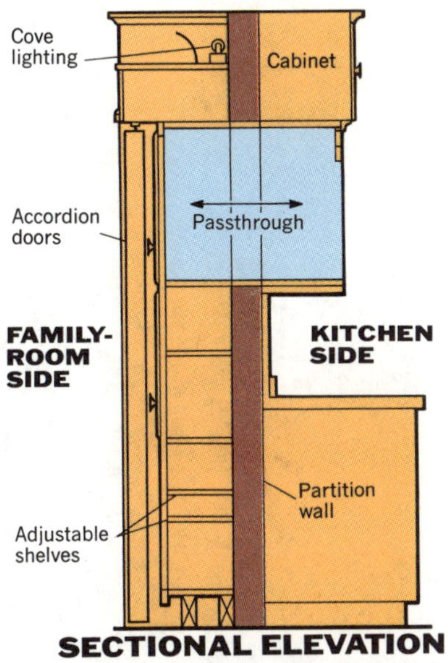

FULL-DEPTH wall gives ample storage required by a large family. Accordion doors hide it all when desired.

The unit shown was constructed entirely of ¾-in. plywood (except for cleats, nailers and the like). To withstand abuse, the unit was finished, inside and out, with a primer and semigloss paint.

To hide the unavoidable clutter of toys that always seems to be present on the toddler's open shelves, accordion doors were installed in front. Then, when the room is used for adult parties, the paraphernalia behind can be quickly removed from view.

If the wall is to be used primarily by adults or teen-agers, the face of the unit could be built of cabinet-grade plywood and stained for a natural finish. Another method would be to treat the facing with either ½-in. plywood or particleboard, and then glue and nail prefinished paneling over.

How to light a freestanding wall

SEE ALSO

Electrical wiring . . . Entryways . . .
Fluorescent lamps . . . Remodeling ideas

■ WHEN ARCHITECT Juris Curiskis of Edina, MN, wanted to add a light fixture over a freestanding wall he built, he found that what he needed would cost about $200. Even at that price, selection would have been a compromise, so he designed and built this handsome fixture.

Instead of the usual fluorescent fixture, 10 incandescent ceiling receptacles are used. These provide the warmer lighting the owner wanted. Conventional wiring is used to build the fixture. Receptacles are mounted on 4-in. junction boxes and BX cable runs from box to box.

Fixture length is determined by need. In the 7-footer shown, 10 *low-wattage* bulbs were used, spaced equidistant and staggered on opposite sides. The frame consists of two 2x6s held together by ¾x1-in. strips on the bottom and ends. The translucent sheet plastic simply rests on the strips. The end piece, of course, is secured with cleats.

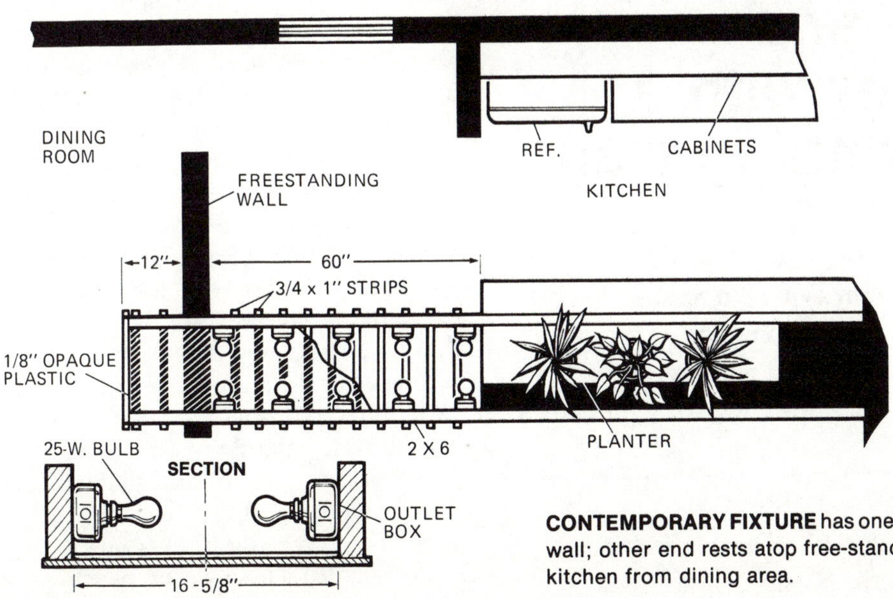

CONTEMPORARY FIXTURE has one end fastened to the wall; other end rests atop free-standing wall shielding kitchen from dining area.

Divide and conquer with a freestanding wall

By HARRY WICKS

Get more from available space: This easy-to-build wall doubles the use of a bedroom and minimizes the disputes when it's shared by two youngsters

SEE ALSO

Bookcases . . . Children's furniture . . . Closets . . . Remodeling ideas

A PERFECT "space-doubler" for youngsters sharing the same bedroom, this freestanding wall clearly draws the line between activity and sleeping areas. Gone will be the nightly squabbles over the right time for lights out—and your role as arbiter, happily, will be vastly diminished.

Don't get discouraged about building this project because you have never built a wall before. You needn't be a master carpenter nor own any special tools to test your do-it-yourself skills on this project. The wall consists of a 2x4 framework covered on one side with plasterboard and wallpaper, and on the other side with a durable ¼-in. plywood paneling chosen from U. S. Plywood's Weldwood Prefinished line.

As in conventional house building, the easiest way to build a wall is to assemble it flat on the floor. To prevent the wall from racking (going out of square), the plywood paneling should be applied to one side while the wall is still in the horizontal position. The wall can then be tilted upright and held with diagonal braces while the plasterboard and wallpaper are applied to the second side.

There are two slight differences between this wall and the walls of your house. First, it is *not* fastened to the floor. This means that you will not be tied down to one furniture-layout scheme. Instead, a piece of ¾-in. plywood, which is attached inconspicuously to the bed frame, is in turn screw-fastened to the wall (see the inset drawing on the next page).

The second important thing to keep in mind is that the wall should stop short of ceiling height by about one foot in most homes. If it did not, the

A BRIGHT, SOPHISTICATED bedroom becomes more functional when space is divided into logical-use areas. Here, wall facing study-play area carries a durable, prefinished plywood paneling (facing page); its other side (below) is plasterboard, wallpapered to match the bedspread and the draperies.

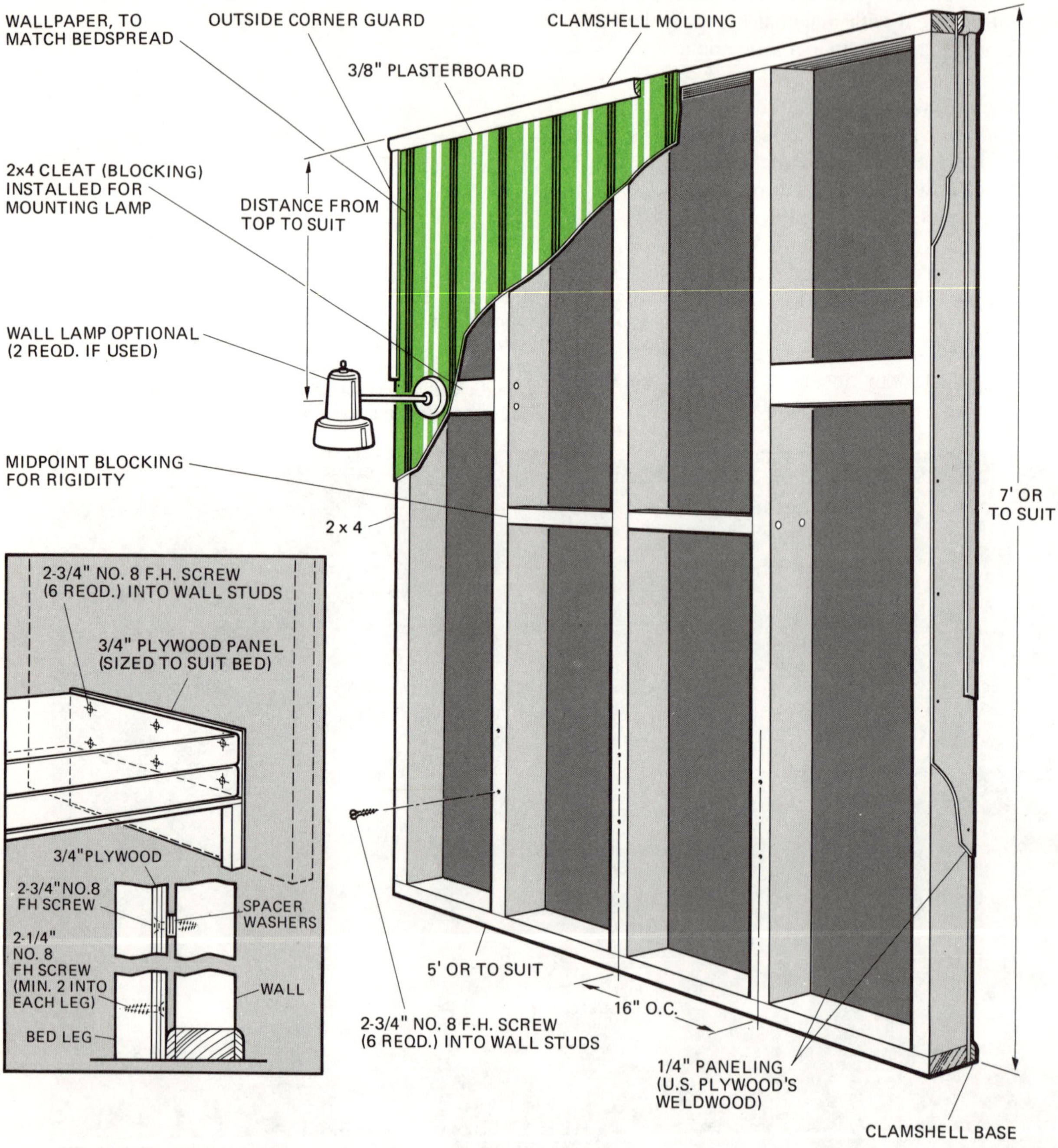

resulting look would be wall rather than divider. Before starting construction, make certain you measure bedroom floor-to-ceiling height and scale your divider to it (as well as scaling the divider width to bed width).

The wall facing the active area is most likely to receive some punishment from lively youngsters. Thus, it is clad with the same plywood paneling used on the bedroom walls. Paneling here also gives a feeling of continuity—that the wall is an integral part of the room. Lacking such coordination, it might look like an afterthought.

The second side is covered with 3/8-in. plasterboard. Joints and dimpled nailheads are hidden with two applications of joint compound and the wall is finished with wallpaper to match bedspread and draperies. Conventional molding at top, base and corners supply the finishing touches. If desired, battery-powered pin-up lamps can be installed on the divider over the bed.

Quiet that floor

Every time we move, the floors squeak underfoot. I have a full basement, can reach the floor from underneath, but what can I do to stop the squeaks?—Paul Hanlan, Detroit

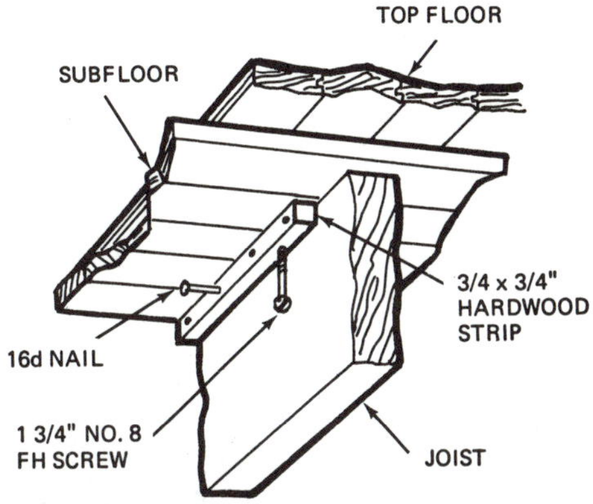

One way that seems to be effective in nearly all instances is shown in the illustration above. First, locate the squeaks from the basement by having someone walk about on the floor. Then nail strips to the joists, spanning the areas of the squeaks, and making sure that the strips are pressed tightly against the floor as you nail them in place. Then have someone stand on the spot while you drive screws through the strips, through the subfloor and into, but not through, the top floor.

Loose register vanes

Two wall registers in my warm-air heating system won't remain open. The vanes drop to their closed position as soon as the control level is released. Can these be repaired?—R. Hanscom, Joplin, Mo.

Chances are the pivots at the ends of the vanes have become worn through usage. Turn out the two screws holding the unit in place, lift it out and you'll see the vanes are pivoted on rivets that normally are set with just enough friction to hold them in place at the desired setting. Stand unit on end with heads of several rivets resting on a sturdy metal surface and tap each lightly. Test for free movement as you go to make sure you don't overtighten them, which would make the vanes difficult or impossible to adjust.

60°F. basement

The temperature in my basement stays at 60°F. all winter, so my workshop is always cold and damp. How can I eliminate this condition? My furnace is in a separate room on a different floor.—F.L., N.Y.

If it is not possible to tap into ducts or pipes to conduct heat into the basement, then the only practical solution remaining is to go to a vented gas heater (which can be suspended from the ceiling or installed between studs in a conventional framed wall). Such heaters are quite efficient and come with a circulating fan for more uniform heat distribution.

For summer months, you might consider the installation of an automatic dehumidifier to keep the moisture content of the air at a given level.

Quick drawer fix

I have an older chest in which the drawers have been heavily loaded at times. As a result, the bottom edges of the drawer sides are somewhat worn, making them difficult to slide in and out. There are no center guides. What can I do to make them slide more easily?—Mrs. J. Tenney, Fort Worth, Tex.

First, pull the drawers all the way out and check to see that the sides have not spread—that is, that the corner joints have not opened; if they have, add glue and tap the sides until the joints are tight. Then drive a large-headed thumbtack in the position shown in the illustration, the head centered under the lower edge of the drawer sides. Spray the lower edges of the sides with a silicone lubricant, which you can buy from your paint or hardware dealer.

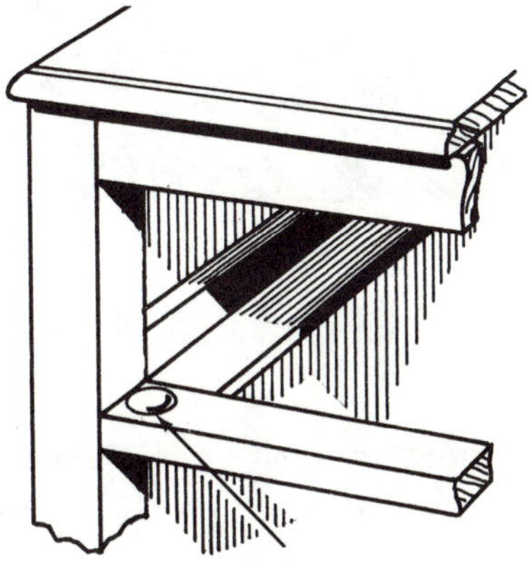

Orienting your new house

We plan to build a new house on our lot next spring. Can you outline briefly how to place a house to gain best advantage of sunlight, air circulation and privacy?—A.L., Tex.

Consider first your local building restrictions, then plan window sizes and exposure to sunlight the year round, direction of prevailing winds, location of plantings and use of fencing or shrubbery or both to attain the desired privacy. A simple penciled plotting of these various features will help you plan your home.

How to use a router

Many home craftsmen mistakenly consider a router to be a difficult tool to work with. Though it gives sophisticated results, it is actually easier to master than you would guess

By HARRY WICKS

SEE ALSO

Discs, wood . . . Drawers . . . Joinery . . . Laminates, plastic . . . Moldings . . . Motors, shop . . . Power-tool maintenance

I'D BE WILLING to lay odds that the screeching and whining of a router will be music to your ears (if not your wife's) after you have had your first crack at pushing the tool through a piece of stock. If you haven't already tried one because you felt—as many workshoppers do—that a router is beyond your skills, be advised it's one of the greatest power tools you can get your hands on.

Undeservedly, the router has the reputation of being difficult to handle. The plain fact is that it's one of the easiest-to-use and most satisfying power tools you will ever handle.

Mechanically, the router is simple; it consists of two pieces, a motor with a chuck mounted on one end and a base that holds the tool in a vertical position for routing. A bit or cutter is mounted in the chuck and protrudes down to do the cutting. The maximum depth of cut is determined by length of the cutter being used. The high speed of the router—anywhere from 20,000 to 28,000 rpm—teamed with a clean, sharp cutter will generally produce a cut so smooth that further sanding is unnecessary.

In essence, a router does much the same work as a stationary shaper *with two differences;* the tool is carried to the job, instead of the other way around, and a router can be used for on-the-job tasks such as hinge-mortising and trimming plastic laminates. (In my opinion, the router is the only way to go if you do a lot of plastic laminating.) If equipped with the proper bit(s), a router can be used on nonferrous metals.

router safety

General power-tool safety rules apply to the router. For example, make certain that the tool is properly grounded if it's not of the double-insulated variety; keep the tool, motor and cutters clean (always being sure that the motor's air vents are not clogged by sawdust), and, because of the flying chips that the tool creates, always wear safety goggles.

Good safety habits you should acquire include: 1) always disconnect the electric cord when installing or removing a cutter; 2) make certain that the piece to be worked is securely clamped; 3) double check to assure that *all* adjustments are tightened before turning on the motor—you should *never make any adjustments while the router is running;* 4) hold the router firmly at all times; 5) though it may seem obvious, as you finish a job and turn off power, place the router on its side on your workbench and hold it until the cutter stops spinning.

router bits and accessories

The first rule regarding bits and accessories—and it's a must—is to use only those cutters and accessories specifically designed for use in high-speed routers. Much of the router's versatility comes from the variety of bits and cutters now available. (One major manufacturer claims there are more than 170 cutters on the

Typical routers and accessories

SIMPLEST OF ALL power tools, the router consists of two basic pieces—the motor with a chuck on one end of its shaft and a base to hold it. These are from Stanley Tools (left), Rockwell (center) and Black & Decker (right).

MOST ROUTERS have a quick-read depth indicator plus a method of adjustment for precision settings.

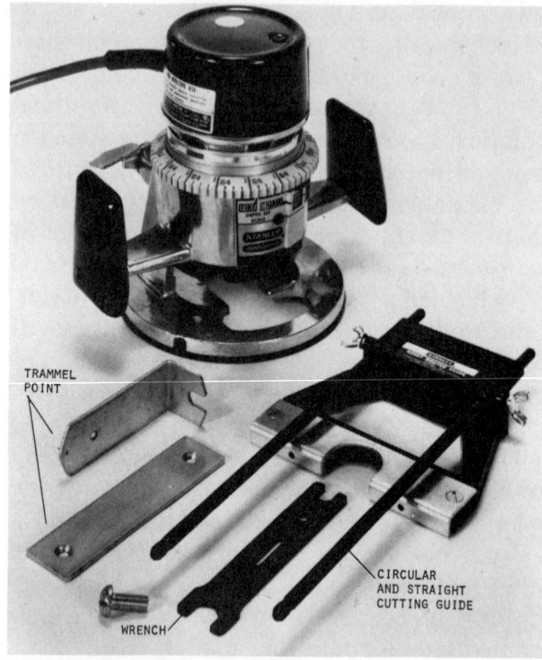

TWO NECESSARY accessories are a trammel point (left) for circle cutting and a straight cutting guide.

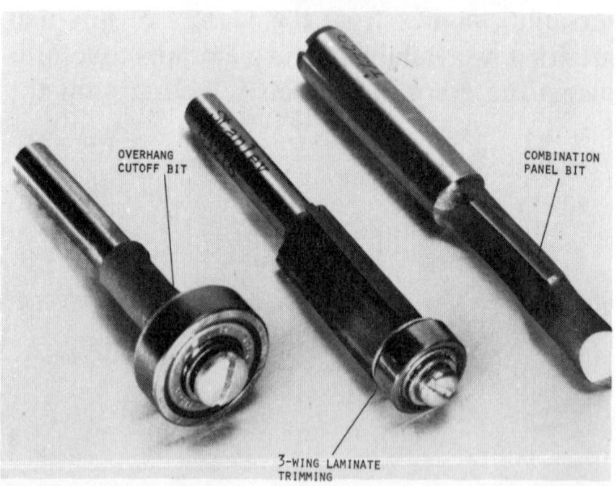

THREE BITS from Stanley Tools aren't cheap but well worth the investment for a steady router user.

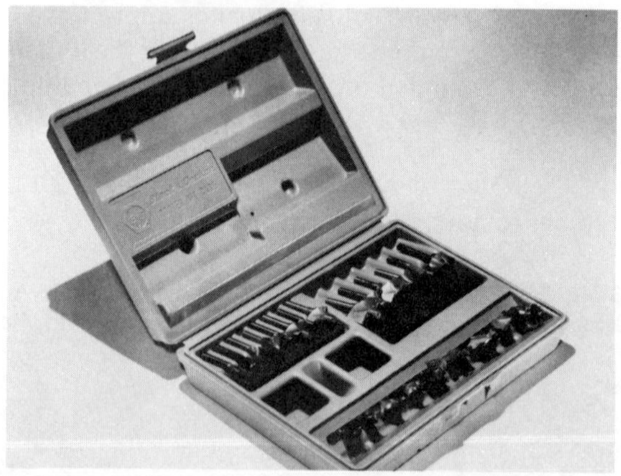

ROUTER-BIT case from Black & Decker keeps bits where you can find them and protects the cutting edges.

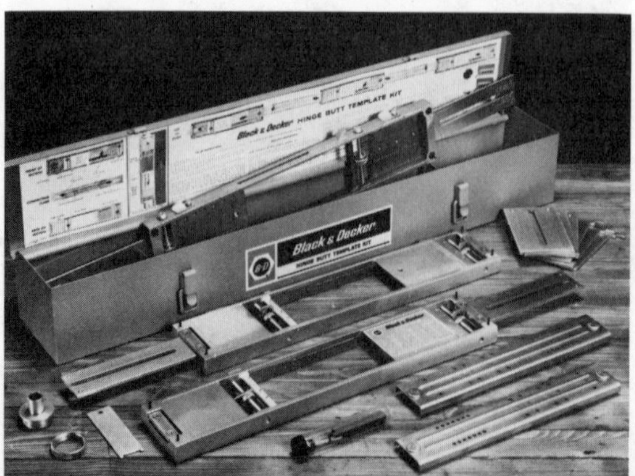

DOOR-AND-JAMB butt template is a timesaver for a professional who wants to hang many doors in a hurry.

market.) Many bits sold today are originally designed to suit specific commercial needs. Ultimately, these special-purpose bits found their way into home workshops.

In simplest terms, there are three types of bits:

• *Pilot type* (such as the edge-rabbet cutter shown on page 2472) is a one-piece bit that has a cutter portion and a pilot at bottom which rides against the work edge while the cutter does its chore. Bits for decorative edge-trimming are of this design.

• *Cutters used for grooving* (mortise-type). These do not have a pilot, and the cutting edge(s) extends full length of the cutter. To use these bits (except when freehand cutting), it is necessary to use a guide: either an improvised clamped-on piece of wood or the factory-made version which is attached to the router.

• *Panel bits,* which have a drill-type tip. These are used when it is desirable to plunge through the workpiece and then commence routing the design.

As mentioned above, variations on the basic cutters are almost endless. And now most makers are offering almost all types in a carbide version. Like saw blades, these cost more initially, but for the frequent user, they are worth extra cash outlay. If your shop production is limited however, you are probably better off buying noncarbide bits and having them sharpened occasionally.

A router without accessories could be compared to a bench saw equipped with a combination blade only. For example, you need attachments to guide the machine for straight and circular work (when using nonpilot-type bits). The straight guide is invaluable when making grooves and dadoes. And using a trammel point,

Installing the cutter

AFTER DISCONNECTING the power, insert the bit fully into the router chuck and then back it out ⅛ in.

TOOL is placed on bench and one wrench is slipped onto the chuck while second wrench tightens the locknut.

Correct way to feed a router into workpiece

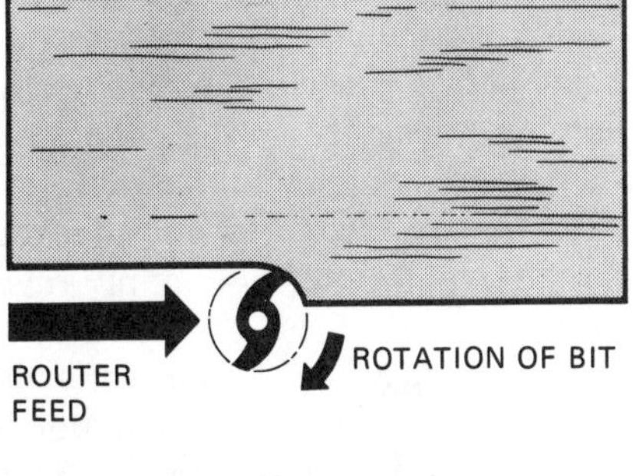

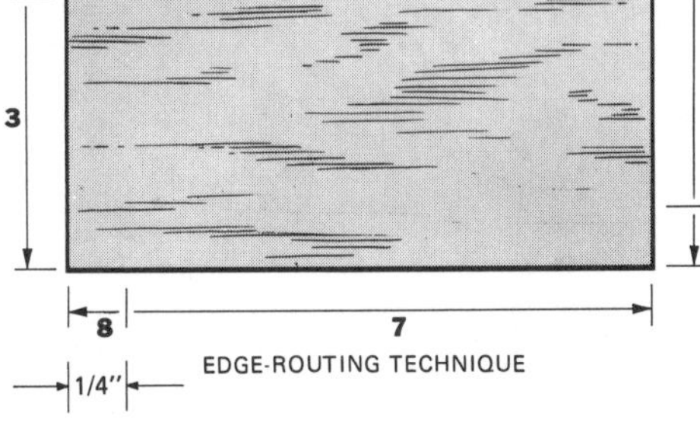

SINCE MOTOR rotates clockwise, move the router from left to right. The sequence at right saves splintered corners.

Cutting grooves and dadoes

TO CUT groove, it is necessary to guide the router. Here, a commercially made guide is being used.

IF CUT must be farther away from the guide, a clamped wood strip—which handles clear—works well.

EDGE-RABBET cutter (foreground) has a pilot that rides against workpiece edge while rabbet is formed.

you'll find you can quickly cut the neatest, most accurate circles in the least time.

You can—and in many cases you must—make your own accessories. For example, a long board fitted to the router shoe will let you safely straddle the cut portion when you are cutting an extra-wide groove. But, generally, the manufactured accessories are in such an economical price range that it makes good sense to buy them.

installing the cutters

After selecting the bit you are going to use, loosen the collet locknut. Insert the bit all the way into the collet, finger-tighten the locknut, then back out the bit about ⅛ in. (This procedure is to prevent the collet from shattering.) Place the motor on the workbench and slip one wrench over the chuck and hold its end against the benchtop. Holding the chuck with this wrench, tighten collet with the second wrench. (Note: Some routers are designed so the collet can be tightened with one wrench. On these, the arbor is locked by means provided on the router motor.) To remove a router bit, simply reverse the procedure.

Loosen the locking nut on the base and install the motor. Adjust the motor so the cutter is at desired depth and tighten the base locking nut. All quality routers have a ring or other means for making fine, precise depth adjustments. Consult

FOR WIDE grooves, tack two boards to limit the router's travel and clamp work to bench for safety.

TO CUT groove in narrow piece, clamp work between two scrap pieces of wood that provide shoe support.

the maker's manual to determine how to make fine adjustments on your router.

direction of feed and thrust

Viewed from above, the router cutter spins in a clockwise direction. Thus, the router should be moved from left to right; this allows you to cut against bit rotation. Feed rate and depth of cut to use will depend a great deal on the material being worked. If possible, make test passes on scraps of the same stock. Keep feed pressure constant, and do not force the router because you will slow down the motor excessively. This will give a poor cut—rough and, in all likelihood, cutter-burn spots. More important, it's unfair to the tool and will shorten its life.

On particularly hard woods or problem materials, your best bet is to make the cut (or cuts) in several passes, lowering the cutter for each successive pass.

When edge-routing with a pilot bit, follow the sequence as shown in the drawing. That is, start the first side ¼ in. in from the corner and feed through to the right-hand corner. Then return to the starting point and plough off the ¼ in. at the left-hand corner. Repeat these steps around sides two, three and four. The first four passes are across the end grain and the next four with the grain. By using this sequence and feeding the router slowly when going left, you'll have splinterfree corners.

grooves and dadoes

Two of the most basic cuts in woodworking can be easily, quickly and neatly made with a properly handled router and accessories. The important points to remember are that the router cannot be allowed to drift or walk away from the guide. And the shoe must always have ample, solid surface to ride on (so it won't rock on the workpiece). As can be seen in the photos, these are easy-to-make cuts. In all probability, these will be the first that you will attempt with your new router.

After you have familiarized yourself with your router by making some test grooves and dadoes, you will probably want to try some different cuts.

The simplest and most common cutting done with a router (right behind the two cuts mentioned above) is decorative edging. It's about the quickest, surest way to add a professional touch to any project.

decorative edging

A shaped edge, whether Roman ogee, beaded or simply rounded-over (quarter round), improves the looks of just about any cabinet door, tabletop or drawer front. Actually, doing these edges goes so effortlessly that it is easy to give in

VIEWED FROM the bottom the shoe of the router sits squarely on the wood surface with the bit cutting out a groove. The shoe should have enough solid surface to ride on so that it won't rock. Cutting grooves and dadoes such as this is the most common and simplest use for a router.

to the temptation to put an edge on just about everything in sight. To avoid the mistake of *over-routing,* decide *which* edges will receive *what* treatment—and stick to the plan.

Bit versatility can be increased by simply raising or lowering the cutter. You can put decorative edges on circular workpieces, too. To do it, use the circle-cutting guide and counterclockwise feed.

When in doubt, feed the router extra slowly. As you gain experience, you'll find that many woods have a tendency to splinter off large pieces ahead of the cutter. A slow feed rate and sharp cutter usually prevent this happening, but if it still happens, you should make the decorative edge with several passes. Lower the bit for each succeeding pass until the desired shape (depth) is achieved.

A lipped door is easily made using the dingover and rabbet-cutter bits. But sequence is important: Make the rounded edge first, then the rabbet. Since the rabbet cutter's pilot will not have a surface to bear against, affix a guide for the router sub-base (shoe) when cutting the rabbets.

circular work

Circles cut with a router will be absolutely accurate, as can be seen in the pair of photos at top of page 2476. The first is a perfect circle being cut from plywood using a trammel point and panel-type bit; the other is a decorative plaque created by routing concentric circles with trammel point and core-box bits of various radii set at a different depth for each circle. Variations on this type of design are almost unlimited; each bit at a different cutting depth will provide a visual difference.

plastic laminates

Because of looks and durability, plastic laminates are now commonly used by do-it-yourselfers. But plastic-laminate fabrication requires precise workmanship. Since plastic laminates are not cheap, it makes good sense to practice on scrap before you put your router to an actual project.

Since conventional steel bits won't hold cutting edges if used on plastics, *always* use a carbide bit. Cutting edges on carbide-tipped bits hold up indefinitely and, more important, give neat, chipfree cuts. Of two types—one-piece solid and self-contained ball-bearing—you'll need two (of either design): a straight cutter for overhang trimming and a bevel bit (varying from 15° to 22°) to finish-dress the joint.

If you prefer the one-piece solid (as I do), smear petroleum jelly on the laminated self-edge to avoid any chance of the cutter creating a scorch mark. But if you have the ball-bearing type, acquire the habit of frequently disassembling parts and cleaning them with lacquer thinner. Then oil and reassemble. If you don't, the bearing eventually clogs with contact cement

How to cut decorative edges that improve your projects

PILOT BIT (here, a beading cutter) can be used around the edge of either a square or free-form workpiece.

TYPICAL EDGES shaped using a pilot-type bit: rounded-over (quarter round) at top and beading.

ROMAN OGEE illustrates how flutes do the cutting as the pilot at bottom rides against the work edge.

LIPPED DOOR is formed using rounding-over bit on the outside edges and ⅜-in. rabbet cutter on inside.

How to handle circular work with no chance of error

TRAMMEL POINT is affixed at the desired radius on guide bar secured in router shoe; straight bit does the cutting. The decorative plaque (right) was created with a core-box bit set at various depths for the concentric circles.

Working with plastic laminates

1. SELF-EDGE is applied to the top and trimmed with a straight carbide bit. Type shown is solid, one-piece.

2. LAMINATE TOP is placed and trimmed, using the same cutter. See text for ways to prevent burns.

and spins at the same speed as the cutter—and then it will leave a burned line along the self-edge. The bearing *must* be free-spinning so it will rotate at the speed of router movement—*not the cutting flutes*.

Make sure that edges of the material to which the laminate will be cemented are square and true.

The self-edge is cut slightly larger than the surface to which it will be adhered; then affixed to the wood with contact cement. With the workpiece clamped to the workbench, the excess laminate is trimmed off with the straight bit.

Next, the top is bonded (again with slight

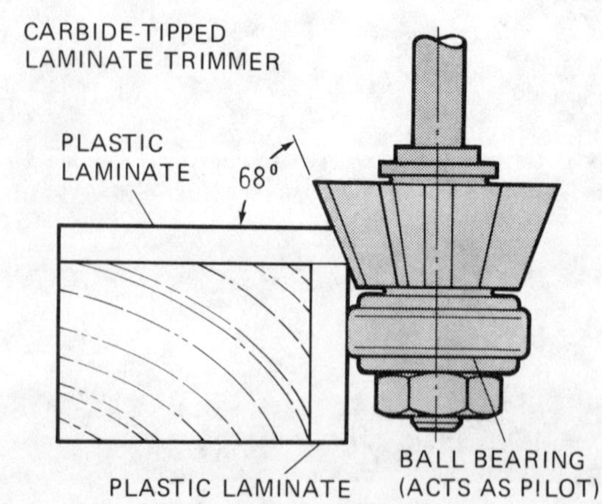

3. EDGE is finish-dressed with bevel. Ball-bearing type bit is also fitted with a carbide tip.

Dovetailing the easy way—with power

TO CUT DOVETAILS, you need a dovetail bit and template guide in router shoe and the dovetail template (below).

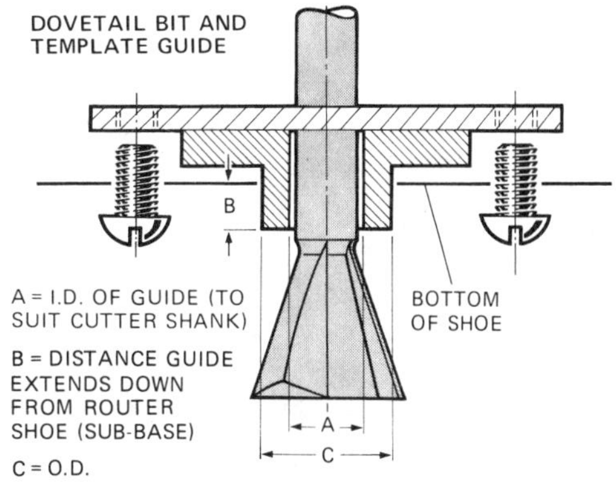

TEMPLATE GUIDE must be securely fastened to the router shoe and the bit set at the precise cutting depth.

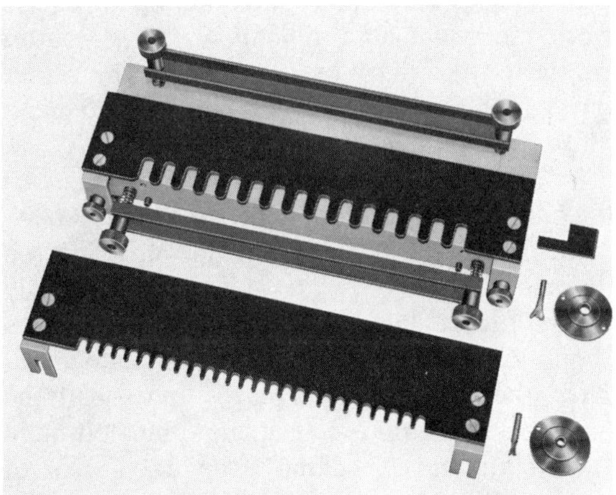

DOVETAIL TEMPLATE component parts: Notice that the main base is fastened to wood to provide clamping area.

overhang all around) and trimmed with the straight cutter. Finally, all edges are dressed with the bevel cutter. Beveling requires only a slight pass since very little stock is removed.

dovetail joints

One of the strongest joints in woodworking, the dovetail is widely used in commercial furniture-making. With the help of a dovetail template and a suitable template guide, your dovetail joints will soon rank with the best. No matter which brand of template and guide you buy, make certain you read and understand the manufacturer's instructions.

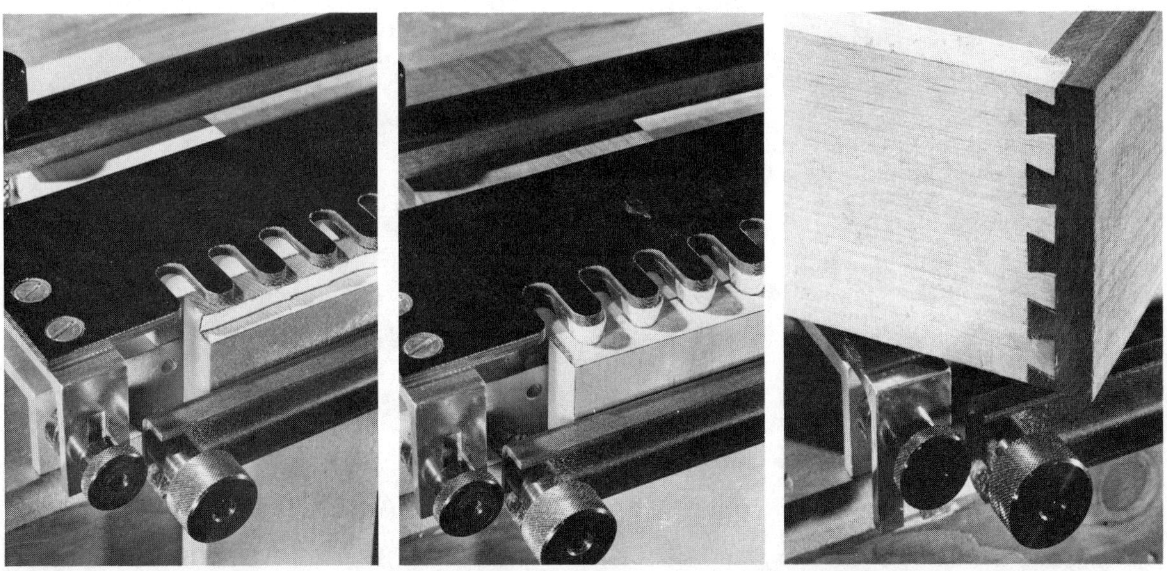

WITH BOTH PIECES clamped in the template, router is moved left to right along complete edge (to prevent splintering). Second pass is also left to right, following fingers. The work is then test-fitted (right).

Template routing

TEMPLATE CUTTING is done using a template guide and pattern cut slightly under the finish-work size.

Freehand routing

A REAL CHALLENGE for a creative craftsman, freehand routing is done without guides or templates.

To make dovetail joints, first install the template guide in the router sub-base. (Note: Since the method of affixing guides varies from maker to maker, buy guides of the same make as your router.) Next, with the router installed in the sub-base (shoe), insert the dovetail bit so it extends exactly $^{19}/_{32}$ in. below the router base.

The base of the dovetail template is always affixed to a piece of wood (or the workbench). Use fh screws in screwholes provided in the base. When clamped in position, the front (overhanging) apron of the base should butt against the front edge of the workbench or board (see photo, page 2477) fastened to the base.

With the template set up as instructed by the maker, always make a test dovetail joint first on scrap of the same material with which you will work. Make no mistake, dovetailing is precise work, so solve all problems—settings, cutter depth and the like—before pushing the router through your work. After obtaining a perfect cut on scrap, you can proceed on the work.

Since the boards are reversed after you make the cut, both boards are placed in the template with inside edges facing out and up. The top (horizontal) piece is first placed temporarily against the left-hand stop with its end extending about ½ in. beyond the main template base. Then, the second piece is placed underneath the finger template and against the other left-hand stop. At the same time, move the first piece until it is flush with the second (see photo, page 2477). When both pieces are perfectly lined up, tighten all template thumbscrews.

When making the dovetail cut, never move the router on or off the template with motor running; there's too high a risk of damaging the template with the cutter. And always make your first cut along the entire edge of the workpiece—without sliding in and out of the fingers—to prevent chipping the edge.

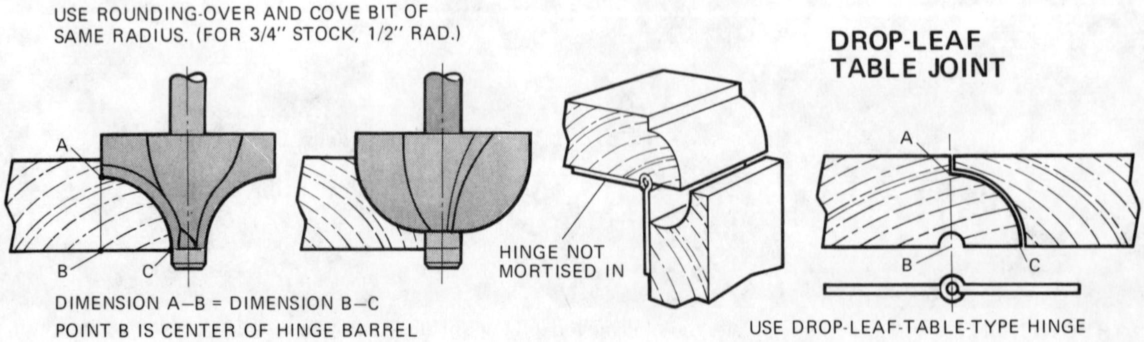

After moving the router from left to right for this first cut, shape the dovetails carefully, moving in and out of the fingers. Again, the router should be walked from left to right. After the cut is completed, turn off the router. When the cutter stops spinning, remove router from the work.

Remove the boards from the template and test the joint. If your test work on scrap was accurate, you should have a perfect joint. But if fit is loose, lower the bit slightly (perhaps 1/64 in.), replace boards in template and re-rout. (If tight, raise the bit by that distance.) Once the template and router are set to produce a perfect dovetail joint, any number of dovetails can be cut accurately. Rabbeted drawer fronts, as well as the joint shown in the photos on page 2607, can be dovetailed, too; it is necessary to reset the template stops, and you should refer to the manual packed with your template.

Special-purpose bits for experts

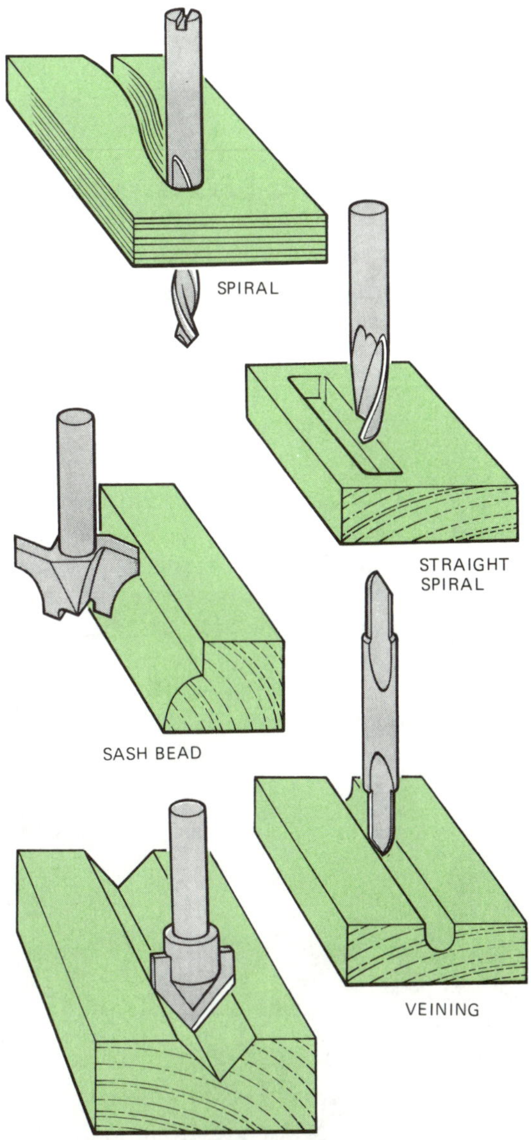

Technical Art by Peter Trojan

template routing

Template guides are available in various sizes. A typical one is shown at the top of page 2477. The B dimension of the guide must be less than the thickness of the template you are using or the router will not sit flat on the template. The i.d. of the guide (A) should be slightly larger than the diameter of the router bit to assure clearance. Work being cut will vary in size, by the distance between the cutting edge of the bit and the o.d. of the guide (C). Be sure to allow for this offset when cutting your template (master pattern).

To make the cut, clamp the template to the piece to be routed. With a straight bit in the router, plunge the spinning cutter into the work until the router base is flat on the template. Then, follow the pattern, making certain that the template guide is *always in contact with the pattern*. Since there is no wear and tear, the template can be saved for future use.

freehand routing

Once you've gained experience and confidence, you'll find the router an extremely efficient shaping and carving tool when used freehand. It can be used to turn out decorative items, lettered signs and the like in minimum time. Remember that the deeper the depth cut, the slower the rate of feed (there's more resistance to your movements).

You can rout out the design proper as illustrated in the photo on page 2478 or raise the design by routing out the backround. Frequently, in freehand routing it is a must to affix a long board to the router base so that the router will straddle the routed-out sections in the work. Simply cut the board to desired length, drill two holes to suit the router shoe and countersink them for screws.

drop-leaf table joint

A cove bit is used to make the concave cut on the table leaf; a rounding-over bit—of the same radius properly extended—makes the cut in the tabletop. Use a core-box bit for the barrel hinge mortise; its location must be precise. This is a tricky joint, so first test on scrap before routing the work.

How to repair body rust

There are two secrets to keeping your car's body looking new—keep it clean to prevent rust from starting and spreading, and patching to hide any rust spots which do show up

BODY RUST can make a car old before its time. This is particularly a problem in northern parts of the country, where ice and salt combine to rob a car of useful years of service.

Washing and waxing the body periodically will help get rid of elements that cause rust. In washing a car, play a heavy stream on the underbody, especially inside fender wells and underneath rocker panels. This will wash away road salt, a leading cause of rust.

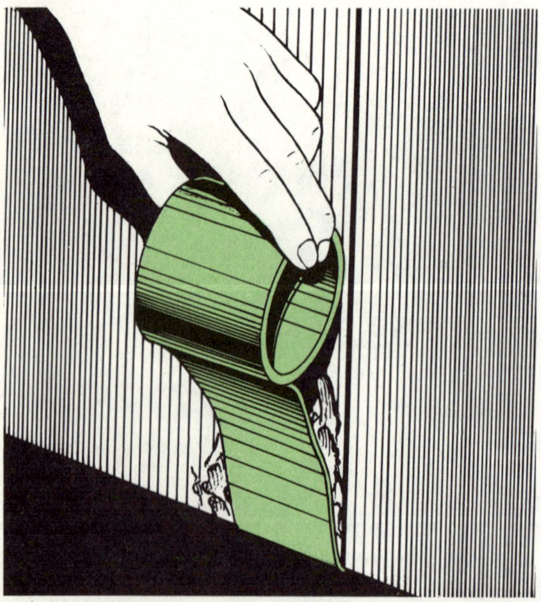

ALUMINUM TAPE and other material make possible body repair in the home garage.

SEE ALSO
Autos, body repair . . . Autos, maintenance . . . Body care, auto . . . Ramps, auto repair

If rust appears, it should be eliminated as soon as possible to keep it from spreading. Sand it down and touch up the spot with matching paint. In the case of extreme rust, where metal is eaten away, one of three repair methods may be employed, as follows:

1. Grind the rusted area until the rust is eliminated. Cover the spot with aluminum tape, which comes in 4-inch widths. See that the tape extends at least 1 inch beyond the damage and that edges of the tape adhere to the body.

Using a piece of 100-grit sandpaper, roughen the tape. Apply plastic body filler as directed in the instructions accompanying the body repair kit. Kits may be obtained at auto supply and accessories counters.

Use a Surform tool to mold the plastic body filler into shape. Then, sand the spot with 40-grit sandpaper which is held in a sanding block. Follow by sanding with a 100-grit sandpaper, again using a sanding block. Continue the sanding until the plastic material is even with the surface of the car body.

Using a piece of 220 wet-or-dry sandpaper and sanding block, feather the repaired area; that is, sand from the center of the area into the body. Keep the sandpaper wet and continue sanding until the repaired spot is just as smooth as the body. Paint the spot.

An auto supply and accessories dealer can help you match the color of the paint if you supply the correct code number. This number is included on the vehicle identification plate, which is attached to the firewall or door pillar.

This repair can be done by the home mechanic. It is effective, but not as long lasting as the other two methods.

2. Get a piece of sheet metal that is of the same gauge as the metal of the body (usually 20 or 22-gauge). This piece should be large enough to extend 1 inch beyond the rust area.

Grind the rust area until rust is eliminated. Attach the piece of sheet metal to the body. This can be done with Pop rivets.

Roughen the sheet metal with a grinding disc. Then, use a plastic filler kit and paint to complete the repair. When applying the plastic repair material, pay careful attention to the edges of the sheet. Use enough filler and feather it into the body. Otherwise the lines of the sheet metal will show.

Most home mechanics are capable of performing this repair, which is more effective than applying aluminum tape, but less effective than the third method.

3. Have a piece of sheet metal welded over the area after grinding off rust. The metal should be the same gauge as the body. A machine shop or auto body shop can do this for you.

With the metal in place, complete the repair yourself using a plastic filler kit and paint.

Use touch-up paint to cover any nicks as soon as you spot them, and keep a good protective coating of wax on your car's body and you'll minimize the time you have to spend on body repair!

This is the only way to stay ahead of the corro-

APPLY PLASTIC body filler and use a Surform to mold materials and remove excess.

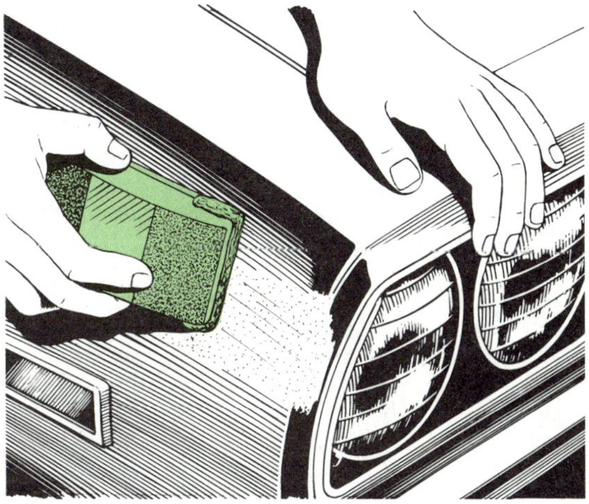

METICULOUS SANDING is critical and you should use a block to prevent raggedness.

sion that shortens your car's life. You've got to become a fanatic about body care! Wash your car at least once a week to get off the surface dirt that holds pollutants against the finish. When you make it a habit to keep your car free of dirt, you'll find that it's easier to detect spots of tar, bird droppings, nicks and other road crud before they get their teeth into your finish.

Simply keeping your car *clean* will preserve its life, and preserve its appeal to you as the years go by. For some, washing is all the care they give the modern finishes on their automobiles. Others, however, use cleaners and waxes to take off the oxidized layer of paint, expose the car's true color and lay on a protective film that will shape those raindrops into big beautiful beads.

You've got your choice of various cleaners and waxes to do the job—from liquids, sprays and presoftened pastes to wax-impregnated cloths. Many car owners have tried all of these types at one time or another, looking for the best one to suit their needs. Many car buffs stock several different types of waxes so they can do a quick job or a real elbow-grease job depending on how much time they have.

You should polish one section at a time using a circular motion to apply the wax and making sure to overlap sufficiently. Your cloth will slowly become the color of your car as you rub off dead paint, so turn the cloth over frequently. When the wax is dry, it will haze on the surface and is then ready to be removed with a clean cloth and the surface buffed to a high shine. Again, fold the cloth frequently, as it becomes glazed with dead paint.

If you don't keep a clean machine with a regimen of "spit and polish" you'll soon find yourself driving a rust bucket.

How to use a sabre saw

By ROSARIO CAPOTOSTO

THE VERSATILE sabre saw can do practically any cutting job that can be done with a handsaw, jigsaw, bandsaw or even table and radial-arm saws—within limits of course. Circular-type saws can only cut in straight lines, while band and jigsaws can only handle materials as wide as the depth of their throat permits. In fact, certain jobs can only be done effectively with the sabre saw.

A wide variety of blades is available for cutting ferrous and nonferrous metal, wood, plastic, mineral and composition materials. For problem materials, such as ceramic tile, slate, cast stone and brick, a special blade edged with tungsten carbide grit is available. There is also a knife blade for cutting fibrous and rigid foam insulating materials, leather, rubber, cardboard, ceiling tile and wallboard. Most blades will fit all brands of saws.

SEE ALSO

Bench saws . . . Circular saws, portable . . . Power hacksaws . . . Power-tool maintenance . . . Power-tool stands . . . Radial-arm saws

For cutting woodwork, there are two basic kinds of blades: set tooth and hollow ground. Set blades have teeth which point alternately to each side. The set serves to cut a kerf wider than the back of the blade to allow it to pass through the cut without binding. Teeth of a hollow ground blade have no set—they're all in a line. However, the sides of the blade are tapered towards the back to provide clearance. Set teeth cut fast, but leave a rougher edge than the slower cutting hol-

BLADES—number is teeth per inch. From left: 32 light gauge metal, 24 standard metal, 14 nonferrous metal, 20 wood scrolling, 7 wood roughing, 10 taper ground-wood, 12 reverse tooth-wood, flush cut, 3 wood rough, knife.

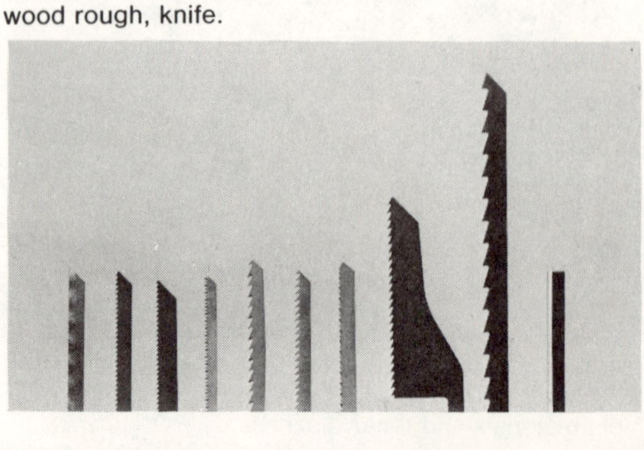

FLUSH-CUT blade aligns with shoe front, lets you cut to a vertical plane; especially good for floors.

A 6-IN. BLADE with 3 TPI (teeth per inch) is good for cutting through a 4x4. Use medium speed.

AT HIGH SPEED, A 32-TPI blade cuts sheet metal much quicker than could be done with snips.

LONG CURVES can best be cut with a flexible guidestrip (about ½ x ¾-in.) tacked in an offset position.

MAKE A pivot guide for cutting circles. This long one will reach beyond range of accessory guides.

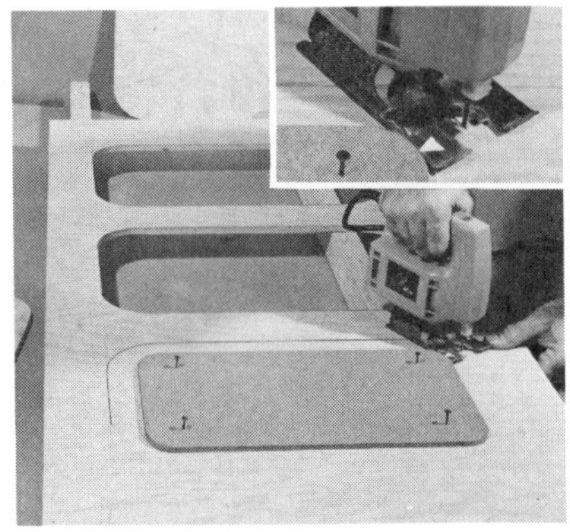

MASKING TAPE arrow on shoe (inset), aligned with blade teeth, keeps constant radius on curves.

low ground blade. The number of teeth per inch (TPI) is another factor—the more TPI, the slower and smoother the cut.

When working with wood heavier than ¼-in., it is advisable to use a blade of ample width because narrow blades have a tendency to flex and drift off vertical. For any guided saw techniques shown, a set tooth blade is strongly recommended to get true cuts.

Cut with the wrong (back) side of workpiece facing up whenever possible. This is a good policy because blades usually cut on the upstroke, causing slight splintering—especially when sawing plywood. The exception is when using a reverse tooth blade—it cuts on the downstroke and makes right-side-up work possible.

Always clamp small pieces of work for safety and accuracy. The nature of the cutting action sets up considerable vibration.

It's wise to start your saw before touching the blade to the work. If the saw has variable speed, start the cut at low speed. It is often possible to start the cut by entering from the edge of the workpiece. When an inside or pocket cut is desired, the blade can be started in a predrilled hole. For a rectangular-shaped pocket, drill a hole at each corner and then make straight cuts from hole to hole. If a straightedge (or pivot guide for circular cutouts) is to be used to obtain a precise outline, the size of the blade entry hole must be big enough to let the blade rest almost flush to the circumference of the hole.

Making a plunge cut is the alternative method for starting an interior cut and doesn't require a predrilled blade entry hole. Use a short, stout blade and tilt the saw forward so it rests on the front of the shoe with the blade not touching the work. Hold the saw firmly, turn to full speed and then slowly pivot the saw back to allow the blade to cut its way in. When the arc is completed and the base rests firmly on the work, advance saw to make the cut.

Intricate scrollwork calls for a narrow scrolling blade with 12 to 20 TPI and 3/16 in. width. To support the work best, place it onto two lengths of 2x4 (set on edge) on the worktable. The 3½-in.

BASIC FREEHAND CUTS WITH VERSATILE SABRE SAW

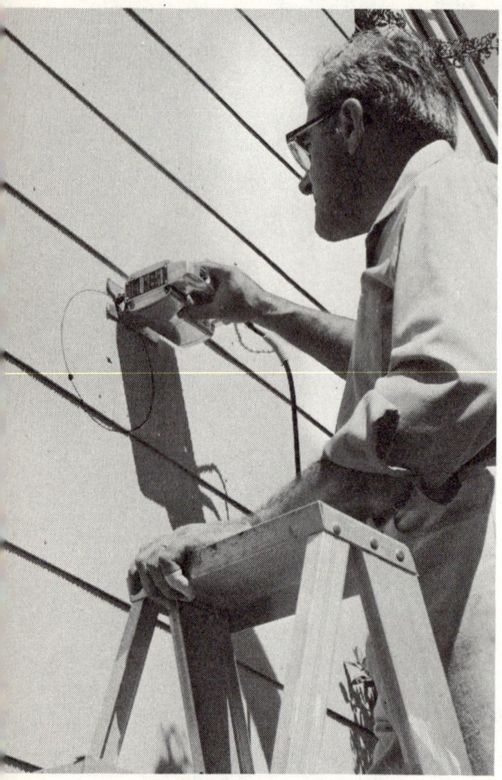

CUT ROUGH openings for soffit vents, louvers, stovepipes and more.

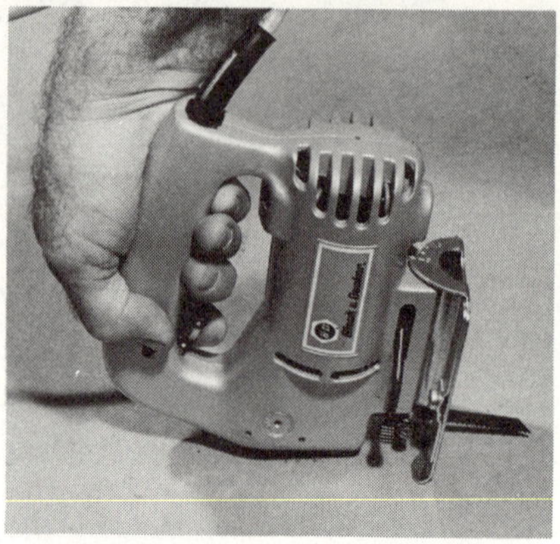

FOR PLUNGE CUT, use short, stout blade. Pivot blade into wood.

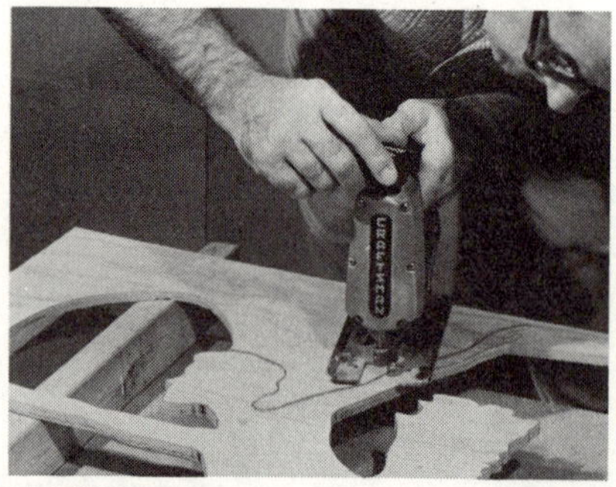

TO MINIMIZE vibration damage, hands and feet of figure are cut last.

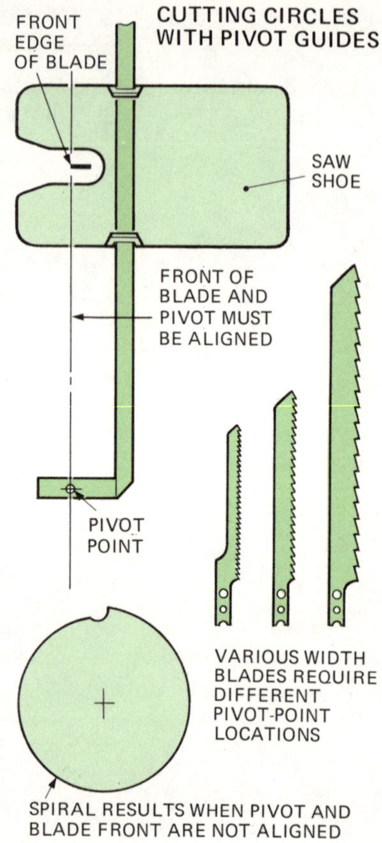

TO MAKE GUIDE for oversize circle cut, use steel with same thickness and width as bar of accessory guide. Fold to form at one end and drill the pivot holes for various blade widths.

standoff allows clearance for the blade. If the work has a delicate pattern, try to leave some uncut bridges in the waste area until the main parts have been cut.

Handy cross lap joints are advantageous for assembling large structural members and easy to make with a sabre saw. If the parts are to cross at other than right angles, determine the angle and tilt the saw shoe (or base) accordingly. Lock base into position and make double parallel cuts equal to the thickness of the stock, halfway through the planks. Chisel out the waste.

For smaller assemblies such as partitions for cabinets and built-ins, the same joint at right angles can be used. This should not be done freehand. Tack or clamp two straightedge strips of wood to the work, separated by the thickness of the work plus width of the shoe, less thickness of the blade. Run the saw along both sides of the guide strips halfway through the work and then remove the waste.

Making accurate rip or cross cuts requires an accessory guide for narrow widths and a straightedge guide for wider cuts. Clamp or tack-nail straightedge guide parallel to the line of cut (see photo).

Perfect circles are a cinch to cut with a sabre saw, but imperfect ones can easily result if you're not careful. T-shaped accessory rip guides are designed to also serve as circle guides. A nail driven through a hole in the crossbar support allows the saw to pivot in an arc. A blade entry hole tangent to the line of cut and in the waste area gets the blade started. Circle guides will work properly only if the front edge of the teeth and pivot point are equidistant from the support bar (see diagram).

The best way to cut *long sweeping curves* is with a sabre saw and a flexible wooden guide. Use a thin strip of wood, about ½ x ¾-in., bent to desired curve and tacked (on edge) to the workpiece. Position the guide so the saw will ride against the inside of the curve. Keep front and rear corners of the saw base in contact with the guide as you saw.

Template sawing economizes on both labor and lumber—and at the same time produces perfectly fitted flush doors or drawer fronts on plywood constructions such as bunk beds, cabinets and built-ins. Lay out the area to be cut by first measuring the distance between the shoe edge and the side of the blade. Double this figure and subtract it from the length and width of the desired opening.

Use these new dimensions to make the template from ¼-in. hardboard or plywood and round the corners to the desired radius. Next, center and tack the template over the opening area. Bore a blade entry hole equal to the thickness of the blade and centered on a straight segment of the line to be cut. Elongate the hole with a coping saw blade, just enough for the blade to be inserted. Place a masking tape arrow on the shoe's edge precisely opposite the blade teeth. Insert the saw blade and start the cut with the saw base pressed against the template edge. When you get to a corner curve, do not sharply pivot the saw. Instead, slowly advance it, keeping arrow point in contact with curved edge of the template.

Mortising jig is made by cutting an opening in a piece of hardboard or plywood. The width is determined by adding the saw base width to the width of the desired mortise and subtracting the thickness of the blade. The length of the jig opening is determined by adding the length of the mortise to the length of the shoe and subtracting the width of the blade. The rectangular jig can be made in two sections consisting of a U shape and a straight back piece. Bore a blade entry hole as wide as the slot near one end of the proposed mortise. Tack the jig into position so it will put the blade on one of the lines of cut. Insert the saw and make two forward cuts with saw base alternately pressed against each side of the jig. Make repeated cuts to clear out waste.

To square the end, slide the saw laterally against the jigs front. To cut out back of slot, reverse the blade so teeth point to the rear. Return saw to the jig and repeat cuts by pushing the saw backward.

CUTTING BEVELS—EVEN IN HEAVY STOCK

SHOE PLATE on most saws rotates between 45° and 90°.

ANGLED CROSSLAP joint is strong, easy to cut. Chisel away waste.

CONTROLLED CUTS WITH GUIDES AND TEMPLATES

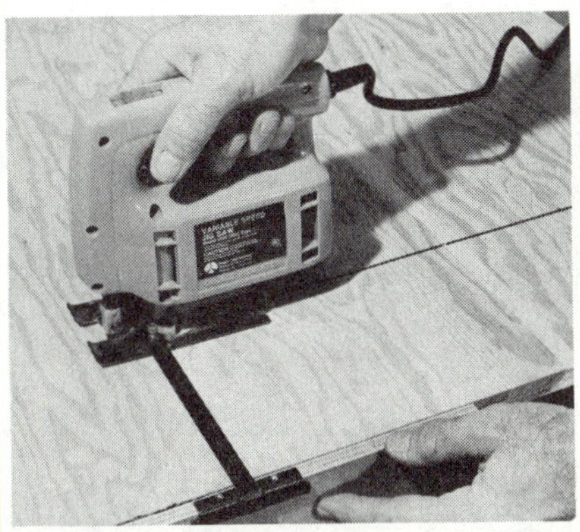

TO MODIFY accessory rip guide, add wood strip for sure contact with work.

CLAMPED-ON straightedge guides should extend beyond both ends.

MORTISING TECHNIQUE WITH TEMPLATE

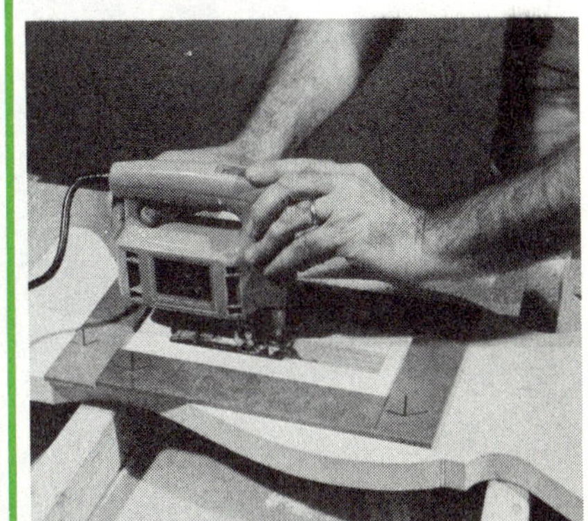

RECTANGULAR hardboard jig permits accurate mortising in table leg.

WITH BLADE reversed, saw is pushed backward to complete mortise.

A 'table saw' from your sabre saw

By WALTER E. BURTON

NUMEROUS SMALL sawing jobs often create handling problems that are as large as those you face when you're single-handedly maneuvering a 4x8 sheet of ¾-inch particleboard. From time to time, many woodworkers are challenged with the task of sabre-saw cutting a piece of board that's just too small to be clamped or to be held securely by hand. And for such small jobs as cutting thin strips from veneers and plywoods less than ½-inch thick a table saw is actually too big. One way to overcome such irritating challenges is with the use of the shop-built sabre-saw table shown below.

While this fixture was designed to accommodate a Model 68 Rockwell tool, you can alter the dimensions to suit any make and model of sabre saw (also known as a portable jigsaw).

Because a portable jigsaw cuts on its upstroke, the material being sawed must be held firmly against the saw platform. This is accomplished by a screw (bolt) that operates a parallel-bar arrangement, and through "cushioning" by a coil spring.

This ingenious table is built mostly of plywood. You'll find it easy to assemble if you follow the construction details shown.

First, attach the parallel-bar unit to the base panel with No. 8 fh screws running downward. Notice that the screwheads are flush with the bar surface. Secure the saw-platform supporting block with four ¼ x 5-in. carriage bolts (you may find that three bolts will be adequate). Wood screws installed from the bottom anchor the block in which the table-control screw operates.

The size of the saw cleanout opening is not critical; a 4x6-in. aperture will be adequate. The table is supported on furniture glide "feet," thus there is no need to countersink the screwheads into the bottom.

SEE ALSO

**Bench saws . . . Motors, shop . . .
Power-tool stands . . . Table saws**

Glue together several 3⅞ x 7-in. pieces to form a platform supporting block that is about 3¹/₁₆ in. high. You'll find that a little testing will be in order to determine the height preferable for you. (When the table is at maximum height, it can be no closer than the thickness of the work-guide bar: on the stand shown, ⅛ in.)

Attach the four 10-in.-long bars to two pivot blocks with four wood screws. It's important to space these screws uniformly to assure accurate movement of the parallel bars. Fasten the work-support table to the parallel-bar unit with screws that run upward through the top bars, but not through the tabletop. The saw slot should be positioned after the stand has been assembled with the sabre saw in place.

The saw rests in a rectangular opening and is supported by a thin metal plate. Cut the plate slightly longer than the width of the plywood platform so that the front and rear edges can be bent slightly upward. Then you can anchor the saw in its recess with four L-shape clips secured with screws. The shorter ends of the clips will press downward on top of the saw base when the screws are tightened.

The table-height control was made from a ⁵/₁₆-18 x 4-in. bolt, with a rod crosswise through the head for easier turning without a wrench. The coil spring between the head and the block enables the table to "give" slightly and serves as

HOLES ARE BORED simultaneously through the saw platform and through the supporting block. The platform is secured temporarily with two nails.

COMPONENT PARTS, parallel-bar unit, saw-platform-supporting block and adjusting-screw block are all firmly attached to the baseboard of ¾-in. plywood.

BY REMOVING two pivot screws from the parallel-bar unit, the upper bars can be easily swung up for installation or removal of the table.

WORK GUIDE BAR is adjustable across the table and is locked in position with a special wingbolt which presses against front edge of the table when tightened.

SHEET-ALUMINUM plate that supports the sabre saw is fastened to the bottom of the saw platform with eight tiny fh screws turned into countersunk holes.

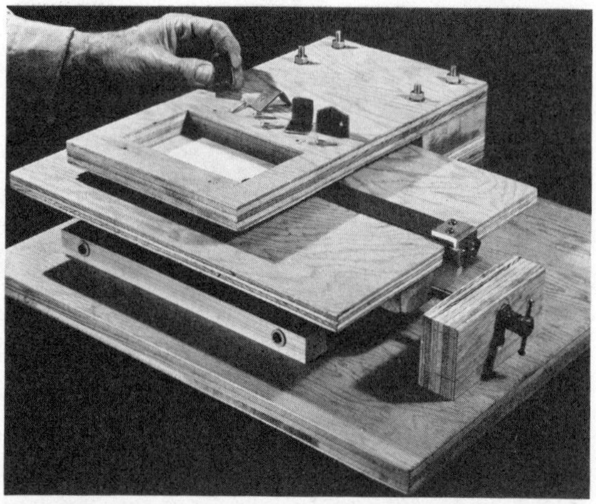

SABRE-SAW BASE is anchored to the platform with four L-shaped metal clips spaced along the sides of the rectangular recess. Clips are attached with rh screws.

HERE'S HOW work is fed into the saw by passing it under saw-supporting platform and along the guide bar. Saw handles work to ½ in. thick and 6 in. wide.

an aid in preventing binding. A dab of oil or grease will lubricate the bolt in the threaded hole of the maple block. By turning the bolt in or out, you can raise or lower the table. The bolt moves up or down with the table and automatically adjusts itself in the slot of the block that's fixed to the base.

To use the stand, push material past the saw blade much the same as on a conventional table saw. Overhang of the saw platform and the table helps to shield the blade, while pusher sticks are used to move the work past the blade and out the rear of the opening between table and saw platform. The work-guide bar must be clamped securely enough not to yield under pressure applied to workpiece.

BASE

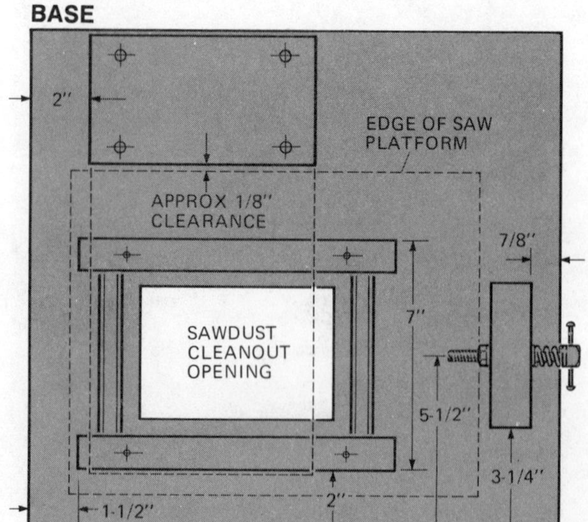

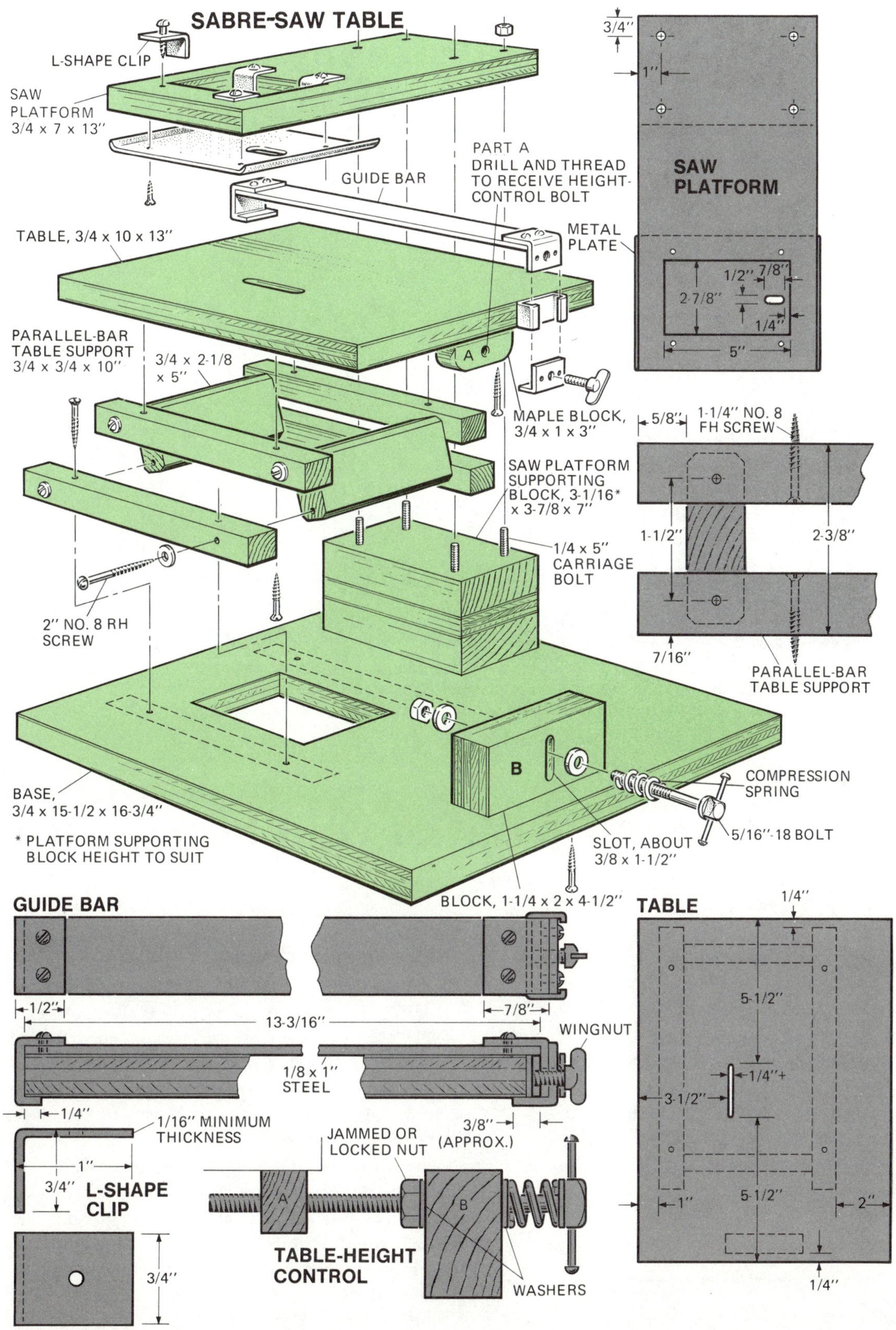
SABRE-SAW TABLE
L-SHAPE CLIP
SAW PLATFORM 3/4 x 7 x 13"
GUIDE BAR
PART A DRILL AND THREAD TO RECEIVE HEIGHT-CONTROL BOLT
TABLE, 3/4 x 10 x 13"
METAL PLATE
PARALLEL-BAR TABLE SUPPORT 3/4 x 3/4 x 10"
3/4 x 2-1/8 x 5"
A
MAPLE BLOCK, 3/4 x 1 x 3"
SAW PLATFORM SUPPORTING BLOCK, 3-1/16* x 3-7/8 x 7"
1/4 x 5" CARRIAGE BOLT
2" NO. 8 RH SCREW
B
COMPRESSION SPRING
5/16"-18 BOLT
SLOT, ABOUT 3/8 x 1-1/2"
BASE, 3/4 x 15-1/2 x 16-3/4"
* PLATFORM SUPPORTING BLOCK HEIGHT TO SUIT
BLOCK, 1-1/4 x 2 x 4-1/2"
SAW PLATFORM
3/4"
1"
1/2"
7/8"
2-7/8"
1/4"
5"
5/8"
1-1/4" NO. 8 FH SCREW
1-1/2"
2-3/8"
7/16"
PARALLEL-BAR TABLE SUPPORT
GUIDE BAR
1/2"
7/8"
13-3/16"
WINGNUT
1/8 x 1" STEEL
1/4"
3/8" (APPROX.)
1/16" MINIMUM THICKNESS
1"
3/4"
L-SHAPE CLIP
3/4"
JAMMED OR LOCKED NUT
A
B
TABLE-HEIGHT CONTROL
WASHERS
TABLE
1/4"
5-1/2"
1/4"+
3-1/2"
1"
5-1/2"
2"
1/4"

FOLLOW GOOD SAFETY practices with a radial-arm saw: Use goggles to protect eyes from flying particles; wear earmuff-type protectors to reduce saw screech to a safe level; keep sleeves buttoned, and hold work securely. Keep your thumb clearly out of the way as you slowly and steadily pull the saw blade through the work.

Take the hazards out of your home shop

By JOSEPH R. PROVEY

■ HIGH-SPEED cutting edges, kicked-back objects, short circuits and slippery floors do not cause shop accidents—*you* do. Realizing this fact is the biggest step you can take toward making your shop a healthy place in which to work. Once you begin to adopt safe practices and a positive attitude toward safety, old accident-prone habits will begin to die. Your work will probably become more accurate and you will enjoy your time in the shop more.

SEE ALSO
Alarms, smoke . . . Fire extinguishers . . . Wiring, electrical . . . Workbenches . . . Workshops

living with power tools

According to the U.S. Consumer Product Safety Commission (CPSC), 17,000 persons each year are treated for injuries associated with electrically activated drills, sanders, routers, lathes, grinders, jointers, planers, shapers, welders and soldering guns. Power saws, however, are by far the most likely power tool to be involved in a severe shop accident—approximately 37,000 injuries are reported by hospitals annually. Most are a result of either contact with the blade, electrocution and shock, or projectiles from the material being worked with, usually wood. Investigations prove that most of these mishaps didn't "just happen." Only *you* can take the precautions necessary to prevent them. Learning a few simple rules and techniques and then following them

SET BLADE depth as shown for safe cutting. The guard is removed for photo clarity only.

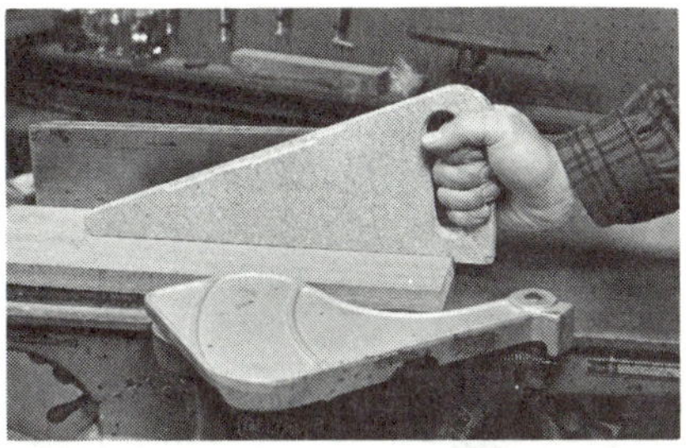

A PUSH BLOCK is a must for safety when planing the face of thin stock. It will also improve your work.

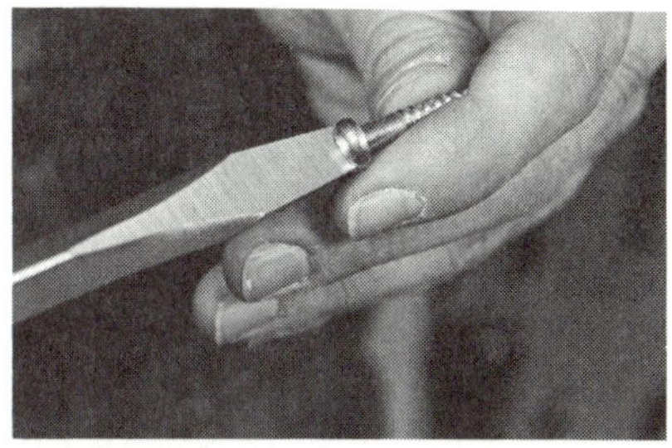

CHOOSING the right screwdriver prevents damage to workpiece, blisters and unnecessary strain.

CLAMPING workpieces securely in a vise or to the workbench will make cutting them easier and safer.

WHEN USING sidewall of grinding wheel, protect your eyes and face from flying fragments.

CARRY PORTABLE power tools with fingers off the activating switch to prevent inadvertent start-ups.

PERSONAL SAFEGUARDS

The most expensive tool imaginable is worthless next to you—and yet the most mistreated and abused "machine" in many home shops is the human body. The products shown here (and throughout this article) represent a small investment when compared to the money you are apt to pay for health care and insurance. It's foolhardy not to acquire a basic inventory that includes such items as goggles, face shield, a supply of lens cleaner and tissue, muff or plug-type ear protectors, dust mask and respirator with appropriate filter replacements, work gloves and other specialty items necessary for jobs you're likely to do.

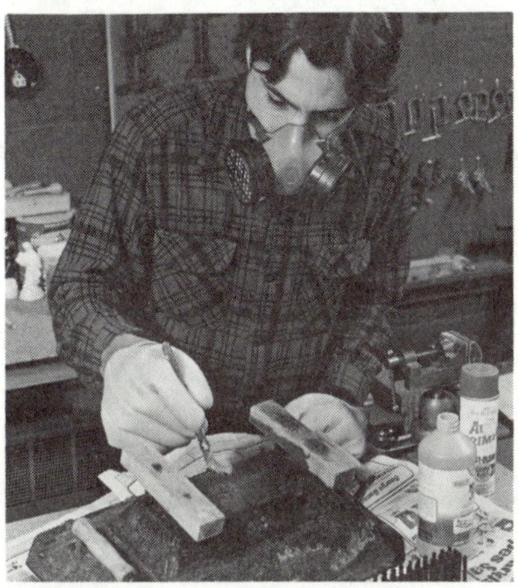

RESPIRATOR and neoprene gloves prevent lung and skin absorption of toxic mists, vapors and compounds.

DUST MASK keeps dust from sanding operations out of your lungs. Wash and/or replace filters as needed.

COMMON SHOP eye gear is most important (clockwise from top in near photo): face shield, impact goggles, welding cup goggles, chemical splash goggles. Far right, plastic box keeps shop first-aid kit dry and dust-free. One like it should be found in every shop. Included in this one are tweezers, scissors, rubbing alcohol, disinfectant, bandages.

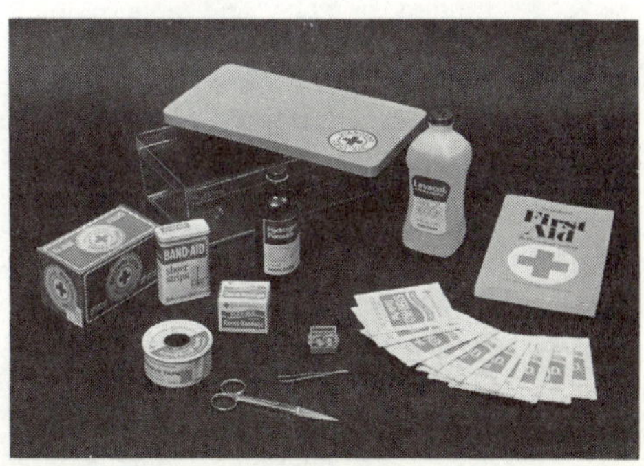

every time will help take the hazards out of your shop.

1. Study the rule box that is part of this article and post safety reminders wherever you feel they may help. For instance, a sign saying, REMOVE CHUCK KEY, posted at your drill press—may keep you from being hit by a ricocheting key if you pay attention and notice it after tightening a bit in the drill chuck.

hand tool savvy

Hand tools are involved in the majority of shop accidents. More than 30,000 people received hospital emergency room treatment for hammer injuries last year alone. Screwdrivers, manual saws, drills and chisels were not far behind. Aside from hammer-and-thumb type slips caused by miscalculation or loss of concentration, many were the result of misuse and poor technique.

2. Choose the right tool for the job. Improvisation, however ingenious, can lead to danger. Study your hand tools' capabilities and learn their limitations as well. Read relevant literature and make practice runs when performing an unfamiliar operation. Seek personalized instruction when necessary. Three booklets on the *Proper Uses and Common Abuses of: Striking and Struck Tools; Screwdrivers, Vises, Clamps, Snips, Tool Boxes;* and *Wrenches and Pliers,* can be obtained from the Hand Tools Institute, 331 Madison Ave., 10017 for a small charge. Take the time to send for these and read them. Most important of all, practice the safety hints given in them.

3. Well-maintained hand tools shorten job time and are safer to work with. A modest investment in a grinder—or even just in manual jigs for sharpening twist drills and chisels—will keep you from forcing a dull tool to accomplish a task.

4. When things start going wrong, take a break. Don't let yourself be pressured into trying a quick, often disastrous, remedy. Impatience causes accidents. Fatigue is another reason to take a break. When you are tired your reaction time is slower and your eye-hand coordination begins to decline.

5. One of the most severe hand tool accidents occurs when metal is struck against metal and a chip, such as a nailhead, flies into the eye. The importance of protective eyewear cannot be overemphasized.

design a safe shop environment

While a good project design is usually the first concern of serious craftsmen, the design of their shops is often given little thought. Check the following safety criteria.

6. Comfort is critical to safety and efficiency. Keep your shop at a good working temperature. I prefer about 60° F. A shop that's too warm tends to make you drowsy and tire more easily. Choose a shop heater with care and follow the maker's instructions when installing. Some gas-fired garage heaters, for example, must be vented to be safe.

7. Adequate lighting also raises your shop's comfort—and safety—index. Use at least two 33-in., 25-watt fluorescent tubes, mounted about 4-ft. above each work station. Baffles and louvers, like the egg-crate designs, reduce glare. As an alternative to fluorescents, use a 150-watt, R-40 flood or spot lamp (with reflector built in) with an adjustable holder. Clamp it so no glare or shadows fall on the work.

RULES FOR AVOIDING POWER TOOL ACCIDENTS

- Be sure electric tools are double-insulated or grounded. A ground fault interrupter is the best protection.
- "Idiotproof" your shop—if it's accessible to untrained persons and young children—by keeping blades and other sharp accessories out of reach. Install central switch for turning off power to shop circuit and lock it when you leave.
- Wear appropriate personal protective equipment. Dress comfortably in snug fitting clothing or use a shop apron. Remove jewelry and secure long hair. Do not wear gloves—they can be snagged by cutters, blades and drive belts.
- Plan your setup carefully: Jigs, clamps, fences and guides, used correctly, make the job easier and safer.
- Keep all guards, shields and antikickback devices in place and in operating condition. Replace fatigued springs which no longer snap guards back.
- Remove chuck keys and wrenches before turning on power. To make this a habit, create a handy place to hang or store them.
- Be aware of your hands and body. Use a push stick or planing block on narrow or thin work. Never overextend your reach. Stand aside while starting motors—and stand clear of the path of potential kickbacks.
- Keep power cords out of the way. Keep (and store) extension cords away from oil, heat and sharp objects.
- Wait until blades or bits are completely stopped before making adjustments. Unplug tool to prevent inadvertent start-ups.

ANTIFATIGUE mats placed at work stations are great leg savers—especially if your shop has a concrete floor.

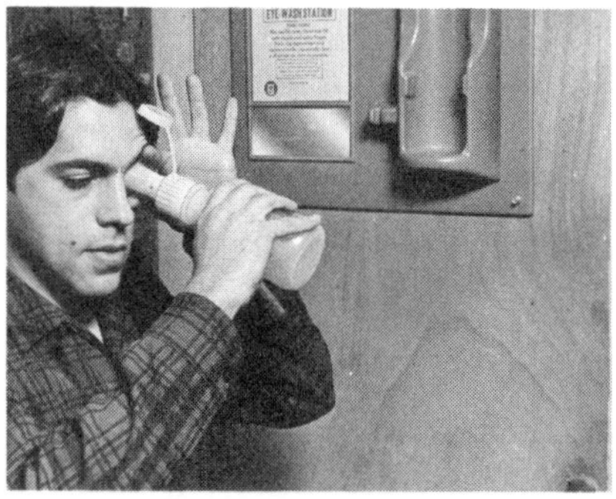

AUTHOR demonstrates eyewash bottle—a precaution in addition to goggles.

CONTAINER for oily wastes confines highly combustible material until it can be safely removed from the shop.

KEEP BARE bulbs from shattering with clear or low-glare safety globes.

PRESSURE GAUGE on extinguisher (left) indicates when it needs to be recharged. Remote signaling detectors (right) with bedside alarm are ideal for shops that are out of earshot. A smoke detector is a must in any shop.

Paint walls and ceilings with light, low-gloss washable colors. Keep bulbs and bulb covers clean. Add protective plastic sleeves to fluorescent tubes to contain glass fragments and gas should the tube be broken.

importance of fresh air

8. Place wall-mounted louvers or an exhaust fan opposite an operable window. A power vent and a supply of fresh air are musts in rooms used for painting and finishing to prevent fire or explosion. Be sure pilot lights, for a gas furnace or hot-water heater, are off when spraying or using flammable materials. Good ventilation (and an appropriate respirator) also prevent inhalation of toxic fumes. Many chemical products are very hazardous—so heed manufacturers' cautions. For example, an ingredient in some paint removers, methylene chloride, forms carbon monoxide in the blood if inhaled.

9. Empty sawdust and combustible waste at the end of every workday. Remember to keep all oily rags in a covered container to prevent spontaneous combustion.

10. Obtain two all-purpose fire extinguishers. Mount one in a central location and the other near an escape route—not next to flammable materials where you might not be able to reach it during a fire.

11. Study your shop floor plan. Does the traffic pattern allow easy, free movement? If not, can it be rearranged? Can unnecessary clutter be removed? A real danger is being startled while you work. Can you rearrange power tools so you face the direction of likely approach? If not, consider locking the door while you work—although this has drawbacks if you work alone.

In any case, act now to take the hazard out of your shop. Don't leave your welfare to chance.

Sailboat from a pram

Convert your pram to a mini-sailer. The result is an easy-to-sail trainer that is ideal for any age

By STUART JAMES

■ MINIMUM EFFORT and expense can quickly convert an 8-foot plywood pram from rowboat into a sailing yacht. No major modifications are necessary, and the result can be fun for a skipper

ANY AGE can get sailing satisfaction from this mini-rig on an 8-ft. pram.

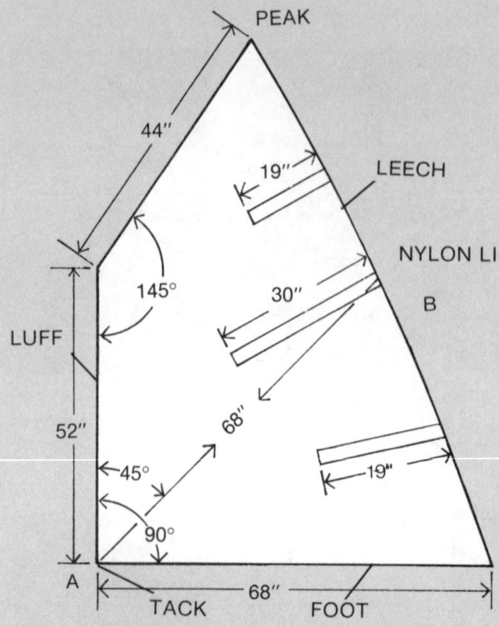

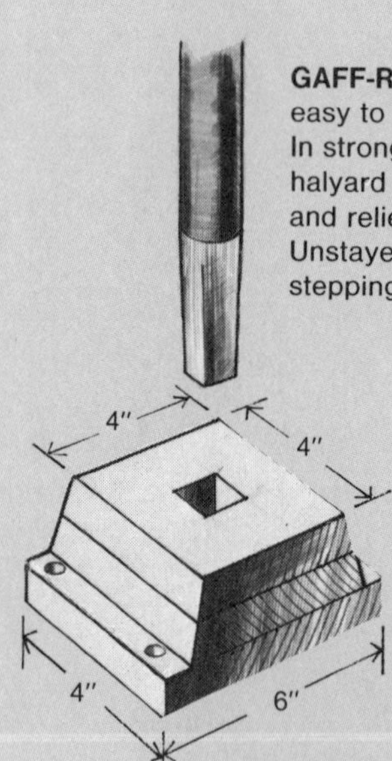

GAFF-RIGGED sail is easy to cut and control. In strong winds, peak halyard can drop gaff and relieve pressure. Unstayed mast simplifies stepping and rigging.

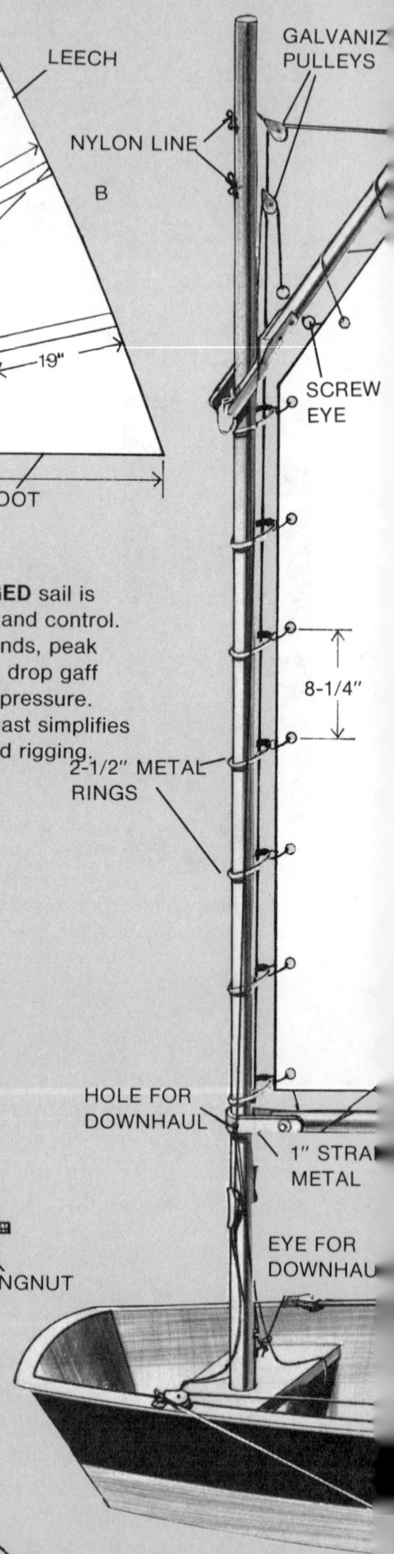

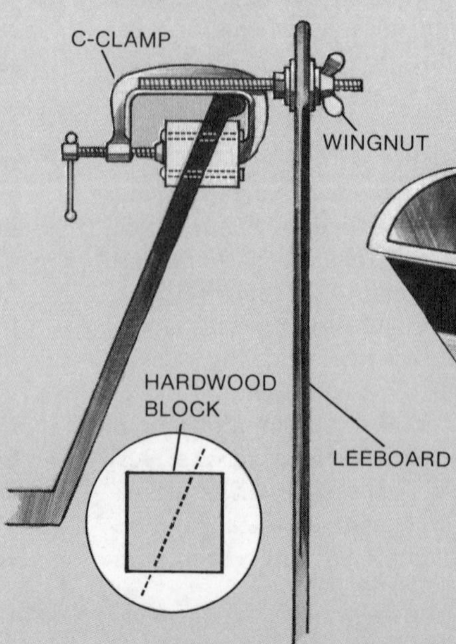

SEE ALSO

Accident prevention, water . . . Boat camping . . . Boating, safety . . . Boating, storage . . . Planing speed, boats . . . Pontoon boats . . . Repairs, boat

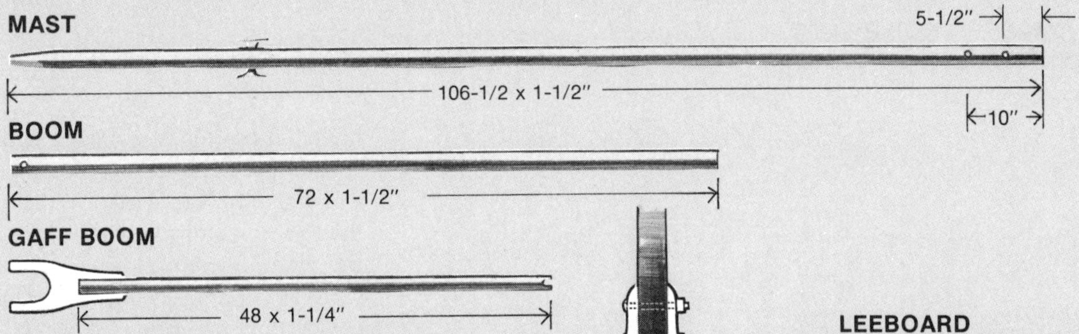

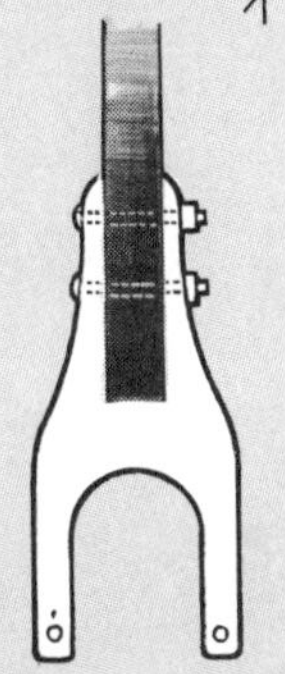

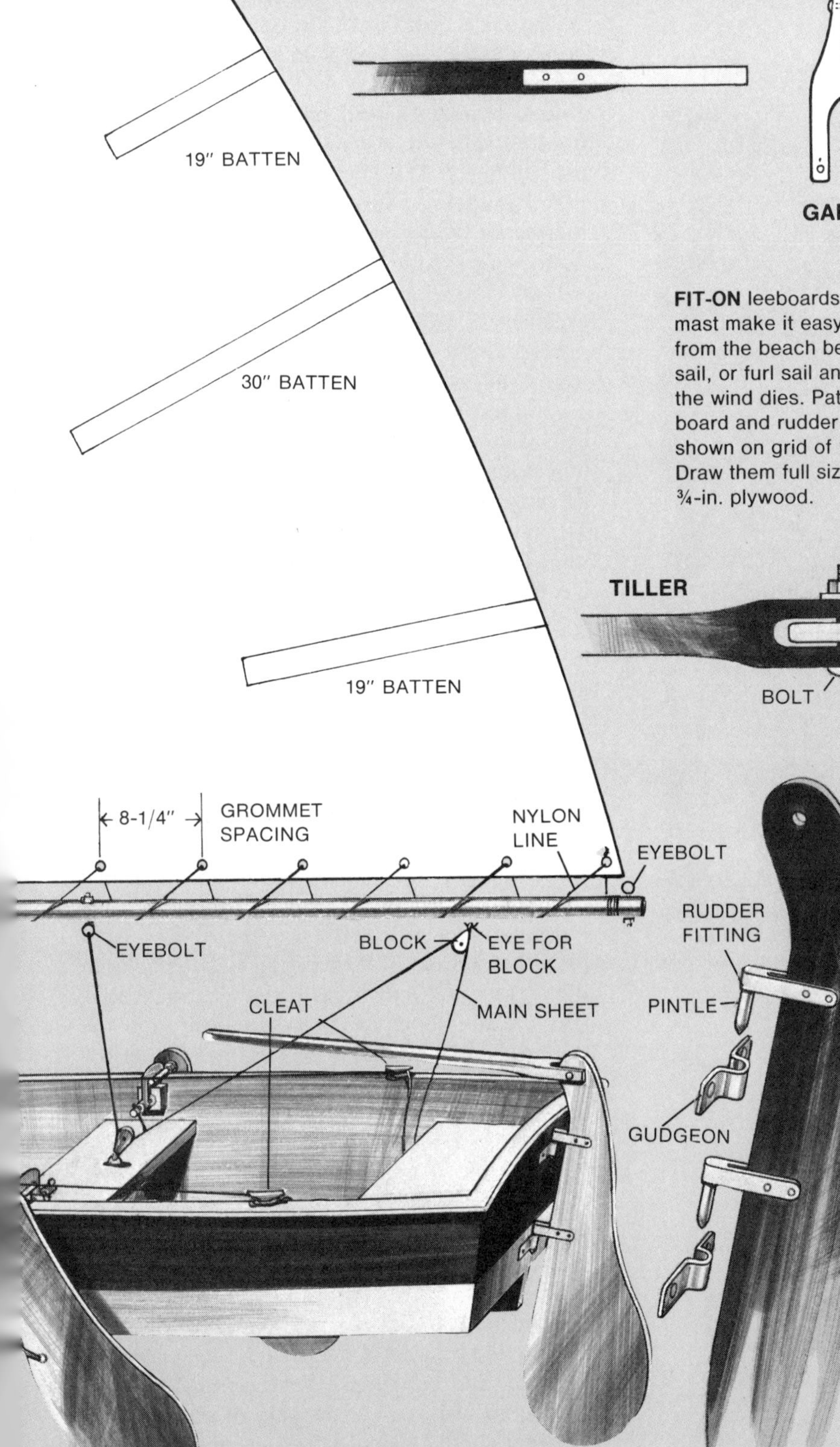

FIT-ON leeboards, rudder and mast make it easy to row out from the beach before setting sail, or furl sail and row home if the wind dies. Patterns for leeboard and rudder (right) are shown on grid of 1-in. squares. Draw them full size for cutting ¾-in. plywood.

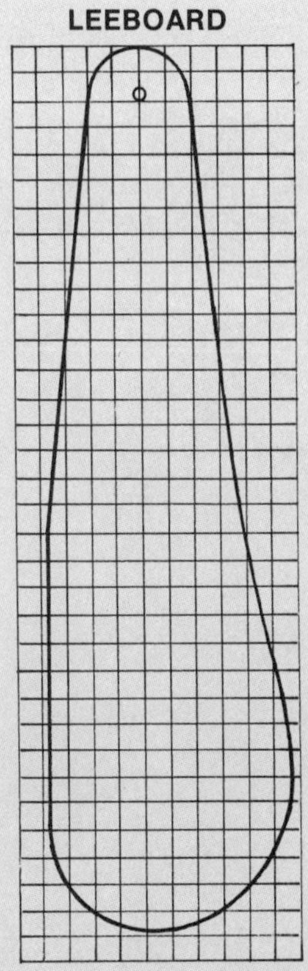

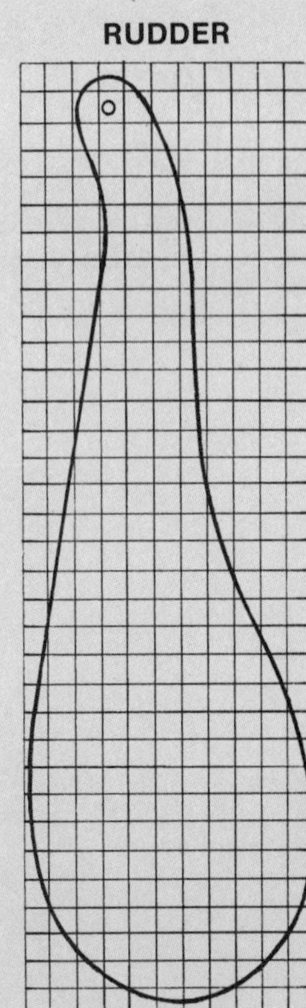

CONVERTED PRAM rivals ready-builts costing nearly $1000. It's a stable, sprightly sailer.

of any age and particularly useful for a youngster learning the sport.

Total time required for the project was four days for gathering hardware and materials, building, assembling and painting. The Dacron sail was cut and sewn by a local awning and boat cover shop, and took one week.

The little boat is gaff-rigged for safety, delivering a large sail area with a low profile. In a strong wind which a young sailor might be unable to handle, the sail can be collapsed in seconds by simply releasing the line that will drop the gaff boom. Tested in 15 to 20-knot winds, the pram was remarkably stable with a 10-year-old helmsman. Performance drops when the sailing pram is pinched too close to the wind, but she is stiff and forgiving with little heel, and makes an excellent learning boat for kids and adults alike.

Mast and boom are made of 1½-in. curtain rod from a hardware store. The gaff boom is 1¼-in. curtain rod and the gaff jaws were cut from ¾-in. exterior-grade plywood. The mast is 106½ in. long with two holes drilled at the top to receive galvanized pulleys for main and gaff halyards. The bottom is shaped square to fit into the mast step. Two small galvanized cleats are attached to the mast for the two halyards, and an eye is mounted for the downhaul.

spars

The boom is 72 in. long with a hole drilled in one end. A piece of 1-in. strap metal is bent into a U-shape, with edges rounded and smoothed, and is attached with a bolt through the hole. This holds the boom to the mast and allows it to move up, down and sideways. A second hole is drilled through both sides of the metal U and, when the boat is rigged, a line (the downhaul) runs from the eye below on the mast up through the holes in the strap metal and back to the eye. With this, you pull the boom down and secure it after the sail has been hoisted. An eyebolt installed at the top of the other end of the boom serves to secure the outhaul for the sail. A second eyebolt, about two-thirds from the end and on the bottom, is for tying on the mainsheet. A second bottom eye, one-third from the end, holds one of the mainsheet blocks.

The 48-in. gaff boom fits into the slot cut in the jaws and is held in place with two through-bolts. A wood rasp and sandpaper shape the gaff end down to the contour of the jaws. A notch is cut in the outer end of the gaff for the peak outhaul. Two screw eyes, one at the jaws of the gaff and the other about 18 in. out, hold the main and gaff halyards. A third screw eye, near the bottom of the jaws, secures the sail lacing.

sail

The sail itself is white Dacron, strong and weather-resistant. It's available from marine supply houses. To simplify fabrication, we drew the outline of the sail on the Dacron and then took it to an awning and boat-cover maker. To sew it yourself, you'd need an industrial sewing machine. Spread the material on the floor and mark a starting point near the lower right-hand corner. You will need excess material on all sides so that the edges can be triple-folded before they are sewn. Draw a 90° angle at the starting point (tack or bottom front corner), a 52-in. luff (leading edge) up from it and a 68-in. foot (bottom of the sail) from the tack out to the clew. From the top of the luff (throat), measure a 145° angle and draw a 44-in. line to the gaff peak for the sail head.

To get the correct curve to the leech (trailing edge), mark a 45° angle at the tack starting point and run a line 68 in. out from the tack along this 45° angle. Bend a long, flexible batten with one end at the peak, the other at the outer clew end of the foot and the center sprung out to the midpoint mark for the leech. Then draw the leech line along the curved batten. Have one 30-in. and two 19-in. strips of material sewn on as indicated to form pockets for holding wooden or plastic battens. When having the sail sewn, indicate you want all edges triple-folded and all corners reinforced.

Installing grommets along the foot, luff and gaff head is a simple job you can do in an hour with a grommet kit from a marine store or mail-order supplier. The holes along the foot and luff are on 8¼-in. centers and at 7-in. intervals along the head.

rudder and leeboards

Pieces of scrap ¾-in. plywood can be used for the leeboards, tiller and rudder. Template patterns can be traced on construction paper using a grid of 1-in. squares as shown. Secure the tiller to the rudder with a stainless-steel bolt with washers and nut to allow to pivot up and down freely. The pintles and gudgeons (pins and sockets that hold the rudder to the transom) are attached with bolts backed with wide washers under the nuts. Slide the pintles up and down for proper position before bolting them on the rudder. Pintles with forks to fit ¾-in. stock and matching gudgeons can be purchased at marine supply dealers.

Leeboards rather than a dagger-board are used to avoid modifying the hull. We bought two C-clamps, a length of ½-in. threaded rod, nuts, large washers and wingnuts from a hardware store. At a welding shop we had lengths of the threaded rod welded to the backs of the C-clamps. To assemble, we roughened the threads close to the clamp with a file and then threaded a nut on until it jammed. Next comes a series of washers, the leeboards, more washers and the wingnut. The sides of the boat were angled so we cut hardwood blocks to the angle and bolted them inside and outside at the clamp position to keep the clamp level and allow each leeboard to pivot vertically down into the water.

To keep the leeboards from being pushed back by the water while underway, a line is rigged forward from each leeboard to a block (pulley) on the gunwale near the mast and back to a small cleat near the helm position. Windward leeboards can then be raised while tacking or both can be raised for launching.

rigging

The mast is stepped by drilling a 1½-in. hole through the center of the bow seat and mounting a step below made of three pieces of 1-in. stock glued together after a square hole has been cut in the center of each. By tapering in the top two blocks, a flange is left on the bottom block through which screws can be run when the step is screwed and glued to the sole.

Mast hoops are 2½-in. galvanized rings slipped onto the mast before the gaff halyard pulleys are installed. These are attached with nylon line run through mast holes and knotted outside washers to reduce hardware weight.

By laying the mast, boom and gaff on the floor, it is easy to lace the foot of the sail to the boom and the head to the gaff using small nylon line. Using sailmakers' thread, the galvanized rings are then attached to the grommets in the luff. Drill holes near the jaw tips and thread the nylon line through these to keep the gaff jaws against the mast.

With halyards attached to the gaff and run through the pulleys, the mast can be stepped in the boat, the sail raised and the downhaul secured. The mainsheet is threaded from the boom eyebolt through seat and boom blocks to the helmsman.

For transporting, the gaff can be folded down against the mast, the boom swung up, and the sail wrapped around the spars and held with an elastic tie. Rig sail and mainsheet, mount rudder and leeboards and you're ready to go.

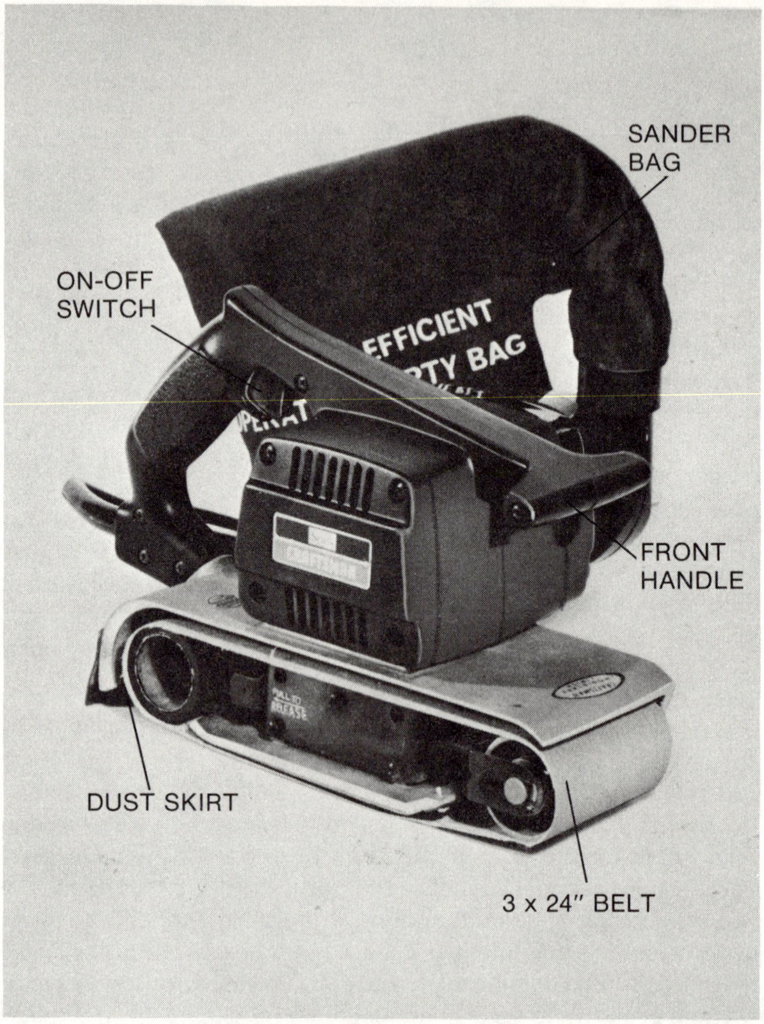

Basics of belt sanding

The belt sander is one of the most useful portable power tools in the homeowner's shop. Unfortunately, it is also one of the most misunderstood tools. Here's some hints on how to get the most from your sander

By HARRY WICKS

■ IF THE STUDENTS in my adult education class represent an accurate cross section of do-it-yourselfers, the portable belt sander is one of the favored homeowner power tools. Surprisingly, though, many people who own the tool do not

SEE ALSO

Abrasives . . . Belt sanders . . . Finishes, wood . . . Pad sanders . . . Sanders, disc . . . Sanding

BELT SANDER SIZE (i.e. 3x24 in., above) refers to the width and length of belt that the tool uses. Size of sander shown is suited for most craftsmen.

know how to get the most out of it. And that is a pity, because a belt sander can save literally hours of hard work, and provide a smoother finish than most of us have the patience to achieve when rubbing by hand.

Though available in a great variety of configurations and sizes, all belt sanders work on the same principle—a loop or belt of adhesive grit travels in a straight line around two drums and across a platen. Platen size is important because this is the actual area of the belt that is sanding when the belt is traveling. Because of the belt sander's power, it is very important that you use the tool correctly:

■ Always keep the platen flat on the work or you will create gouges, bevels and the like.

■ Always keep the sander moving. The test run across the grain (see photo) gives a dramatic example of what results when a belt sander is left running too long in one spot.

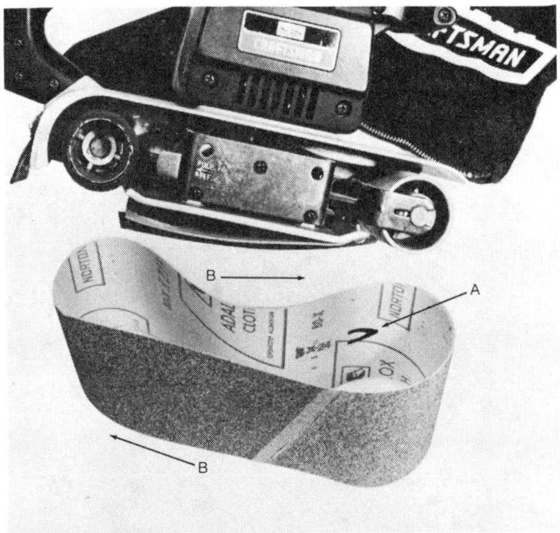

BELTS ARE MARKED for correct installation. Arrow A on the belt should always travel in the direction shown by arrows B or it may rip on the seam.

SMALL STOP—thinner than workpiece—is a must. It frees both hands for managing tool.

■ Always push the belt sander back and forth with the grain of the wood to avoid scratches.

■ Always make sure that you have adequate electrical cord to reach the full length of the work. If you forget to check this out beforehand, you stand a good chance of the line stopping the sander in midstroke—with inevitable gouging of work. If you should require an extension cord, make certain that you use the right size—not a lamp cord.

When you buy a belt sander, your dealer probably will stock the most popular homeowner sizes—3x21 in. and 3x24 in.—as well as some larger professional models. You are well advised to pick one of the homeowner sizes. Greater size also means greater weight you must heft around. Considering the slight increase in platen size, it isn't worth all that extra sweat. (The professionals choose the biggies because of their industrial-rated longer-life construction.)

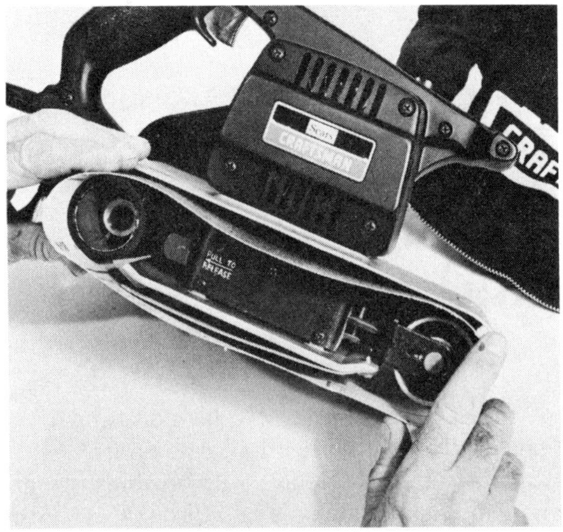

AFTER YOU RELIEVE drum tension according to the instructions, the belt simply slips on.

TEST RUN shows power of a belt sander and why you should keep it moving on the work.

ON THIS MODEL, the tension is created when the small latch is released (bottom photo).

Build this disc and drum sander

■ BESIDES BEING an excellent disc and drum sander, this inexpensive tool can perform other functions, such as buffing, wire brushing, deburring and light grinding. The adjustable table can be removed for buffing large objects.

If you desire, the mandrel speed can be varied by using a two-step pulley on the motor. Operate a 12-in. sanding disc at about 1725 rpm, an 8-in. disc as high as 3450 rpm for the most efficient work.

Start by making and assembling the end members. Install the mandrel support with lagscrews and the way supports with carriage bolts. Make the ways from 1¾-in.-dia. round stock (or the largest available to you) and bore holes in J and K to suit. Slots, cut 1½ in. deep in ends of ways, allow easy insertion.

The table is clamped to the ways with pieces B. These are made by clamping two pieces together and boring for the ways or by boring holes in a 3½ x 3½-in. block first, then resawing to suit on a bandsaw. Plane about 1/16 in. off the inside faces of B after boring to ensure good clamping action. Tilt table is controlled by a miter-gauge head available from many tool dealers.

The mandrel unit must be carefully mounted so it's perpendicular to the miter slot in the table. The unit is available from Prairie Tool Co., Box 332, Prairie Du Chien, WI 53821, for about $15 postpaid. The ½-hp, 3450-rpm motor is mounted to a piece of ¾-in. plywood, which, in turn, is attached to the motor shelf with a standard 3½-in. door hinge.

SEE ALSO

Abrasives . . . Belt sanders . . . Pad sanders . . . Sanders, belt . . . Sanding . . . Wood finishes

CUSTOM STAND boasts a guard for the belt and pulley, and a tilting table.

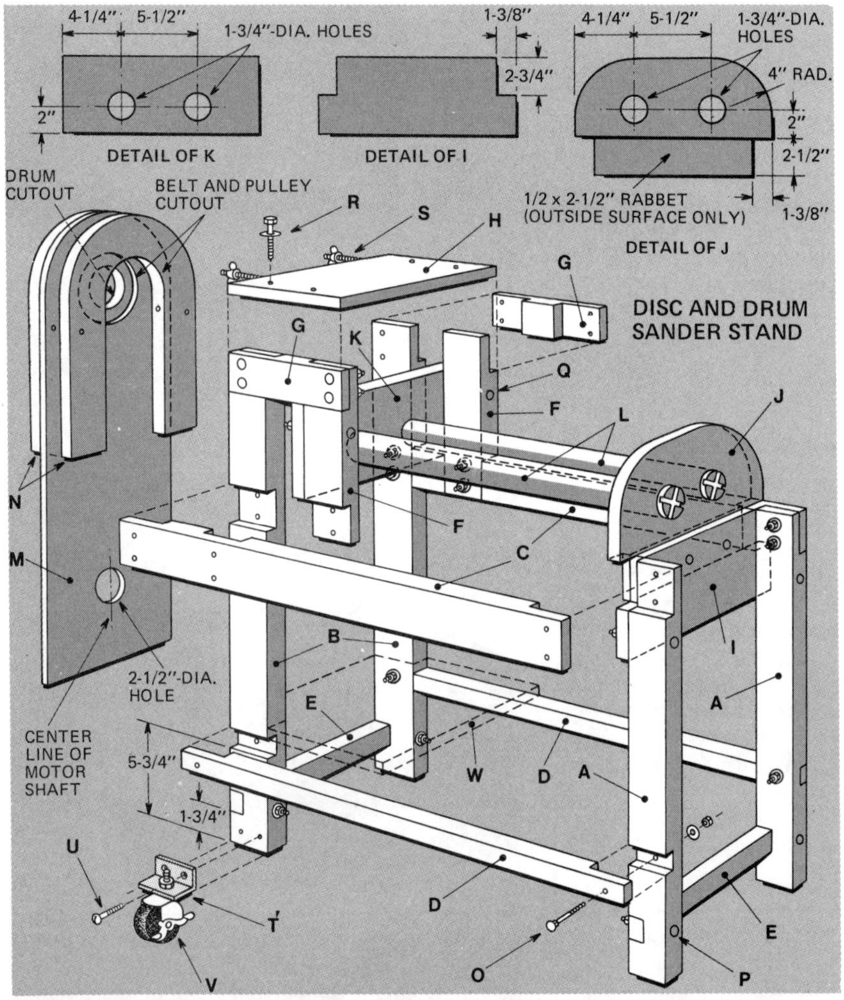

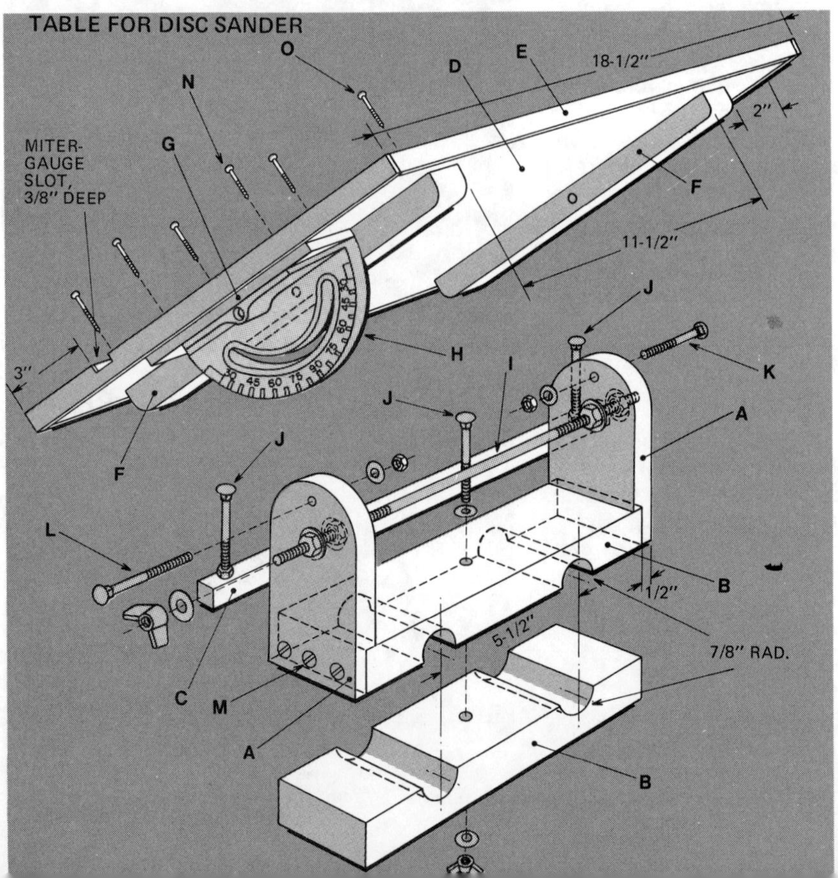

MATERIALS LIST—SANDER STAND

Key	No.	Size and description (use)
A	2	1⅜ x 2⅝ x 21" oak or fir (leg)
B	2	1⅜ x 2⅝ x 29⅜" oak or fir (leg)*
C	2	1⅜ x 2¾ x 28" oak or fir (rail)*
D	2	1⅜ x 1¼ x 28" oak or fir (side rail)*
E	2	1⅜ x 1¼ x 14" oak or fir (end rail)*
F	2	1⅜ x 2⅝ x 11" oak or fir*
G	2	1⅜ x 2⅝ x 7" oak or fir*
H	1	¾ x 7 x 14" oak or fir*
I	1	1⅛ x 5½ x 14" oak, fir or pine
J	1	1⅛ x 8¼ x 14" oak, fir or pine
K	1	1⅛ x 5½ x 14" oak, fir or pine
L	2	1¾"-dia. x 24" round stock (ways)
M	1	¼ x 8¾ x 29½" birch plywood*
N	1	¾ x 8¾ x 14" birch plywood (guard)*
O	24	¼ x 1¾" carriage bolts, washers, nuts
P	4	¼ x 3" carriage bolts, washers, nuts
Q	2	¼ x 4" carriage bolts, washers, nuts
R	4	¼ x 2" lagscrews
S	2	¼ x 4" hanger bolts, wingnuts (guard fastener)
T	4	3/16 x 1¼ x 1¼ x 2⅝" angle iron
U	8	¼ x 2" fh stovebolts
V	4	2" Black & Decker locking casters
W	1	¾ x 14 x 14" plywood (shelf for motor)

MATERIALS LIST—SANDER TABLE

Key	No.	Size and description (use)
A	2	⅞ x 3⅜ x 6" oak, fir or pine*
B	2	1½ x 3⅜ x 10½" oak, fir or pine*
C	1	1 x 1 x 15" oak (leveler, nail to carriage)*
D	1	1 x 15½ x 18½" birch plywood [glue ¼" to ¾" piece]
E	4	¼ x 1" x length to suit birch edging
F	2	1½ x 1½ x 14" oak or fir
G	1	½ x 1¾ x 6½" oak or fir (spacer)
H	1	Cast-iron or oak miter head
I	1	⅜"-dia. x 12½" steel rod
J	3	¼"-dia. x 3½" carriage bolt, nuts, washers
K	1	¼"-dia. x 3" carriage bolt, nut, washer
L	1	¼ x 4½" carriage bolt, nut, washer
M	6	No. 8 x 2½" fh screws
N	2	No. 7 x 1¼" fh screws
O	8	No. 8 x 2" fh screws

* These are overall dimensions; pieces must be cut to fit.

MATERIALS LIST—DISC STORAGE

Key	No.	Size and description (use)
A	4	1 x 1½" x length to suit (space blocks)
B	1	¼" plywood, cut to suit

Misc.: White glue, ¾" brads as required.

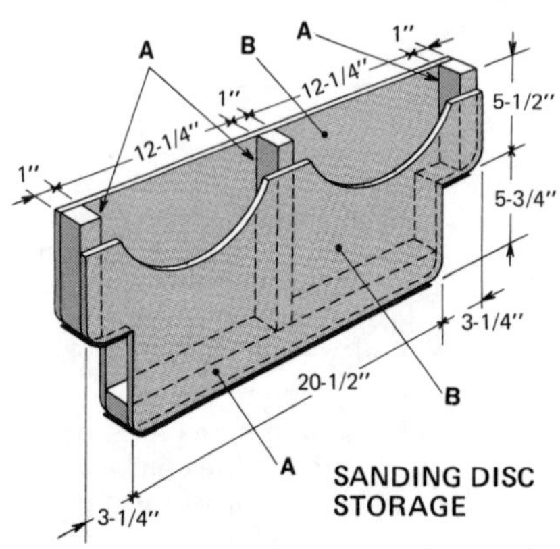

L-SHAPED SOCKET WRENCHES are often easier to use when fitted with handles which convert them to T-shape. One way to do this is to form a short slot in one wall of a 3-in. length of 1/8-in. pipe to accept the short leg of the wrench. With the wrench in place, pack the pipe with autobody filler or epoxy putty to anchor it. A series of overlapping holes will form a suitable slot.

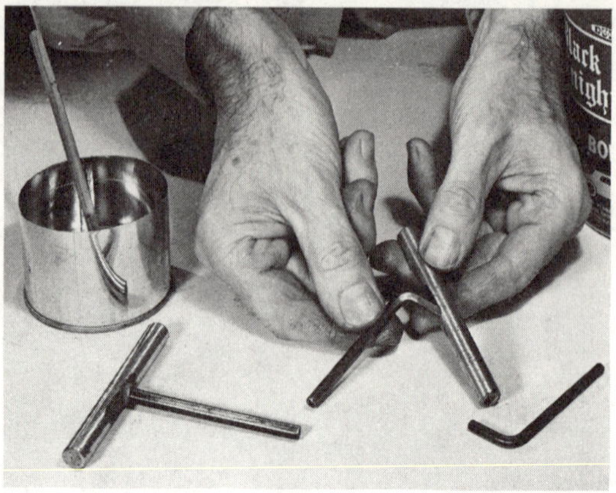

ONE OF THE NEATEST pouches for storing tiny tools and delicate shop instruments is a discarded eyeglasses case and there's hardly a home that doesn't have one going to waste in a drawer. Whether it's a pouch or buttoned-flap type, you'll find it just the ticket to keep track of small files, cutting pliers, shop tweezers, drift pins and countless other small tools which have a way of "wandering off." Tuck it in your toolbox or workbench drawer and you'll always know where to look for the tools.

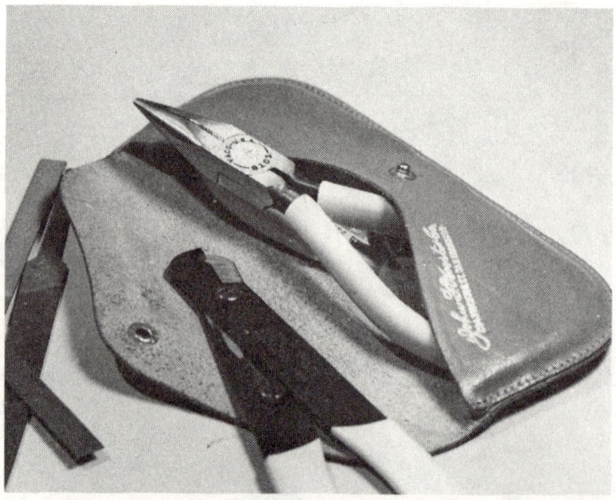

SOMETIMES it's advantageous to reverse a hacksaw blade so the teeth face the frame. When the saw is held with its center of gravity below the work, the blade is easier to hold and seems to cut more smoothly. In this position it is also possible to increase the cutting pressure by adding weight to the frame, such as with the small vise shown. Of course, when the saw is weighted this way, be careful when nearing completion of the cut to avoid letting the saw fall to the floor.

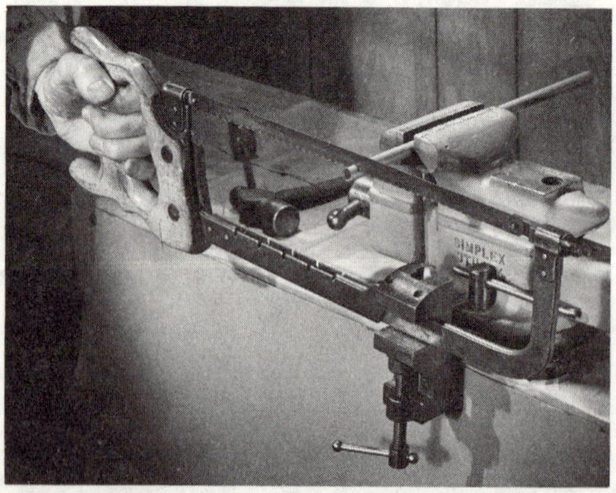

IN A PINCH an ordinary pocket comb can be used as a gauge to space lines in a drawing. Line positions are spotted with fine pencil marks between the teeth and then drawn with the aid of a T-square or straightedge. By placing the comb diagonally instead of vertically you can even reduce the minimum single-tooth spacing. Maximum spacing is determined by the tooth spacing selected in the comb. It's a good stunt to remember when laying out lines for a music staff.

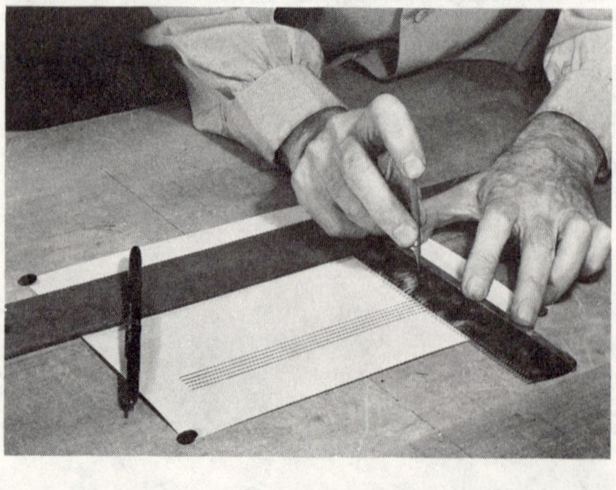

Thorough sanding is one of the hallmarks of the master finishing craftsman. It's that all-important initial step

Sanding from start to finish

By W. CLYDE LAMMEY

■ GOOD FINISHING begins with good sanding. On new work sanding brings out the best in the wood. On old work which has been previously finished sanding should do two things: preserve the aged color of the wood and smooth the surface to take a new finish. Working from new-rough or old-rough is a repeat-step procedure, using sandpaper from coarse to fine through several successive steps. This applies to both hand and power sanding. In power-sanding new work you may produce an acceptable surface in three successive steps. In hand sanding it may take as many as five successive steps, using five grades of sandpaper, to end up with a surface of equal quality. Each time over must remove the "scratch" marks of the step preceding, as otherwise these marks, will show under any finish.

On old work preservation of the color, or patina, of fine woods usually is desirable. Take off the old finish, either transparent or opaque, with a wash-off type remover. Then sand lightly with a medium to fine grade paper and note results closely as you go. Don't use a hand scraper or power sander to remove the finish on old work when you wish to preserve the aged color. Finish with the finest grade of paper, normally 8-0 grade.

The best test you have of smoothness is simply

SEE ALSO

Abrasives . . . Belt sanders . . . Finishes, wood . . . Floors . . . Pad sanders . . . Sanders, disc . . . Scrapers . . . Staining, wood . . . Wood finishes

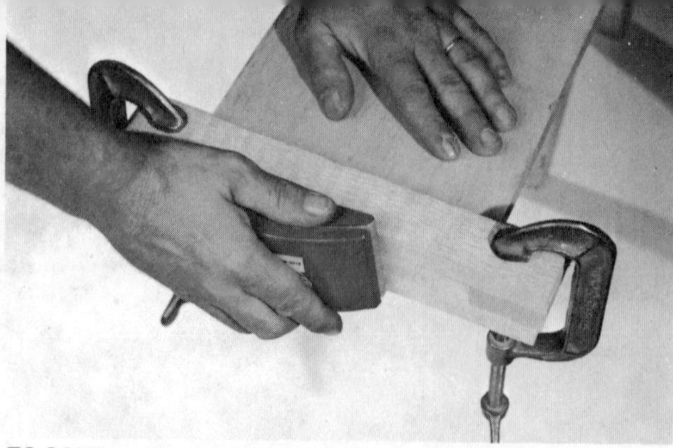

TO SAND end grain by hand, clamp waste strips to work as pictured. This not only keeps end square but prevents rounding edges. Or, alternatively, use an unpadded block.

PAD SANDERS, orbital and straightline types, are used mainly for the finish steps with the finer grades of sandpaper.

"SHOESHINE" sanding is usually best for rounding corners and sanding turnings. Method maintains desired radius and leaves smooth surface.

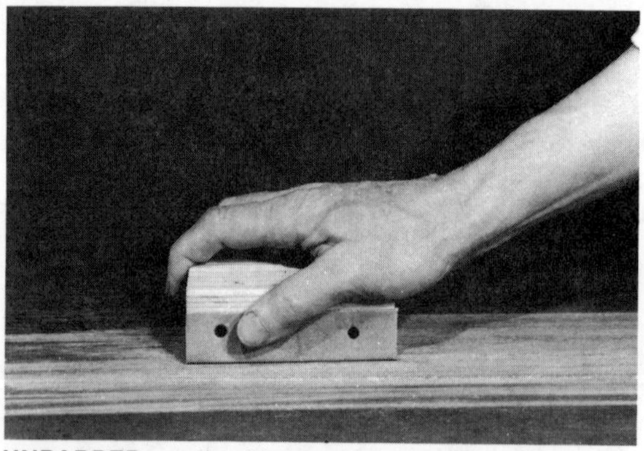

UNPADDED sanding block usually saves time and work on rough surfaces. It cuts down high spots, sands out hollows and leaves a true surface.

to draw your forefinger lightly over the sanded surface diagonally or at right angles to the direction of sanding. Thus you can detect any minor depressions, or even slight roughness. Give these places, if any, a little more attention. But be careful not to cut through that old color acquired only by the aging of the wood.

New work can be handled a little more vigorously. If you are hand-sanding and you discover any slight ups and downs on the surface, make a special sanding block from a 5-in. length of 2 x 4. Cut the ends at an angle of 5 degrees or so, cut a strip of sandpaper to the exact width of the block and to such length that the ends will fold up on the ends of the block where each can be attached with tacks. Don't pad with felt.

Purpose of such a block is to cut down the high spots, ridges and the like and level the surface the first time over. Use a uniform pressure, overlap each stroke about one fourth the width and be especially careful not to round the edges of the workpiece. Don't allow the block to overrun the edges more than about one-fourth its length or width. If there are knots in the surface, to be retained as a decorative feature of the grain, remember these usually are of a different texture, harder than the surrounding wood, causing the abrasive to cut somewhat slower. Such areas usually call for a few extra strokes in each sanding step to hold them flush. Keep a close watch when sanding certain softwoods having a coarse, flat grain. There may be especially soft areas which tend to cut down faster, producing a surface of low ridges and shallow hollows. Changing sanding strokes to a slight angle with the grain usually disposes of this problem. Keep a close check on progress with the finger-tip test.

Should the project you are working on be of

SOMETHING NEW in "sandpapering." Perforated metal forms edges that cut in all directions. Sheet is self-cleaning, removes stock very fast.

FOR BOAT-HULL sanding there's nothing quite like a portable belt sander of husky size with a belt at least 3 in. wide. It saves hours of labor.

veneer construction, either plywood or solid-core type, either old or new, be especially careful not to over-run the edges and cut down to the core stock. On new work the veneers used are likely to be quite thin, usually only about 1/28 in., and may have already been machine-sanded, so you haven't much of the veneer left for the finishing steps. On older work the veneers are usually thicker, but as a rule they've been sanded pretty thoroughly when prepared for finishing.

One disadvantage of the unpadded block is its tendency to score the work more deeply than will a padded block and also it may tilt and slightly ridge the work along the length of the strokes if you don't keep close tab on the uniformity of the pressure you are applying. But it does level the work the first time over, cuts down the more resistant areas, such as knots and vertical grain, and in the end it's a timesaver. After using an unpadded block the first time over most craftsmen go to the padded block (the bottom of the block padded with felt or other soft, flexible material) or they use a flexible rubber block such as supplied by manufacturers of sand-

USE A COARSE grade of sandpaper to bare wood after removing old finish, except on old work where you want to preserve age color, or patina. Use uniform pressure and don't allow block to tilt.

WITH FEW EXCEPTIONS, do your sanding with the grain, even though latter is at angle with workpiece.

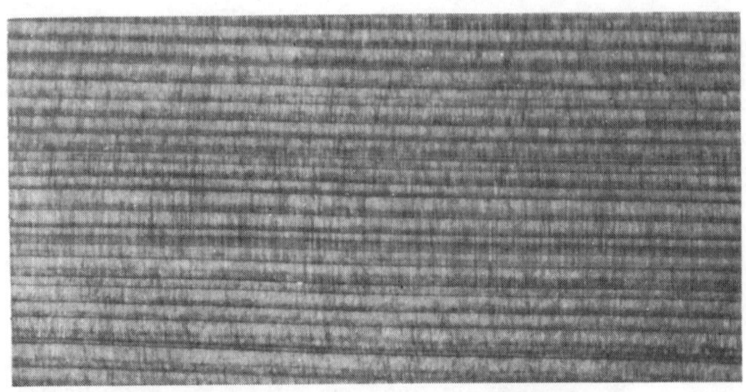

ON OPEN-GRAINED woods such as oak, sanding at a slight angle with grain will prevent enlarging pores.

HAND SANDING, medium to fine grade, is usually done with a felt-padded block unless surface is rough or ridged. Strokes should follow grain and overlap slightly as sanding progresses.

FLEXIBLE rubber sanding block is often best for sanding surfaces originally in good condition. Care must be taken to apply uniform pressure throughout the stroke to prevent block from tilting.

paper. Some even prefer to wrap the sandpaper around a piece of thick, hard felt for the final finish sanding. But in using flexible blocks of any type one should keep in mind that they have a tendency to round the edges and corners of any workpiece which is narrower than the block. For such work, also sanding end grain, a small unpadded block is generally best, especially if the finished job calls for sharp, straight corners with no waves or wobbles.

As a rule blocks don't work well on any type of curved surface that must be hand-sanded. Some types of straight moldings can be sanded quite accurately with flexible blocks but on moldings having irregular or curved shapes such as those on scalloped edges, one generally finds it best to cut sandpaper into small squares, fold once over and use the thumb or forefinger as the "block." Such a simple method is quite effective and much faster than one might suppose. Wear a glove or finger cot if there's much of this kind of thing to do.

The "shoeshine" method of sanding usually works best on turnings, either in the lathe immediately after turning to finish size or with the workpiece held in a vise, or on turnings already assembled, as in old pieces or unfinished furniture. Just tear or cut strips of cloth-backed abrasive from ½ to 1 in. wide, pass the strip around the work and pull on the ends in a back-and-

ON SQUARE PARTS with rounded corners a nylon abrasive pad or fine steel wool often gives that final finishing touch.

forth stroke. When sanding in this fashion in the lathe operate the machine at a slower speed and keep the abrasive strip moving back and forth and simultaneously along the work to prevent undue heating and discoloration of the wood. As a rule you use only the medium to fine grades of abrasives in shoeshine sanding, but you use descending grades from medium to fine to eliminate scratches as you go.

Only the bulb and vase shapes and the concavities of turnings should be sanded by the shoeshine method. Don't pass the strip over narrow beads as it tends to flatten them; use instead a fine V-file or 3-cornered file, touching it lightly to the work in a back-and-forth stroke and rolling it simultaneously to retain the curvature of the bead. In many cases a strip of sandpaper wrapped around a dowel of small diameter

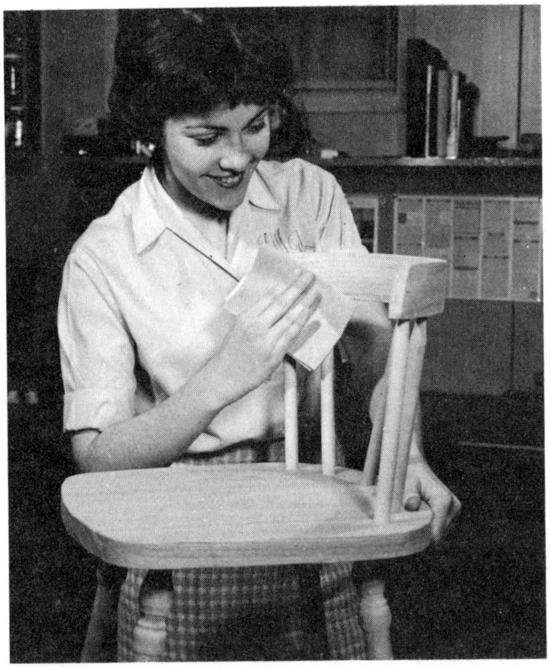

FOR HAND-SANDING curves of short radius, sandpaper folded several times is quite effective. Flexibility of folded "pad" allows it to follow contour of surface without digging in or scoring too deeply.

DISC SANDER of swiveling type makes short work of truing a butt joint such as that pictured. Disc cuts very fast and leaves a smooth, swirl-free surface. Use only light, uniform pressure.

is handy for getting into flutes, round-bottom cuts, also on straight moldings where short-radius shapes are involved. Spread glue on the dowel and wrap the sandpaper strip diagonally with the meeting edges of the strip butted, not overlapped.

how to clean sandpaper

Sometimes there's trouble with the finer grades of paper clogging or glazing, especially on woods of resinous content, or on "oily" woods such as teak. Usually you can clean the abrading surface effectively with a brush having metal bristles; a brush of the type used for cleaning suede shoes is just the thing. When sanding old work preparatory to refinishing, residues of old fillers may tend to glaze the sandpaper and resist cleaning with the brush. When this problem develops just spill a little turpentine onto the work surface. This will usually cut the glaze and "re-sharpen" the abrasive. The turps will evaporate quickly and won't discolor the wood, but one should keep in mind that turpentine is rather highly flammable, that there is always some hazard in its use. Move the job outdoors when possible or have your home fire extinguisher handy. And don't smoke.

Once the initial rough sanding has been finished go to a finer grade of sandpaper, a grade that will remove the scratch marks of the first, and then continue the step-by-step procedure, going to a finer grade of abrasive each time, until the finger test turns up a glass-smoothness over the entire surface. Many craftsmen dampen the sanded surface after initial sandings from coarse to medium grades of sandpaper. Dampening the surface raises the grain, causes surface fibers to stand vertically, or near vertically. In this position they are easily cut off in the next step. On very fine work this procedure is often carried through several steps, to properly condition the wood for a "piano" finish.

sanding by machine

Machine sanding with a portable electric sander is much the same thing except that it's faster and requires a little closer attention to control of the tool. Generally a portable belt sander is best for average work on flat surfaces, one having a 3-in., or wider, belt being somewhat easier to control when using fast cutting abrasives in the coarser grades. If the surface to be sanded is in reasonably good condition, no digs, gouges, dips, or ridges, then use of a coarse-grade abrasive may not be necessary. Make sure that the belt you use tracks properly when in place on the sander and be sure to check to see that it's running in the right direction. All sander

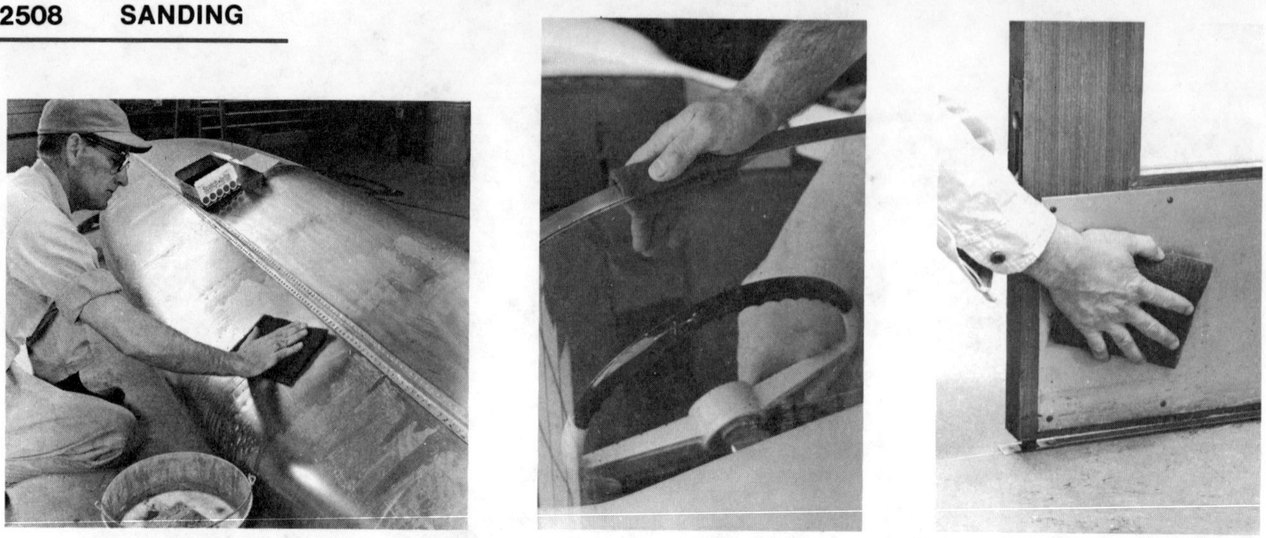

Photos courtesy Minn. Mining & Mfg. Co.

NYLON ABRASIVE PAD works on either metal or wood equally well. Just the thing for cleaning and "shining" up aluminum canoes, boat brasswork, door kick plates, or metal turnings. Fold or cut the nylon pad to a convenient size and use as you would sandpaper.

belts are marked with an arrow indicating the direction they are to be run.

Start the sander before lowering it onto the surface to be sanded and keep it moving after contact in slow, back-and-forth strokes much the same as in hand sanding, the strokes overlapping slightly and working either to right or left. Don't allow the unit to stop on the surface, even for an instant, and be especially careful to prevent it from tipping sidewise. If the unit is stopped momentarily, or permitted to tilt slightly, the coarser-grade abrasives can cut through thin veneers in the wink of an eye, or form a depression that's difficult to sand out. Just as in hand sanding with a block, be doubly alert to avoid over-running the edges and ends of the work.

Don't bear down on a belt sander. Usually the weight of the unit is sufficient to keep the belt cutting freely. If it seems necessary to urge it a little, as in sanding end grain perhaps, bear down only very lightly and keep close watch of results. Bearing down heavily may cause the belt to heat unduly and glaze, thereby greatly reducing its efficiency. Once the surface has been leveled satisfactorily—use that finger test again—change to a finer grade belt, continuing to step down until you finish with the finest belt.

Pad sanders are of two types, the terms, or names, used referring to the action of the pad. In the orbital type the pad moves in a circular stroke. On the second type known as the straight-line sander the pad moves in a straight, back-and-forth stroke. On some later-model pad sanders the stroke can be changed from straight to orbital as desired. Pad sanders are generally used for the finishing steps with fine-grade abrasives as they are capable of sanding to a very smooth surface.

In general, stance is of some importance in both hand and machine sanding. Some prefer to stand at the side of the work when hand sanding as they can keep pressure and stroke more uniform on a relatively large surface. Working with a portable belt sander can be done in much the same position. Hand pressure is not necessary with the power unit, leaving the hands free to control direction and limits of the stroke. On some woods, especially those with a coarse, open grain, you'll get a somewhat smoother job by directing the strokes slightly diagonal to the grain through all the steps from coarse to fine. This will be true of both hand and power sanding. Also, it's advisable to do a little experimenting to determine the grades of sandpaper that do the best job from start to finish on a given wood.

Sawbuck handles long logs

■ THIS SAWBUCK, with add-on support for safe, easy handling of long logs, makes cutting unwieldy logs a one-man job. The buck is assembled with carriage bolts and wingnuts to permit folding for against-the-wall storage. The extension, which is attached with a bolt that acts as a retaining pin, also folds flat.

Building the sawbuck is straight-forward. Cut pieces to the lengths given and cut angles and bevels as required. Then assemble with nails and bolts and waterproof glue as indicated. To attach the extension, glue block F, as shown in the drawing, to leg A and crosspiece E. Don't allow excess glue to seep into the X-joint. When the waterproof glue is thoroughly dry, drill the hole for the retaining pin.

MATERIALS LIST—SAWBUCK

Key	No.	Size and description
A	4	1½ x 3½ x 48″ fir, trimmed to size
B	1	1½ x 3½ x 18″ fir
C	1	1½ x 3½ x 25½″ fir
D	1	1½ x 3½ x 52″ fir
E	4	¾ x 3½ x 22″ pine
F	1	1½ x 2 x 2″, cut from scrap 2 x 4
G	3	⅜ x 3½″ carriage bolts, washers and nuts
H	1	⅜ x 3½″ carriage bolt
I	8	6d common nails
J	1	4″ T-hinge

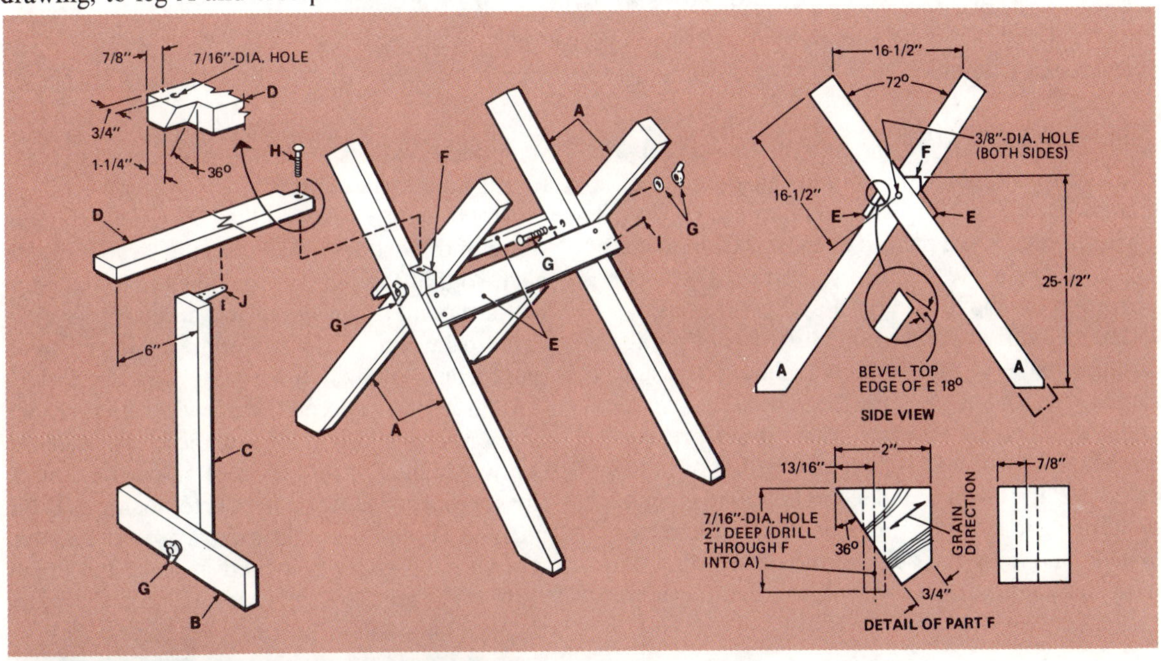

EXTENSION is notched to fit snugly into corner. Bolt serves as a retaining pin.

SEE ALSO

Chain saws . . . Crosscut saws . . . Fireplaces . . . Firewood . . . Log cutting . . . Saws, buck

A simple-and-easy sawhorse

Two twists of your wrist reduce this fine, firm sawhorse to a small bundle of boards you can store anywhere, or tote easily to a remote job

By W. CLYDE LAMMEY

IT TAKES DOWN and sets up in seconds. The legs fold flat in pairs, so you can stand them in a corner where shop space is limited. Or you can toss them into a pickup or the car trunk with room to spare. Set up, these horses will take heavy loads, shoves, knocks and poundings.

The beam is straight-grained hardwood—oak or maple is best—and ¾-in. oak should be used for the legs, or trestles. These are made in pairs, and care must be taken to make quite precise duplicates. Two legs are hinged together as indicated and the beam is dadoed at both ends, each dado being made at an angle of about 7 degrees. When making the dadoes, cut them with square, true shoulders and just a hair's breadth wider than the thickness of the leg stock. And be sure to cut a uniform depth of ¼ in.

After you have shaped the legs, clamp them in place in the dadoes and screw the strap hinge to each so that the pin just touches the lower edge of the beam. Then make the spreader as indicated from flat steel—sometimes referred to as band iron—and screw it to one leg. Then, with the legs in place spread them, swing the spreader down into position and mark the location of the screw which slips into the slot at the free end of the spreader. The trick here is to position all the parts and then exert a little extra pressure so that when the spreader is locked in place the upper ends of the legs in the dadoes will grip the beam tightly. This will assure that when you pick up the horse or move it about, the trestles will stay solidly in place.

The length of the beam, the height of the trestles and the finish are your options. For rough work there need be no finish at all, but for use in a "show" workshop you can stain and varnish to whatever color suits your fancy.

SEE ALSO
Hinges . . . Joinery . . . Workbenches . . . Workshops

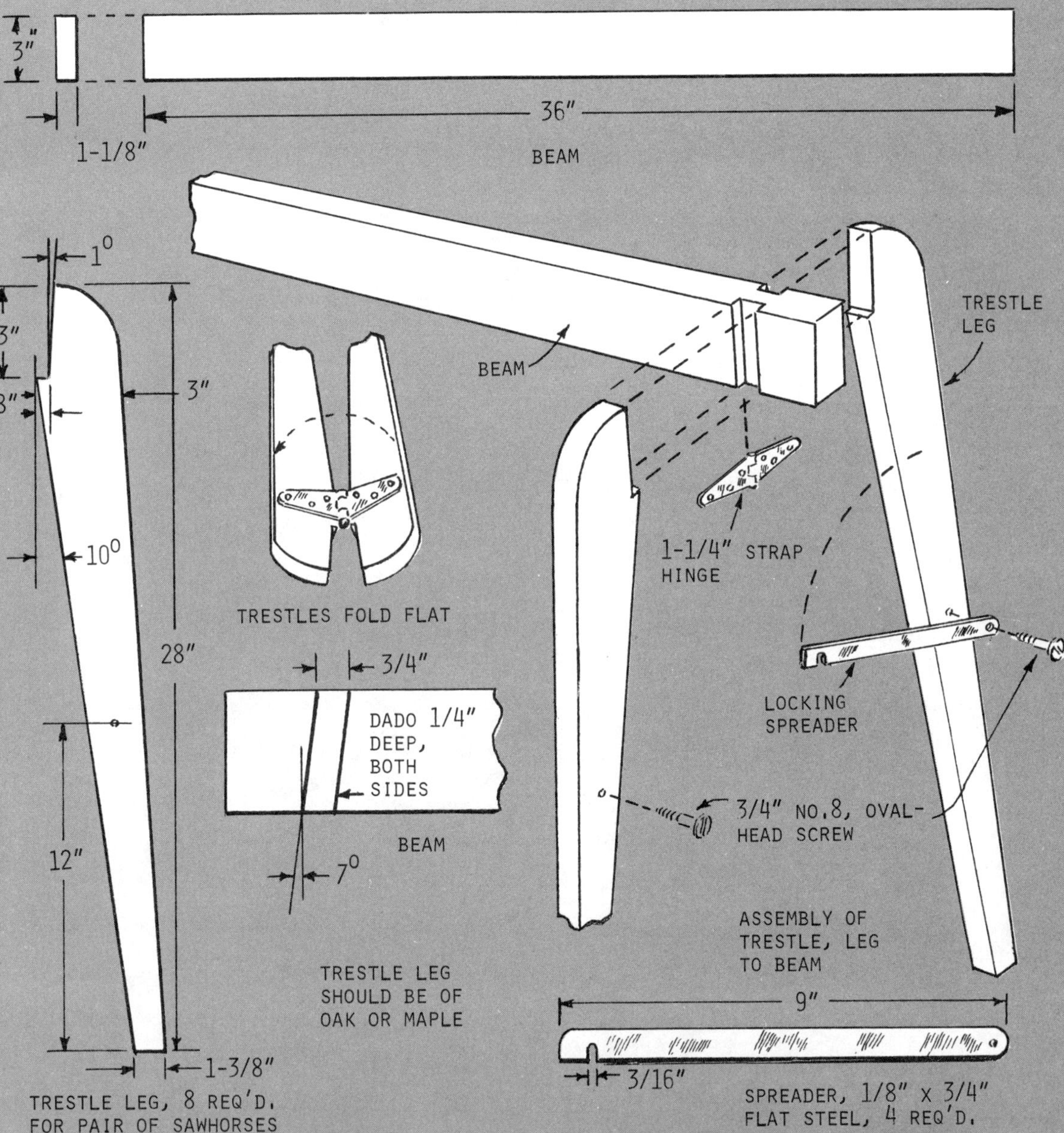
3"
1-1/8"
36"
BEAM
1°
3"
3/8"
3"
10°
28"
12"
1-3/8"
TRESTLE LEG, 8 REQ'D.
FOR PAIR OF SAWHORSES
TRESTLES FOLD FLAT
3/4"
DADO 1/4"
DEEP,
BOTH
SIDES
BEAM
7°
TRESTLE LEG
SHOULD BE OF
OAK OR MAPLE
BEAM
TRESTLE
LEG
1-1/4" STRAP
HINGE
LOCKING
SPREADER
3/4" NO.8, OVAL-
HEAD SCREW
ASSEMBLY OF
TRESTLE, LEG
TO BEAM
9"
3/16"
SPREADER, 1/8" x 3/4"
FLAT STEEL, 4 REQ'D.

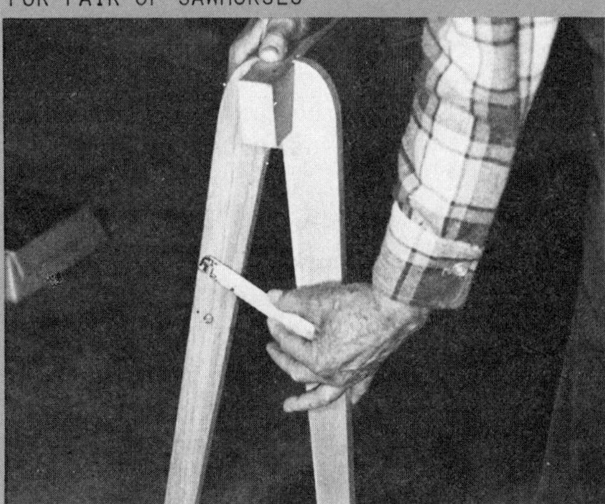

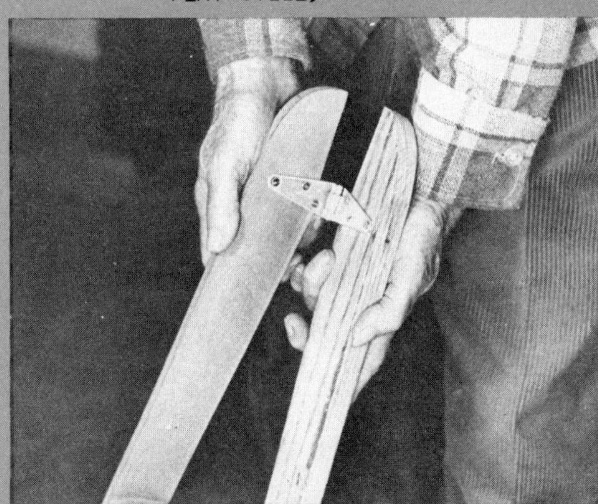

Sawhorse becomes a workbench

You can make your sawhorse do double duty as a workbench. Just add a tray, perforated board, electrical outlet, a top, and you have a go-anywhere workbench

■ A SAWHORSE need not be just a sawhorse; it can be the handiest home-repair "workbench" you ever saw. Fitted with a flat top, it provides a benchtop surface for all kinds of layout work, plus a place to clamp a vise.

When a shallow tray is fitted between the legs, you can keep your hand tools, nails and screws all in one handy place such as a toolbox.

SEE ALSO
Shop techniques . . . Shop tools . . . Toolboxes . . . Workbenches . . . Workshops

When a piece of perforated hardboard is fastened to one side of the horse, you have a built-in tool panel on which to store countless small tools with clips.

And when you install a duplex receptacle in one of the sawhorse legs and wire it to a retractable power-cord reel, you have convenience plus when plugging in power tools.

To add such a receptacle, an outlet box is first installed in the leg in a cutout made to receive it. The female plug is cut off the end of the cord reel and the line is attached to the outlet box with a Romex connector. Finally, the receptacle is installed in the box, which is then fitted with a plate.

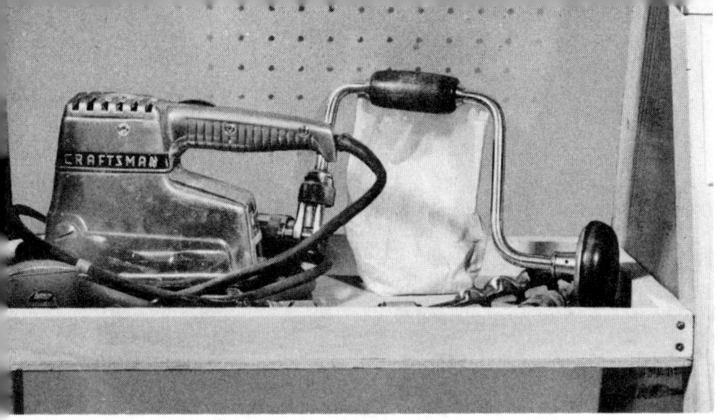

THE TOOL TRAY is permanently affixed—and adds rigidity—to the sawhorse legs. It offers a good storage area for portable tools, small parts, screws and nails.

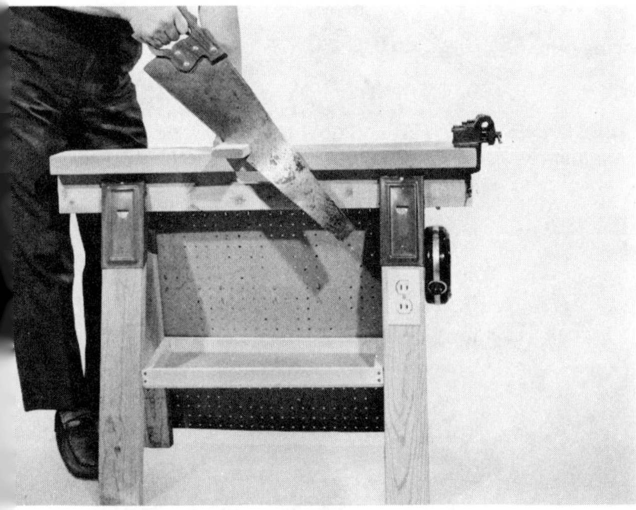

THE TOP WORK SURFACE is simply a bolted-on length of 2x6; ample for drilling, sawing and most other carpentry jobs.

AN ELECTRICAL OUTLET BOX is installed in one leg, with the line from a cord reel connected to the receptacle. The other end of the line is plugged into a power source.

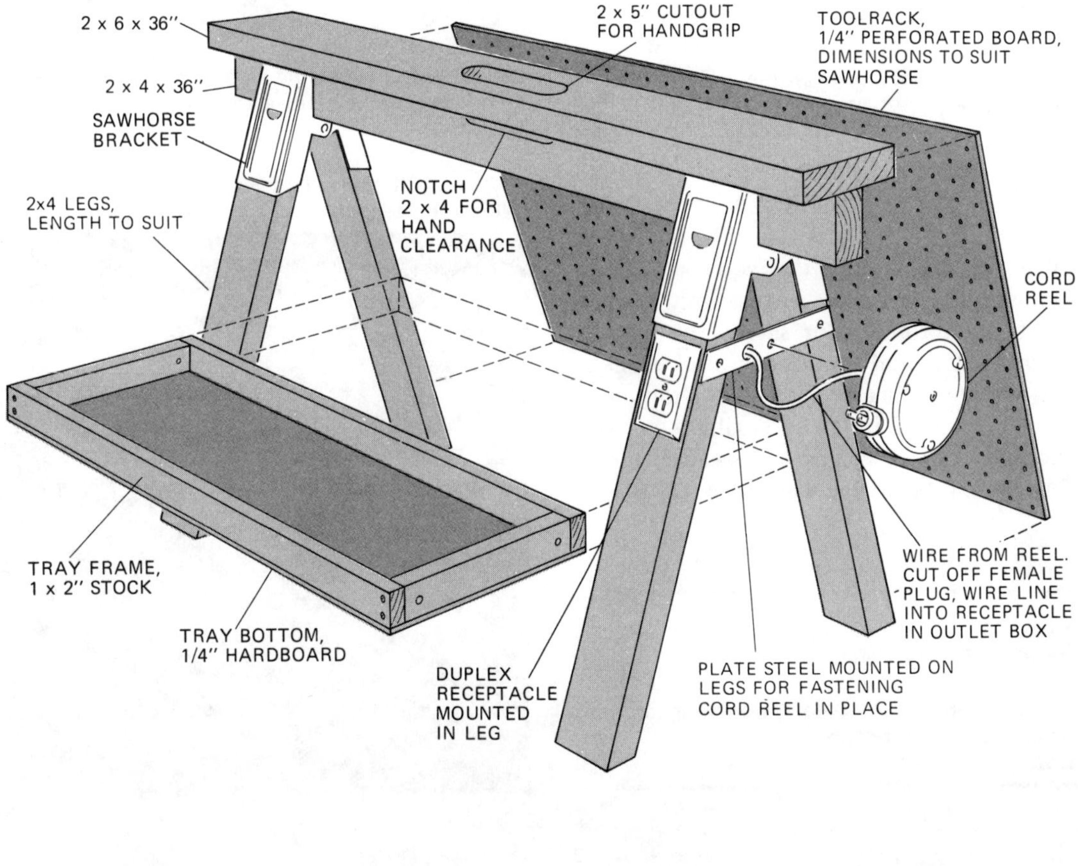

Bench saw basics

By HARRY WICKS

■ WHETHER YOU CHOOSE a radial or table saw for your first shop saw is a matter of personal preference. The major difference is that on a radial the blade moves and the work remains stationary. On a table saw you push the work against the spinning blade. One advantage of the table saw is that you can cut large sheets of plywood or hardboard that you could never cut with a radial saw.

A table saw's capacity is determined by the maximum diameter blade it will hold. A 10-in. saw is handiest in most shops because it will cut through wood 3⅜ in. thick. Arbor size is the diameter of bolt on which the blade mounts.

Always use the rip fence to rip boards and the miter gauge when crosscutting. Never try to cut freehand without one of these supports. Also never use both the rip fence and miter gauge at the same time unless you are not cutting all of the way through the board (for example, a dado). To do so may result in a kickback.

making a chamfer

Cutting a chamfer on a board's edge is one of the simplest sawing techniques. To make the cut, you just tilt the saw blade to the required bevel angle, adjust the rip fence to correct width and push the board through. For safety, the edge being chamfered should be the one *away* from the fence. If the cut must be made along the inside edge, remember to install an auxiliary wood fence, so the blade will contact *it* instead of the metal fence when it exits the workpiece.

SEE ALSO
**Bench saws . . . Blades, carbide . . .
Circular saw blades . . .
Power-tool maintenance . . . Safety, workshop . . .
Shop techniques . . . Stands, bench saw . . .
Table saws**

DISCONNECT POWER and hold block of wood against teeth. Loosen the arbor nut with a wrench.

PUT NEW BLADE on the arbor and then reinstall arbor washer that is provided with the table saw.

WITH BLOCK of wood against blade teeth at rear, install and tighten arbor nut. Don't overtighten.

FOR SAFETY, have minimal saw blade exposure; ⅛ in. is good.

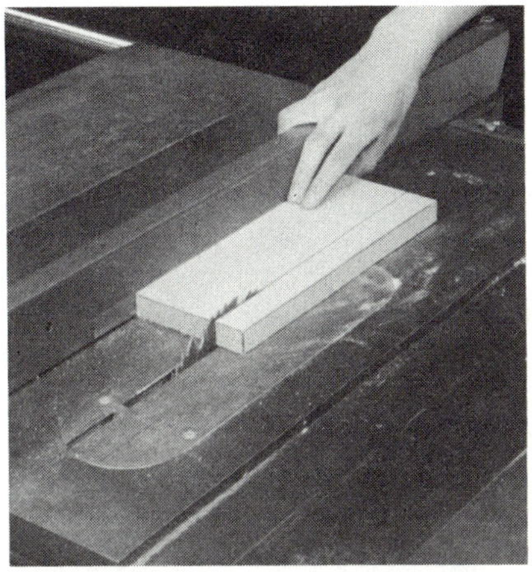

WHEN RIPPING a board that is wider than 3 in., hook two fingers over fence.

WORKHOLDING fingers inside blade guard protect user from kickback.

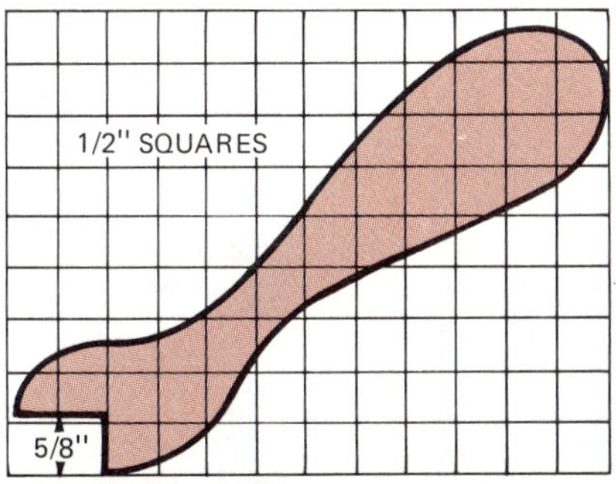

SIMPLE pushstick of ¾-in. plywood can be cut with bandsaw or coping saw.

USE A TRY square to check miter-gauge setting at start of work session.

ALWAYS USE the miter gauge when crosscutting—*never* crosscut freehand.

USE A PUSHSTICK to feed work less than 3 in. wide between blade and fence.

WHEN RIP FENCE is to right of blade, top edge of the workpiece is chamfered.

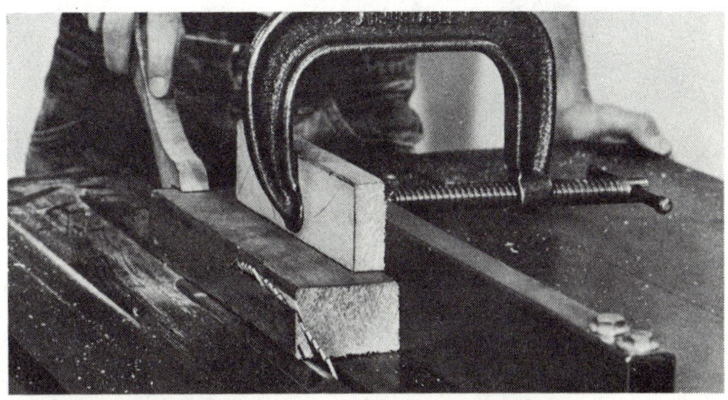

CHAMFER CUTTING is done with cut made along edge of workpiece that is *away* from rip fence.

PUSHSTICK was used while cutting this simple chamfer the complete length of the board.

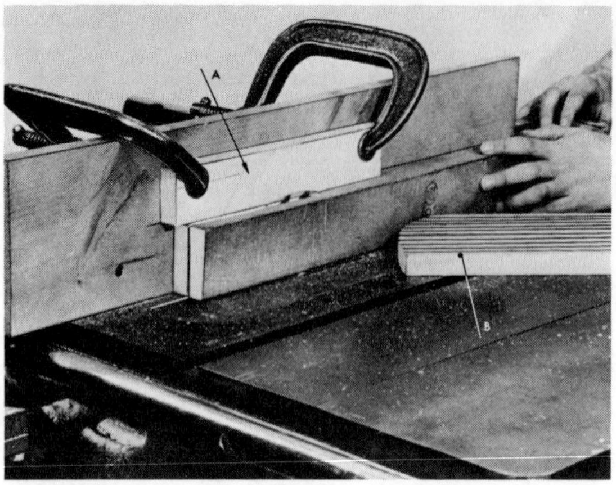

TO INSURE a straight cut when resawing, use both a hold-down (A) and hold-in (B). The hold-in or wood spring is clamped to the saw table.

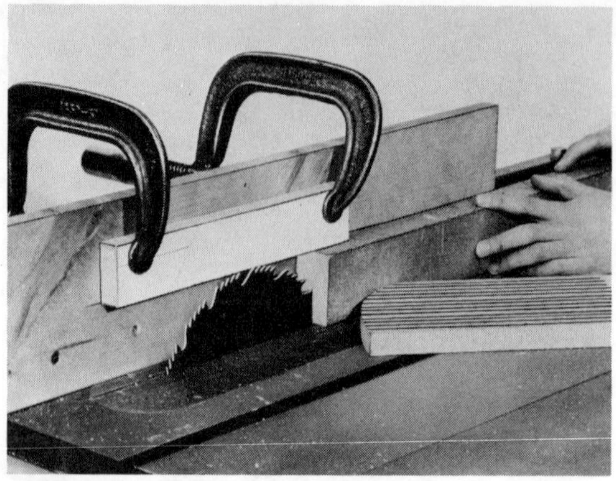

NARROW BOARDS CAN be halved in one pass, as shown. To resaw wider material, flop material 180° after first pass and make second cut.

TO COMPLETE cut, use a pushstick from side of table. Hold-down prevents pushing through with stick; thus you must *pull* work to finish cut.

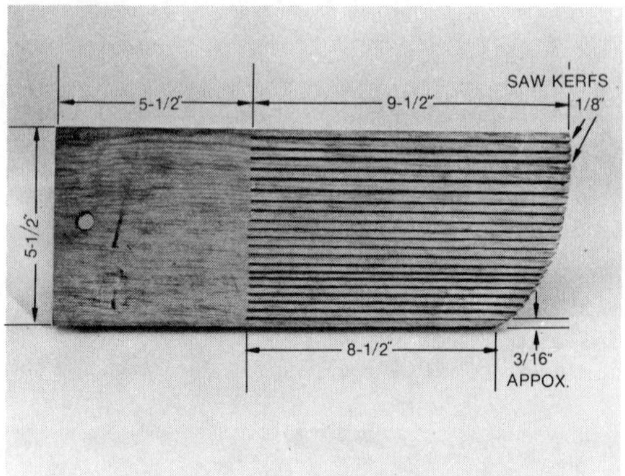

WOOD SPRING is made by running a series of bench-saw cuts into a 15-in. length of 1x6 pine. Shape lower edge as shown on a bandsaw.

You can use a combination blade to cut most chamfers, but if smoothness doesn't matter, switch to a rip blade for quicker cutting. No matter which blade you use, push the work through at a reasonable feed rate and make certain it stays in close contact with the fence so it doesn't bind between the tilted blade and fence.

resawing—with care

Resawing is the technique of making a rip cut through a thick board's edge to create two thinner boards. This sounds simpler than it really is. Make no mistake; resawing is difficult and one of the more hazardous bench-saw cuts because the splitter and guard must be removed.

A narrow board can be resawed in one pass; you raise the blade until it is ⅛ in. above the board's top plane. On wider stock, the blade is raised so it will cut slightly more than half-thickness and the first—and easier—cut is made. The board is rotated 180° for the second, more difficult pass. It is best to use the setup as shown when doing resawing. The hold-down and hold-in jigs enable you to feed the stock without exposing your hands to blade danger. The spring stick's pressure should be on the workpiece, clear of the blade toward the operator (the pressure must not be exerted on the work at or after the blade). The stick shown can be made in 15 minutes or less and is a worthwhile addition to your bench-saw accessories.

If smoothness of cut isn't critical, there is a safer way to resaw a wide board. Elevate the saw blade to slightly less than half-thickness, so that the second pass *will not* separate the two boards. The finish, or separating cut, is made on a bandsaw, where greater operator control is possible. For safety, use the bandsaw's rip fence to make the parting cut.

Build the American bucksaw

■ IT'S A SAFE BET that your grandfather cut a great many cords of firewood with an American bucksaw. In all likelihood, your dad did too. Now you can make a bucksaw and enjoy using it as well.

Handy for cutting up to 8-in. logs, our version is made of cherry, but any hardwood will do. You don't need a great deal of this expensive wood; a piece measuring 1 x 6⅝ x 25 in. will do.

You can order the kit pieces—blade, blade screws, bolts, rod and thumbscrew—from Woodcraft Supply Corp., 313 Montvale Ave., Woburn, MA 01888.

building the saw

To begin construction, lay out the three pieces on the hardwood. Cut out the crosspiece first using a bandsaw or sabre saw. Make certain the two handle pieces are cut on the table saw, because you will need square edges for mortising and to make the blade-holding kerfs.

Cut the handles on the table saw and then lay out the mortises, saw kerfs and holes to be bored. The blade-holding kerf on the long handle is the blade's width by 1$^{7}/_{16}$ in. deep. To make the end kerf on the short handle, use either the tenoning attachment for your saw or rig a setup, with clamps, to straddle the fence.

Bore the holes for the blade screws and for the rod at the handle ends. Shape all edges with a rounding-over bit and router, except for that portion of the edges around the mortises.

SEE ALSO

Chain saws . . . Crosscut saws . . . Fireplaces . . . Firewood . . . Log cutting . . . Sawbucks

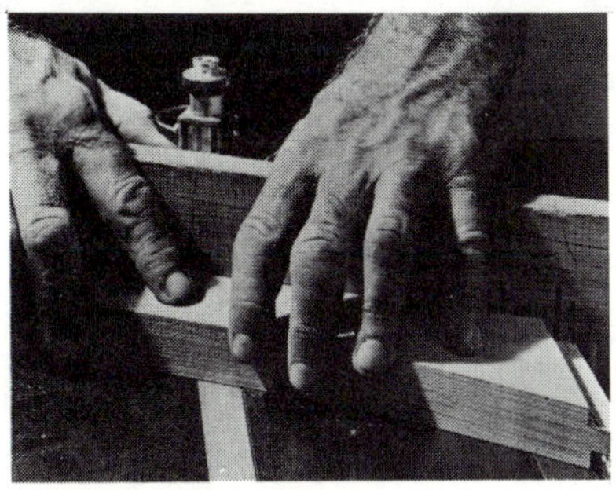

MAKE THE CUTS for the tenon with crosspiece against the miter-gauge (left). To make blade-holding kerf, clamp the stock and slowly elevate blade to 1$^{7}/_{16}$ in.

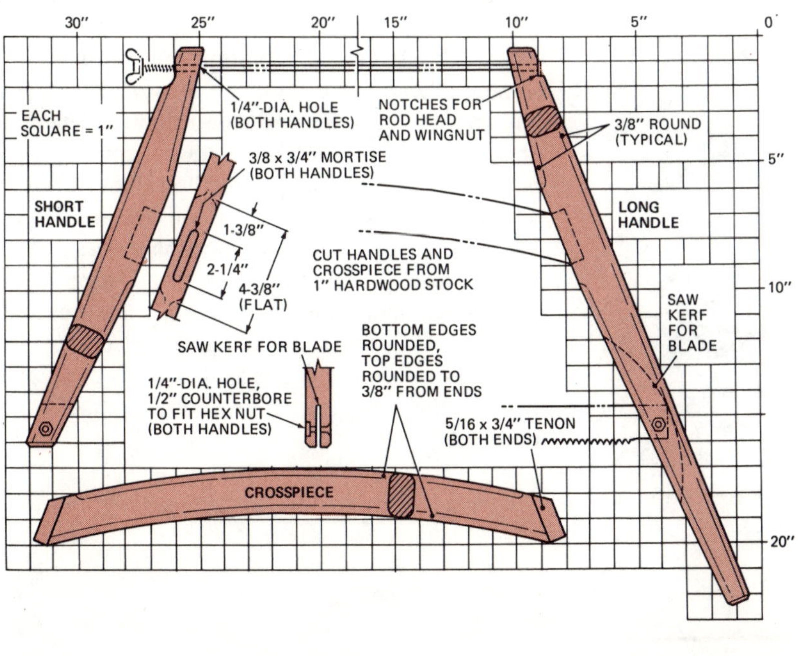

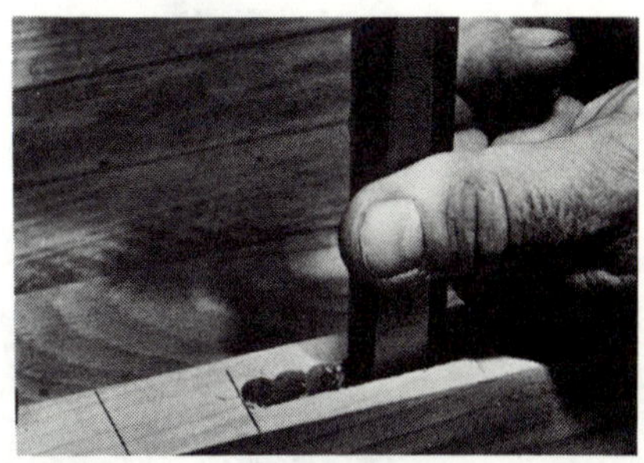

IN HANDLES, bore overlapping ⅜-in. holes within the outline. Square with a chisel.

COUNTERBORE nut hole; chisel to hex shape. Tap the nut in with a hammer.

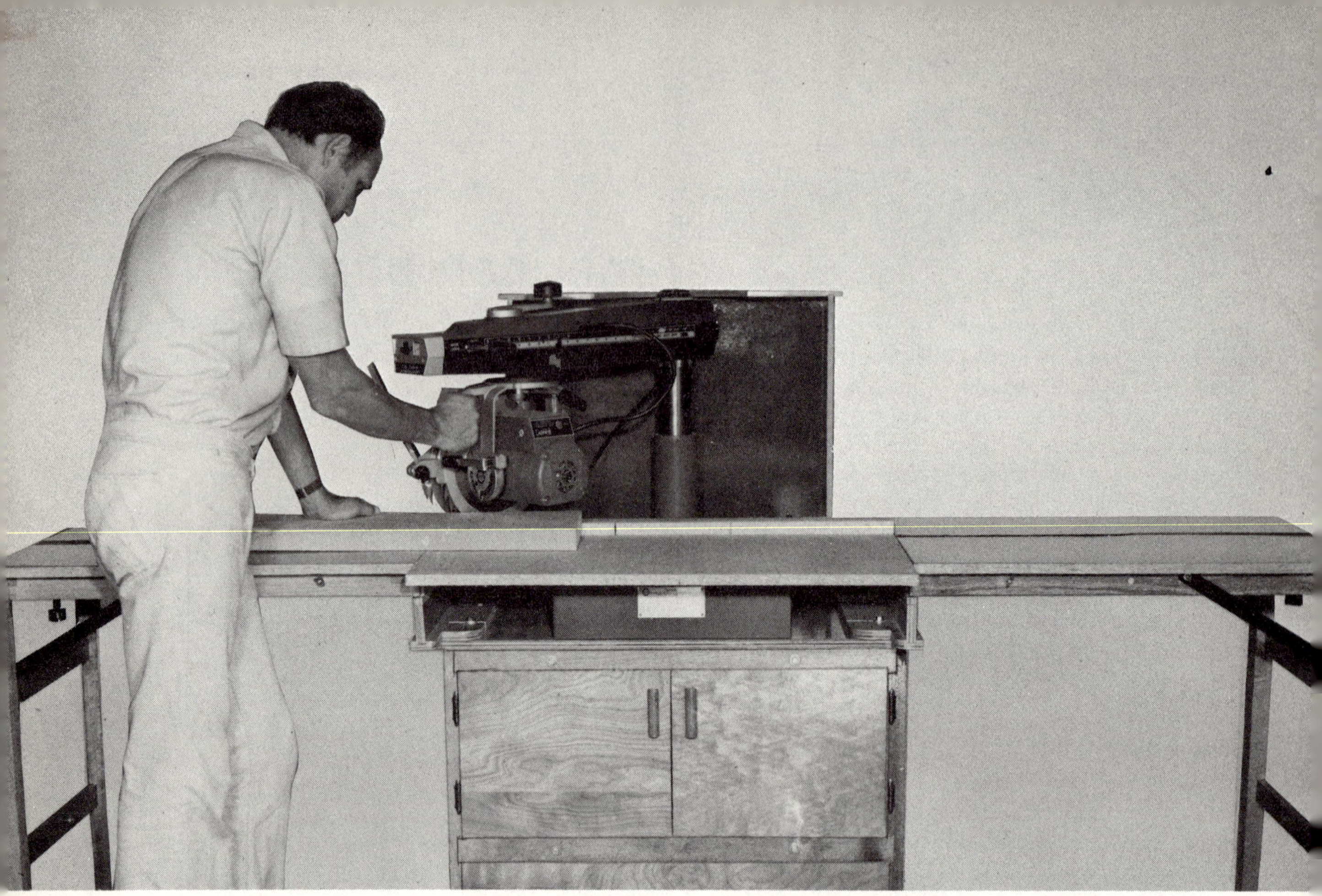

THIS RADIAL-SAW cabinet may be one of the best ones designed. In addition to its folding tables, it boasts a repetitive-stop feature, sawdust chute and drawer, and blade storage (see open doors below).

Compact table for a radial-arm saw

By C. E. BANISTER

SEE ALSO

Blades, carbide . . . Motors, shop . . . Power-tool stands . . . Radial-arm saws . . . Workbenches . . . Workshops

■ THERE ARE SEVERAL reasons why this is one of the best saw cabinets you'll ever see. First, it's really well built. We used oak and birch plywood to construct the prototype, but the design is so sound you can economize by substituting fir and fir plywood. Second, the sawdust deflector chute and easy-to-empty drawer constitute a neat, simple solution to the dunes of sawdust which usually accumulate in and around a saw. Third, the cabinet has a built-in blade organizer. It will store 12 blades, a dado head, a molding head, plus other tools, such as tape measures and squares which you might like to keep at your saw station. Fourth, the entire unit moves on casters, two of which are equipped with locks to make the unit stable.

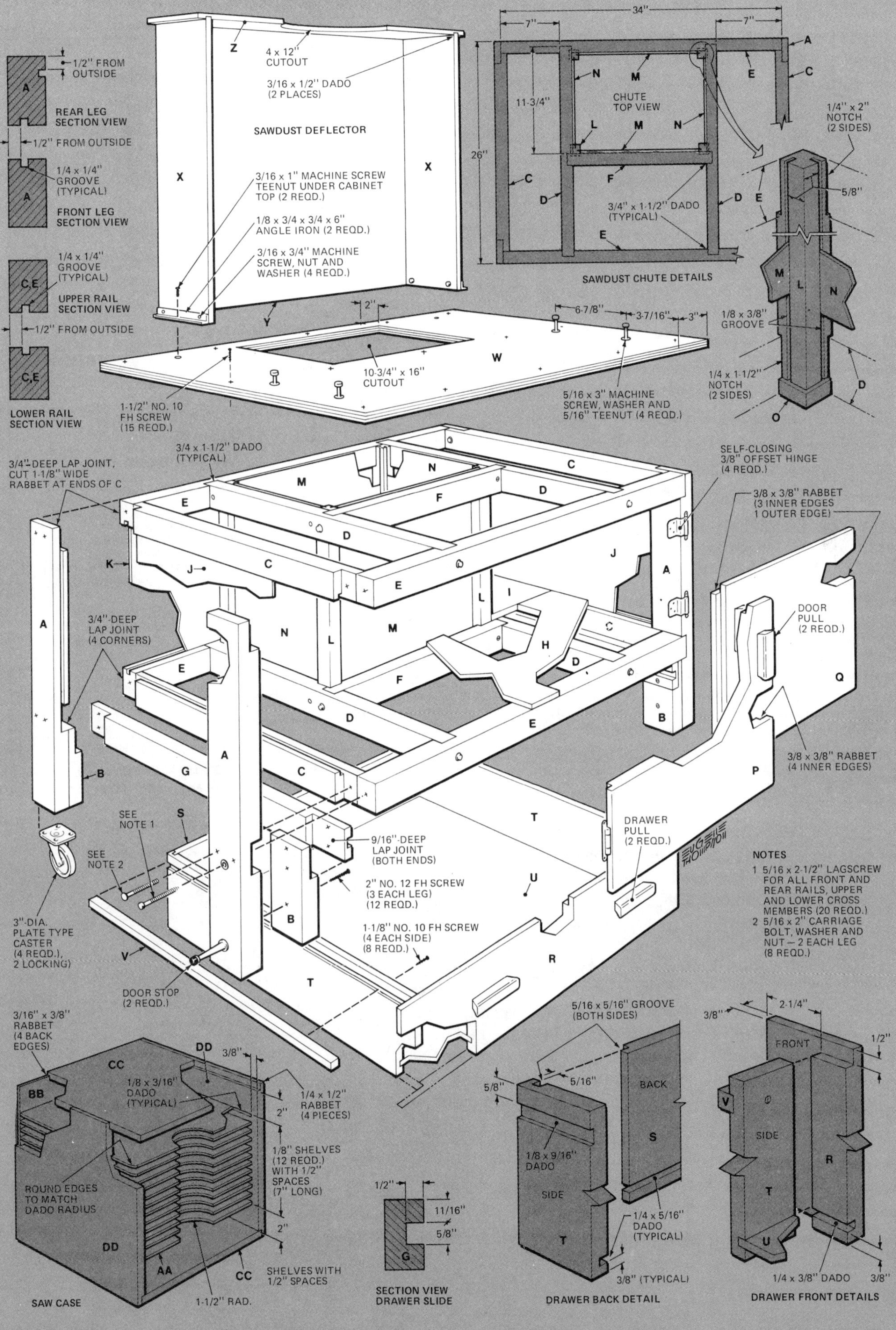

1/2" FROM OUTSIDE
REAR LEG SECTION VIEW
1/2" FROM OUTSIDE
1/4 x 1/4" GROOVE (TYPICAL)
FRONT LEG SECTION VIEW
1/4 x 1/4" GROOVE (TYPICAL)
UPPER RAIL SECTION VIEW
1/2" FROM OUTSIDE
LOWER RAIL SECTION VIEW
4 x 12" CUTOUT
3/16 x 1/2" DADO (2 PLACES)
SAWDUST DEFLECTOR
3/16 x 1" MACHINE SCREW TEENUT UNDER CABINET TOP (2 REQD.)
1/8 x 3/4 x 3/4 x 6" ANGLE IRON (2 REQD.)
3/16 x 3/4" MACHINE SCREW, NUT AND WASHER (4 REQD.)
2"
10-3/4" x 16" CUTOUT
1-1/2" NO. 10 FH SCREW (15 REQD.)
6-7/8"
3-7/16"
3"
5/16 x 3" MACHINE SCREW, WASHER AND 5/16" TEENUT (4 REQD.)
34"
7"
7"
26"
11-3/4"
CHUTE TOP VIEW
3/4" x 1-1/2" DADO (TYPICAL)
SAWDUST CHUTE DETAILS
1/4" x 2" NOTCH (2 SIDES)
5/8"
1/8 x 3/8" GROOVE
1/4 x 1-1/2" NOTCH (2 SIDES)
3/4 x 1-1/2" DADO (TYPICAL)
3/4"-DEEP LAP JOINT, CUT 1-1/8" WIDE RABBET AT ENDS OF C
SELF-CLOSING 3/8" OFFSET HINGE (4 REQD.)
3/8 x 3/8" RABBET (3 INNER EDGES 1 OUTER EDGE)
DOOR PULL (2 REQD.)
3/4"-DEEP LAP JOINT (4 CORNERS)
3/8 x 3/8" RABBET (4 INNER EDGES)
SEE NOTE 1
SEE NOTE 2
9/16"-DEEP LAP JOINT (BOTH ENDS)
2" NO. 12 FH SCREW (3 EACH LEG) (12 REQD.)
DRAWER PULL (2 REQD.)
1-1/8" NO. 10 FH SCREW (4 EACH SIDE) (8 REQD.)
3"-DIA. PLATE TYPE CASTER (4 REQD.), 2 LOCKING)
DOOR STOP (2 REQD.)
NOTES
1 5/16 x 2-1/2" LAGSCREW FOR ALL FRONT AND REAR RAILS, UPPER AND LOWER CROSS MEMBERS (20 REQD.)
2 5/16 x 2" CARRIAGE BOLT, WASHER AND NUT — 2 EACH LEG (8 REQD.)
3/16" x 3/8" RABBET (4 BACK EDGES)
3/8"
1/8 x 3/16" DADO (TYPICAL)
1/4 x 1/2" RABBET (4 PIECES)
2"
1/8" SHELVES (12 REQD.) WITH 1/2" SPACES (7" LONG)
ROUND EDGES TO MATCH DADO RADIUS
2"
SHELVES WITH 1/2" SPACES
SAW CASE
1-1/2" RAD.
1/2"
11/16"
5/8"
SECTION VIEW DRAWER SLIDE
5/16 x 5/16" GROOVE (BOTH SIDES)
5/8"
5/16"
BACK
1/8 x 9/16" DADO
SIDE
1/4 x 5/16" DADO (TYPICAL)
3/8" (TYPICAL)
DRAWER BACK DETAIL
2-1/4"
3/8"
FRONT
1/2"
SIDE
1/4 x 3/8" DADO
3/8"
DRAWER FRONT DETAILS

HARDWARE NEEDED: (1) ⅜x2-in. carriage bolts, Teenuts—for leg-height adjusters. (1-A) ⅜x⅜x2-in. carriage bolt with two sides ground and ⅛-in. hole drilled through thread end to receive ⅛-in. steel pin, ⅜-in. washer and section of extension spring—to make leg-locking device. (2) ⅛x1x14-in. strap iron with screw, washer—for leg brace. Bore 3/16-in. hole in frame and cut locking slot in leg end. (3) Knob, 5/16x3-in. threaded rod, lock washer, nut, 5/16-in. Teenut, ⅞-in.-dia. x ½-in. dowel with nonslip self-adhesive stair tread. Assemble as shown in plans—device functions as friction lock when extension stop bar is in use. (4) 5/16x2½-in. thumbscrews may be used in extension stop bar locking device in place of knob and threaded rod assembly. (5) ½x1½-in. carriage bolt with washer and wingnut. Assemble through stop bar to function as a lock. (6) Drop-leaf table hinges, screws. Hinges allow leg assembly to fold against top of table.

The list doesn't stop here. The extension tables let you handle long boards with ease. Each is equipped with a pair of stops. Repetitive stops, which slide on top of the tracks, are used with boards that do not extend beyond the ends of the tables. Extension stop bars, with dowel catches at outboard ends, slide under the surface between the angle irons and can be used when the workpiece extends beyond the end of the tables. The topside stop will lock at any point along the track when you simply tighten a wingnut. The extension stop-bar locks in place by tightening a rubber-surfaced friction clamp.

Best of all, the extension tables fold up neatly

MATERIALS LIST—SAW CABINET

KEY	PCS.	SIZE AND DESCRIPTION
A	4	1½ x 2⅝ x 23" oak
B	4	1⅛ x 2⅝ x 6½" oak
C	4	1½ x 2 x 23" oak
D	4	1½ x 2 x 24½" oak
E	4	1½ x 2 x 34" oak
F	4	1½ x 2 x 18½" oak
G	2	1⅛ x 2 x 26" oak
H	1	⅜ x 12¾ x 34" fir plywood
I	2	⅜ x 8½ x 11¾" fir plywood
J	2	¼ x 13 x 21¼" birch plywood
K	1	¼ x 13 x 33" birch plywood
L	4	1⅛ x 1⅛ x 16"
M	2	⅛ x 15⅞ x 16" tempered hardboard
N	2	⅛ x 10⅝ x 16" tempered hardboard
O	4	½ x 1 x 1" plywood
P	1	¾ x 13⅛ x 16⅝" birch plywood
Q	1	¾ x 13⅛ x 16 15/16" birch plywood
R	1	¾ x 6¾ x 33¼" birch plywood
S	1	⅝ x 6¼ x 29¼" fir plywood
T	2	⅝ x 6¼ x 25¼" fir plywood
U	1	¼ x 24⅝ x 29¼" fir plywood
V	2	9/16 x ¾ x 25¼" oak
W	1	¾ x 27 x 38" birch plywood
X	2	½ x 6 x 24" fir plywood
Y	1	⅛ x 24 x 27" tempered hardboard
Z	1	½ x 6 x 29" fir plywood
AA	12	⅛ x 10½ x 11" tempered hardboard
BB	1	⅛ x 11½ x 11¾" fir plywood
CC	2	½ x 11¼ x 11⅛" fir plywood
DD	2	½ x 12 x 11⅛" fir plywood

Misc.: 4, drawer and door pulls; 4, ⅜" offset self-closing hinges; 20, 5/16 x 2½" lagscrews; 8, 5/16 x 2" carriage bolts washers, nuts; 2, ⅛x¾x¾x6" angle irons; 2, 3/16 x 1" machine screws and Teenuts; 4, 3/16 x ¾" machine screws, nuts and washers; 4, 3"-dia. plate-type casters (2 locking and 2 nonlocking); 2 stem-type door stops; 4, 5/16" machine screws and 4, 5/16" Teenuts; screws, nails and brads as required.

MATERIALS LIST—EXTENSION TABLE

KEY	PCS.	SIZE AND DESCRIPTION
A	2	1½ x 1¾ x 32" oak
B	2	¾ x 2 x 21¼" oak
D	1	⅛ x ¾ x 13½" strap iron
E	1	¾ x 8 x 17" birch plywood
F	1	¾ x 2¾ x 17" birch plywood
G	1	¾ x 2½ x 17" birch plywood
H	2	1 x 2 x 32" oak
I	1	½ x 1¼ x 31 7/16" oak
J	1	¾ x 2 x 15¾" oak
K	2	1½ x 2 x 17" oak
L	1	¾ x 2 x 6" oak
M	1	¾ x 10⅞ x 32" birch plywood
N	1	¾ x 8 x 32" birch plywood
O	2	¼ x ¾ x 32" oak
P	1	¾ x 2 x 23" oak
Q	1	¾ x 2 x 2" oak
R	1	9/16 x 1¾ x 32" oak

Misc.: 2, ⅛ x ¾ x ¾ x 32" angle iron; 2, 5/16 x 3" carriage bolts, washers and nuts; 2, 1⅝ x 2" butt hinges; 2" hanger bolt, washer and wingnut; 2, ⅜ x 1½" carriage bolt; 2, ⅜" Teenuts; 5/16" Teenut; 5/16 x 3" threaded rod; knob; 2, 3/16" bolts and Teenuts; ½ x 2" carriage bolt washer and wingnut; ½ x 1½" dowel; ⅞-dia. x ½" dowel; ⅞-dia. rubber disc cut from stair tread.

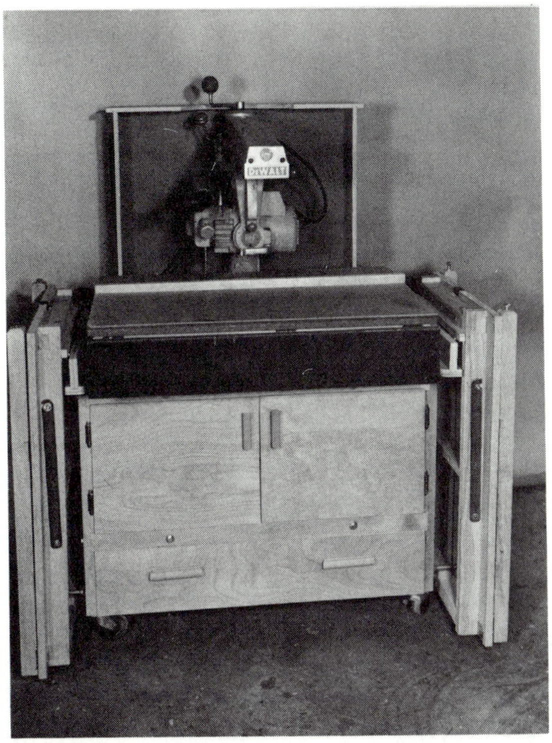

SAW CABINET can be used—or easily moved to a new location—with the extension tables folded.

LEG-LOCKING device holds the leg assembly securely to the angle-iron track when the table is folded.

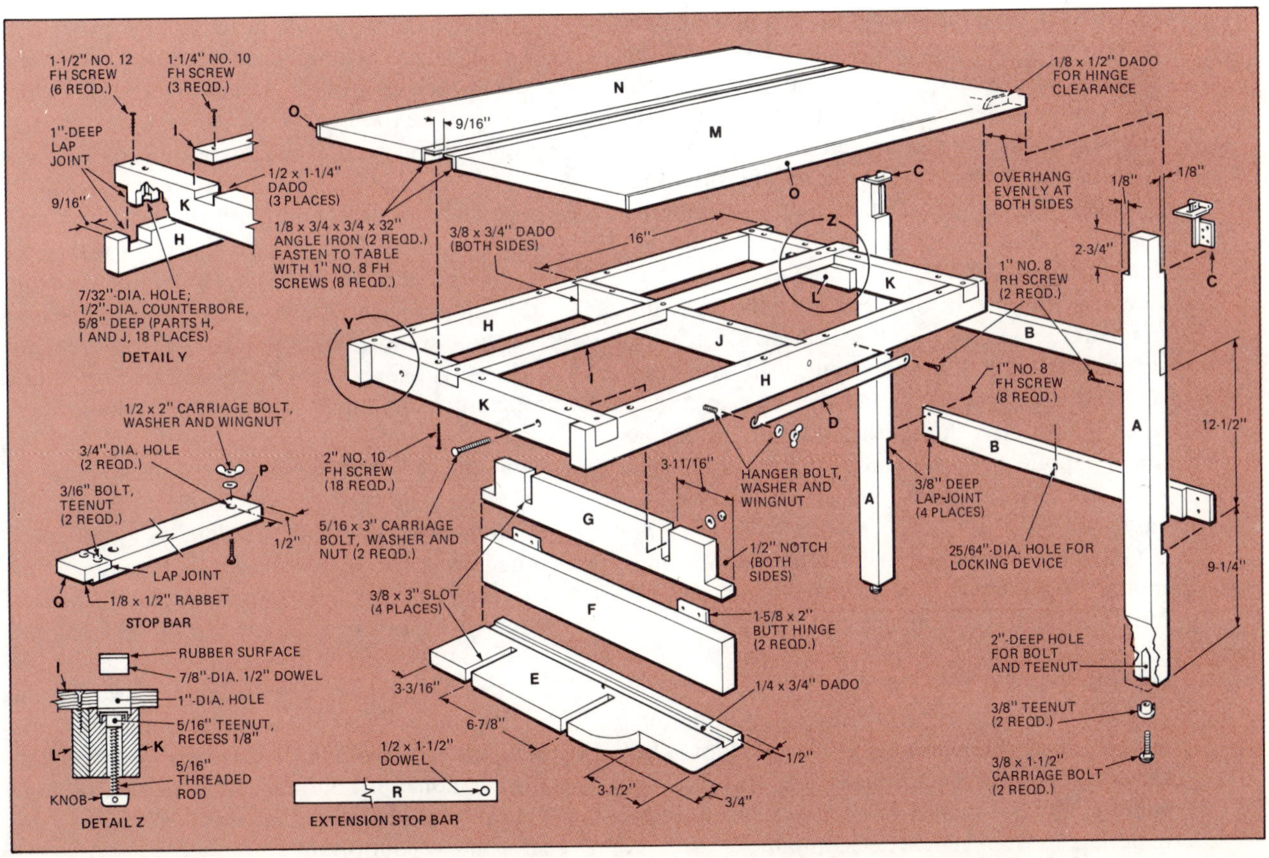

accordion style, freeing up shop space when you need it. In the open position, the extension tables provide a valuable working surface for assembling projects.

The cabinet stiles and rails, along with the dadoes, rabbets and grooves indicated in the plans are cut first. (See materials list for saw cabinet.) Then assemble the sides with carriage bolts and glue. Join the two sides with the rails, using lagscrews and glue. It's a good idea to square and clamp the entire unit before bolting and screwing it together.

Next, make the four corner stabilizers of the sawdust chute and screw them in place. Add panel stops (O) and slip the four tempered hardboard panels into the grooves from the top.

Install the floor of the cabinet around the chute in three sections (I, I and J). Then attach the birch plywood at top; countersink screw heads.

Once the basic cabinet frame is complete, turn your attention to appendages like the sawdust deflector, dust-collecting drawer and the heavy duty plate-type casters. Assemble the housing with nails and glue. Two pieces of angle iron are used to attach the deflector to the cabinet top. Bolt the angle iron to the deflector with machine screws or stovebolts, washers and nuts. Use Teenuts, however, when attaching the assembled deflector to the cabinet top. This will make it easy to remove when the need arises. To install the Teenuts, drill ¼-in. holes in the cabinet top. Hold the Teenut under the hole and thread on a bolt from the topside. Then tighten down on the bolt to pull the Teenut prongs into the plywood. Teenuts can be installed in the conventional manner if you lay out, mark and drill holes before fastening the top.

When building the drawer, fasten the oak runners to the grooves in the drawer sides with screws driven from the inside out. Add oak slides (G) and slide supports (B) to the front and rear stiles. Later, after the finish has been applied, a liberal application of paraffin to the slides will make the drawer move with a good deal more ease.

Cut the rabbets for the cabinet doors and mount them on the cabinet with self-closing hinges for both convenience and safety.

building the extension tables

You may choose to build one or both extension tables. If you choose one, make it the right side, since it generally gets the most use. As with the cabinet, any good solid wood can be used. (See materials list for single extension table).

Cut the legs and rails first, with notches and dadoes as shown. Note that it will be necessary to reverse one of the drop-leaf hinges—the mortise must be cut accordingly. (Note: Hinges are available from Craftsman Wood Service Co., 1735 West Cortland Ct., Addison, IL 60101.) Bore holes in the ends of the legs for the table height adjustment; install Teenut and carriage bolt. Also bore holes to accommodate the leg lock and extension stop clamp. Next, cut the two surface sections to size and cut slots for hinge clearance. Fasten lengths of angle iron to edges with screws and then install top by driving screws up through the rails.

not necessarily adjustable

The assembly which joins the table to the cabinet does not necessarily have to be adjustable. The attachment may be made with bolts through bored holes instead of slots. Ours was made adjustable, so that it would be possible to change over to a different saw with a different table and base dimensions at a later date.

Make the stop bar and extension stop bar as shown in the plans and install all remaining hardware. Note that the leg lock (see photo, page 2520, parts 1A) secures the table legs to the underside of the table surface. To make the lock, grind the carriage-bolt head flat on two sides. Drill a ⅛-in.-dia. hole in the threaded end of the bolt to receive a pin cut from a 10d nail. When installed, a 90° turn of the pin will lock the unground edges behind the angle-iron track.

The extension stop bar clamp (see detail Z, page 2521) is used only with the extension stop bar. Cover the clamp's pressure plate with a ⅞-in.-dia. piece of rubber—which may be cut from 3M's nonslip stair tread or any similar piece of rubber—to increase its grip.

Finally, a few coats of polyurethane will add a tough, durable finish to the completed unit.

mounting and positioning saw

In the prototype, we installed De Walt's 770, 10-inch Deluxe model radial saw—although other saws with a steel base and column mount can also be used. The radial saw base was centered with its front flush to the cabinet front and then bolted in place through the cabinet top. In this position, the extension table tracks for the sliding stops will be just forward of the saw fence. With different saws there may be a slightly different location for mounting the extension table to the cabinet. There is adequate room to make this adjustment comfortably.

Noisy steam heat

My home is steam-heated and during the heating season I'm bothered with noises in the system—a popping, cracking sound that banishes sleep. This I must correct before another heating season. What's the remedy?—Frederick Mason, Albany, N.Y.

A common cause is a defect that creates a vacuum somewhere in the system, usually in a line that slopes downward toward a radiator. Have your service company check to be sure pipes are correctly installed at the boiler. Then check lines to radiators yourself with a level to detect any that slope toward the radiator (they're supposed to slope away from it). You can then raise the radiator on wood blocks to achieve the correct slant.

Stretching bar clamps

My sofa has a wood front rail, the ends of which are loose in the leg joints; I suppose the glue has failed. I have two 36-in. bar clamps and my problem is how to use them to draw the joints tight.—E. Carlos, Chicago.

If the sofa is a standard size, the clamps will have to span 6 ft. I once solved a similar problem by boring two holes in a short length of ¾-in. plywood, enlarging these to take the sliding jaws of the clamps. With these jaws hooked in the holes, you and a helper could place the clamps so the screw-actuated jaw will engage the legs, then tighten. You could draw the clamps tight enough to close the opened joints on fresh glue. Bore tiny holes in inconspicuous places at each joint and force glue into joints with a glue injector. Wipe off excess glue before it dries or it may discolor the finish. Pad clamp jaws so they don't mar the legs.

Right damper length

I plan to build my own fireplace and I have gotten "yes-and-no" answers to my question of the proper length of the damper. Is the correct installation across the full width? If not, what part of the full width?—Thomas Fell, Nashville, Tenn.

In natural fireplaces of conventional size it's common to install full-width dampers. The damper should be the full width of the smoke opening—the distance measured at the back, often called the "fireback." A damper of shorter length may tend to create turbulence in the updraft, causing the fireplace to smoke—incurably in some instances. I'm assuming your fireplace is to be built into a wall and not the projecting or two-way types. These require a different damper assembly.

Cleaning a clock face

I want to clean an old clock dial, which is soiled and discolored. How do I go about it?—E. Edmund, Oakland, Calif.

Carefully—it's risky at best. If the dial is paper on metal or wood, one way to clean it is to flood it with naphtha—*caution:* naphtha is flammable—and immediately sprinkle it with talcum powder, covering the whole surface uniformly. Wait a minute or two, then brush off the talc. If some discoloration still shows, the process may be repeated. If the dial is enamel on wood or metal, a light washing with mild soapy water, applied with a loose pad of clean cotton, is safest. Be careful not to overwet the surface. Do not use naphtha or any other solvent, as it might soften or remove old enamel.

Removing decal residue

I've managed to scrape old decals off an enameled surface, but how does one remove the sticky residue? No solvent I've tried will touch it.—Edward Hosen, Utica, N.Y.

There is a remover specially made for this purpose. If you cannot obtain it locally, try rubber-cement thinner, available at art-supply and stationery stores. This will soften the residue of decal adhesive so that it may be scraped off, or rubbed off with a fingertip.

Painting new plaster

How long a time should elapse before new plaster (not Spackle) is painted?—J. Horner, Knoxville, Tenn.

New plaster contains moisture which should be allowed to dry out before you paint. Offhand, I'd set 90 days' drying time as a minimum unless the room is heated for part of the drying period. In that case, the time could be shortened to two months.

Insulation for A/C

I intend to install central airconditioning this season. There are 3-in. batts in the ceiling, and I'm told by my airconditioning service people I need at least 7 in. of insulation. I've thought this excessive—Are they correct?—J. Heston, Tulsa, Okla.

I would agree with the suggestion, simply on the ground that most older homes tend to be under-insulated. Ceiling insulation should be R-19 to R-22. These R-ratings (thermal resistance) take the insulating value of structural materials into account; an insulation dealer in your area should be able to determine your needs. Check attic ventilation.

Build a mobile scaffold

By JOHN A. IAMONACO

This simple movable platform not only speeds the job of painting and repairing your house but also cuts the risk of accidents. It can be made easily and inexpensively and disassembles for flat storage

PAINTING FROM a scaffold is both safer and more efficient than trying to do the same job while standing on a ladder. Your footing is more secure. Also, you can cover much larger areas before having to climb down and move the scaffold. With less time spent moving equipment, the job goes a lot faster.

The simple scaffold detailed on the facing page costs very little to build. Basically, it's just two 8-ft. ladder-type sections connected by a pair of X-braces. One section is equipped with wooden wheels to simplify moving the scaffold from one painting location to the next. If available, you could just as well substitute wheels from a discarded wagon or tricycle.

The other ladder section features adjustable legs which make it possible to use the scaffold on uneven ground. Extension units for both ladder sections allow you to increase the height of the scaffold to 12 ft.

The box-type platform shown in the plan has the advantage of being much lighter than a solid plank. Retainer studs on either end fit over the ladder rungs and prevent the plank from slipping. Rung spacing permits placing the plank at height intervals of 2 ft.

When not in use, the scaffold can be disassembled and stored flat. Simply remove the wingnuts from the eight anchor bolts securing the X-braces and fold the braces together. Once you've taken it apart, the scaffold is compact enough to store in your garage.

SEE ALSO
Ladders . . . Painting, exterior . . . Sheathing . . . Siding

PAINTING EAVES of this split-level home is just as easy as ground-level work when the scaffold is used. With extension units added to the ladder sections, the painting platform can be raised as high as 12 ft.

WHEN YOU want to move the scaffold to another spot, simply lift one ladder section and trundle it along on the wheels. While designed for painting, the scaffold is also perfect for construction and repair jobs.

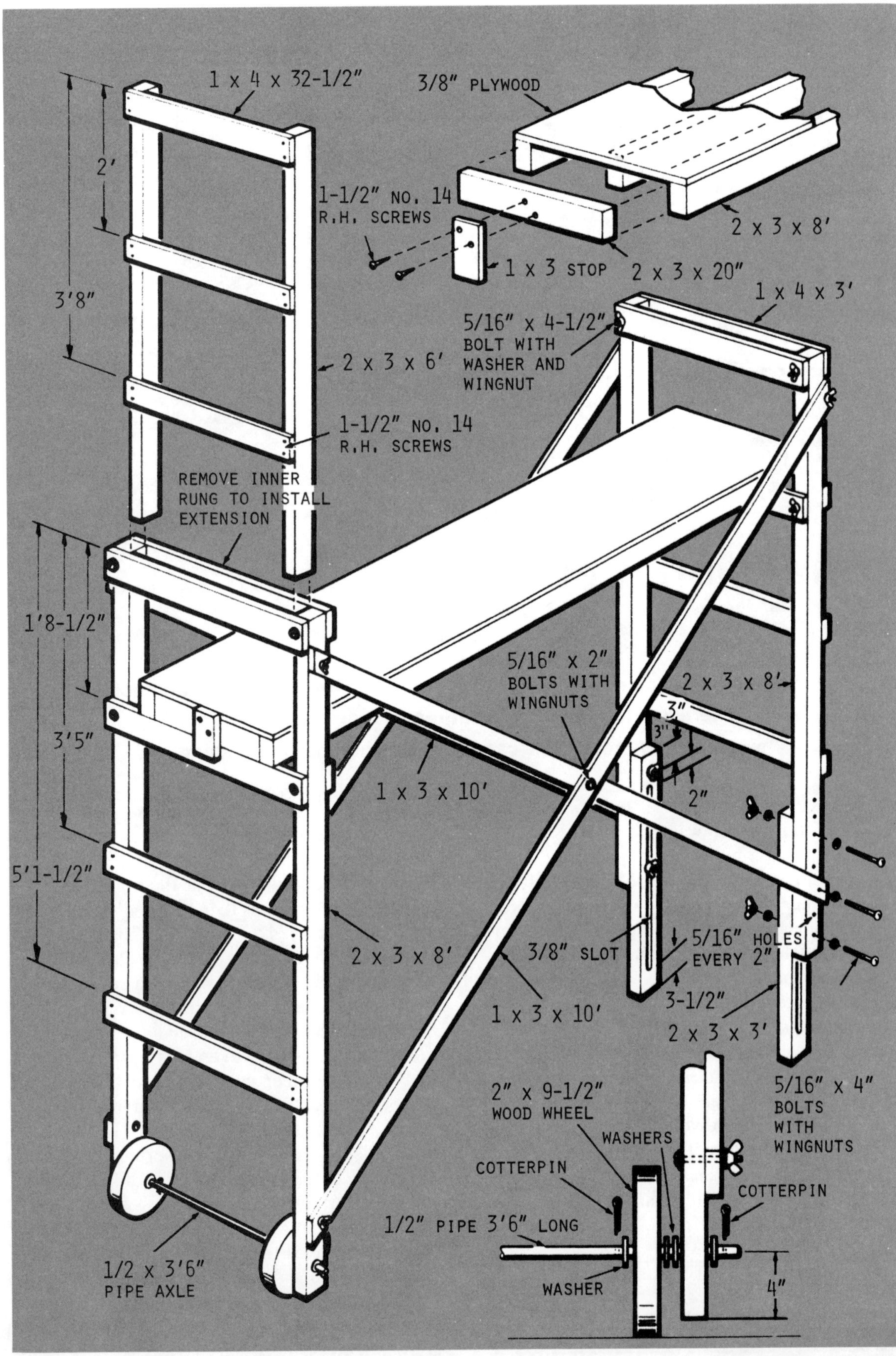
1 x 4 x 32-1/2"
3/8" PLYWOOD
2'
1-1/2" NO. 14
R.H. SCREWS
2 x 3 x 8'
1 x 3 STOP
2 x 3 x 20"
3'8"
1 x 4 x 3'
5/16" x 4-1/2"
BOLT WITH
WASHER AND
WINGNUT
2 x 3 x 6'
1-1/2" NO. 14
R.H. SCREWS
REMOVE INNER
RUNG TO INSTALL
EXTENSION
1'8-1/2"
5/16" x 2"
BOLTS WITH
WINGNUTS
2 x 3 x 8'
3"
3"
3'5"
1 x 3 x 10'
2"
5'1-1/2"
2 x 3 x 8'
3/8" SLOT
5/16" HOLES
EVERY 2"
3-1/2"
1 x 3 x 10'
2 x 3 x 3'
2" x 9-1/2"
WOOD WHEEL
5/16" x 4"
BOLTS
WITH
WINGNUTS
WASHERS
COTTERPIN
COTTERPIN
1/2" PIPE 3'6" LONG
1/2 x 3'6"
PIPE AXLE
WASHER
4"

Professional cabinetmaker scrapers

By JOHN BURROUGHS

Scrapers are some of the most forgotten and misunderstood handtools. There are jobs such as paint removal or smoothing certain surfaces that these tools can do better than power sanders

■ BEFORE SANDPAPER became widely available, the scraper was one of the cabinetmaker's more important tools. It was used primarily to smooth off blade marks left by hand-planing. Today, since most woodwork is now machine-cut and power-sanded, the scraper, unfortunately, has fallen into near oblivion.

But not complete oblivion, for there are some jobs that scraping does better than sanding. Scraping is preferable, for example, if the surface you're smoothing isn't all of equal hardness—such as when you're finishing glue-joints flush or finishing repairs made with wood filler. Carefully scraped hardwood acquires a smooth gleam that's hard (if not impossible) to match with sanding. Scraping is sometimes the fastest, cleanest way to remove old paint or varnish from furniture you plan to refinish.

SEE ALSO
Abrasives . . . Finishes, wood . . . Sanding . . . Tools, hand . . . Wood finishes . . . Wood sculpture

The scraper itself is simply a thin spring-tempered steel blade having either a straight or curved edge. (The rectangular scraper measures 2¼x6 in.) The edge is first filed and oilstoned perfectly square. It is then "turned" with a burnisher—burnished over to form a hooked cutting edge. The burnisher, which is file-hard steel polished glass-smooth, is stroked several times with firm pressure along the square edge of the scraper at gradually increased angles until it has a turned-over sharp, even burr.

While a scraper can be pulled toward you, experienced cabinetmakers, when scraping a flat surface, ordinarily push the tool. The blade is grasped with both hands and sprung into a shallow arc with the thumbs. Then it's tilted forward until the cutting edge cuts and it is canted slightly for shearing action. Scraping with the grain of the wood leaves the smoothest finish; scraping across the grain at an angle removes wood more rapidly. The scraper's cutting edge can be re-formed with the burnisher several times before re-oilstoning is necessary.

THREE CABINET SCRAPERS, plus a burnishing tool are fairly inexpensive. They can be purchased through woodworker's supply houses. Instructions for using the burnisher (far right) are usually furnished with the tools.

UNFINISHED EDGES of new scraper are draw-filed with a single-cut file to prepare the blade for sharpening.

TO TRUE THE edge, slide the scraper back and forth on a wood block against an oilstone set on edge.

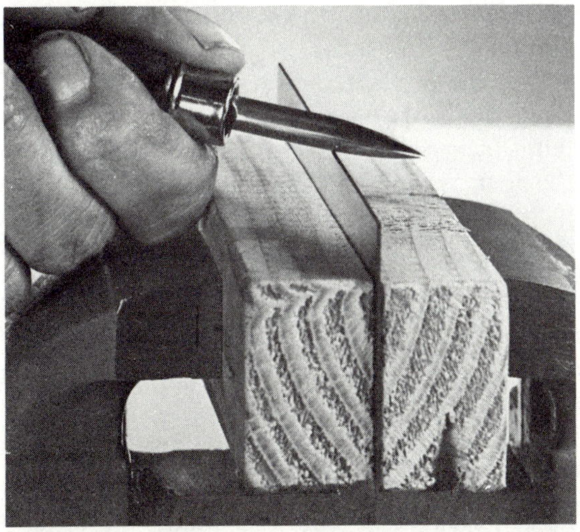

TO "TURN" scraper's edge, burnisher is stroked at an angle with pressure to burnish hooked cutting edge.

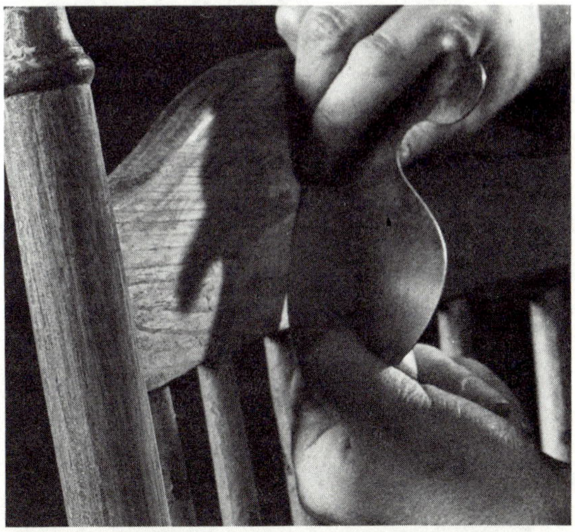

FRENCH-CURVE scraper does a great job of removing paint or varnish from furniture to be refinished.

Add a screened porch

Adding a screened porch to your house can protect your cookouts from the bugs and rain. It also adds value to your house at resale time. Here's how to build a handsome addition to provide comfort for you and your family on those warm summer nights

By DON SHINER

■ WHEN IT COMES to practical outdoor living, you just can't beat a screened porch. Open patios are fine when there are no bugs or sudden showers, but one or the other can ruin a cookout. When you're safe from both within the shelter of a screened porch, summer entertaining and living become twice the fun for family and guests alike.

Adding such a porch is not the major job you may think. It's a project that can be completed in stages to suit both your spare time and wallet. And even before you have it fully screened in, you'll find it usable for a cookout without worrying about getting wet.

SEE ALSO
Cabanas . . . Carpeting, outdoor . . . Concrete . . . Decks . . . Garden shelters . . . Gazebos . . . House additions . . . Lumber . . . Nails . . . Patios . . . Roofs . . . Screens

IF BUGS AND RAIN send you scurrying indoors from a cookout, it may be time to consider a screened porch.

The best spot for your porch is at the back of the house where you have the most privacy, but more important, where it will be accessible from the kitchen. If you are able to build it on the north side of the house, it will be shaded from the hot afternoon sun.

You can tackle the job in three easy stages; 1. Pouring the slab; 2. Framing the roof; 3. Adding the screens, all of which you can do yourself with help now and then from a friend. In most cases you'll be ahead if you have the slab poured. In time saved, you can have your porch completed over a two-week vacation.

If you take on the slab yourself, stake it out to suit and remove 5 or 6 in. of topsoil. Dig down 18 in. along the outer edges to form a trench to provide extra support for the roof. Erect form boards so the slab will pitch slightly away from the house (¼-in. per ft.) and are level with foundation.

Regardless of size, it's best to pour the slab in sections, a day apart. This minimizes cracking and makes it possible, when working alone, to trowel the concrete before it sets. As each divider is pulled out, a ½x4-in. strip of expansion felt is tacked to the green section before pouring the next. When the slab is finished, cover it with building paper or burlap and keep it wet for four or five days, allowing the concrete to cure fully.

Before you start the roof, study the framing drawing. Each rafter is paired with a ceiling joist and the joists are faced on the underside with ⅜-in. plywood before a lintel, supported by 4x4 posts, is placed under it.

Start by spiking a 2x6 nailer to the side of the house at ceiling height. This runs the full length of the porch. Next erect a box-like frame around three sides and prop it up temporarily in a level position. Now install the ceiling joists, 24 in.

SLOPE THE FORM 2 in. to assure proper drainage. Then divide the form in sections for pouring.

AFTER EACH SECTION is poured, smooth it with a trowel, then cover it with burlap and keep it moist.

CEILING JOISTS are toenailed to a 2x6 nailer which is first nailed to the house at ceiling height.

CEILING FRAMING is temporarily supported in a level position by scrap props which rest on the slab.

center to center, and toenail them to the nailer. Spike them through at the front. After this, figure how many rafters are needed (two more than joists if you double up the end ones to make a flush surface) and cut one for a pattern. Taper the end to match the pitch of the house roof. Nail rafters to the roof, right on top of the existing shingles, and spike them to the joists.

Next, you close in the framing by nailing ¾-in. plywood to the rafters and ⅜-in. plywood to the joists. Follow this by covering the roof with tar paper, then with a metal flashing where the new roof meets the old and, finally, with shingles to match the house. All that's left is to install the 4x4 lintel and its supporting 4x4 posts before filling in the ends of the porch roof and adding a 1x8 fascia board across the front and up the ends.

The number and size of frames you need to enclose your porch is determined from the porch itself. If you've planned for 8 ft. between posts, then all screens across the front can be made 48 in. wide. The drawing shows how the screen frames are made from common 1⅛-in. screen stock. Note how members are half-lapped for extra strength.

You have a choice of installing the frames permanently in place or fitting them so they can be lifted out and stored for the winter. In the

TAPERED ENDS of the rafters rest on the roof, to which they're nailed 24 in. o.c. Plywood covers rafters.

WHEN WIRING IS IN, the underside of the joists is covered with ⅜-in. plywood.

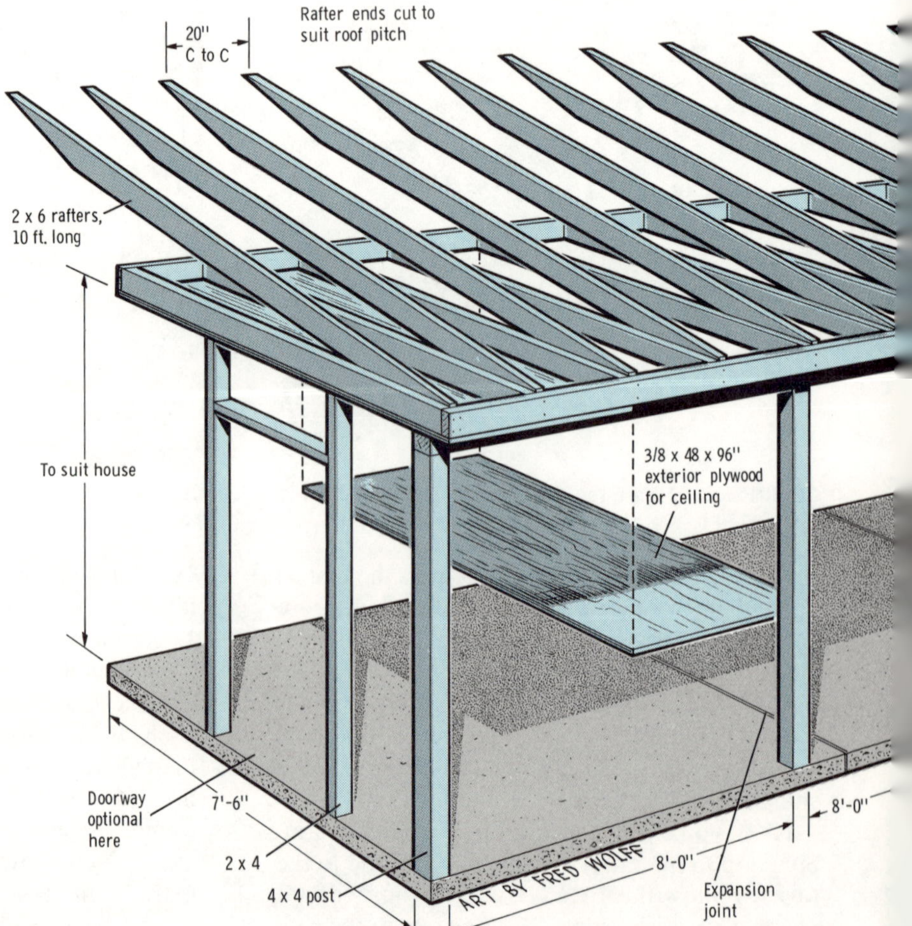

PERMANENT 4x4 posts are anchored to the slab with angle brackets, then a 4x4 lintel is placed on top.

AFTER ADDING FLASHING, roof sheathing is covered with felt, and matching shingles are applied.

please turn the page

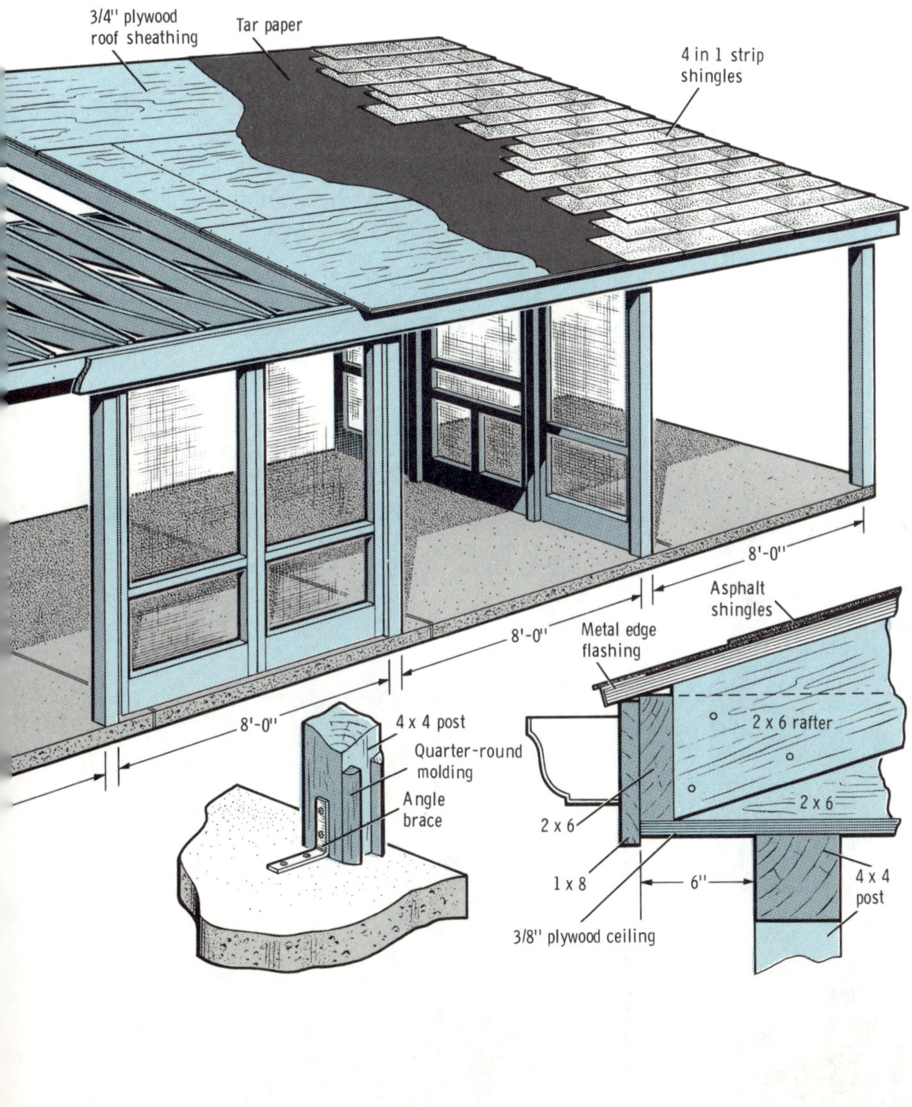

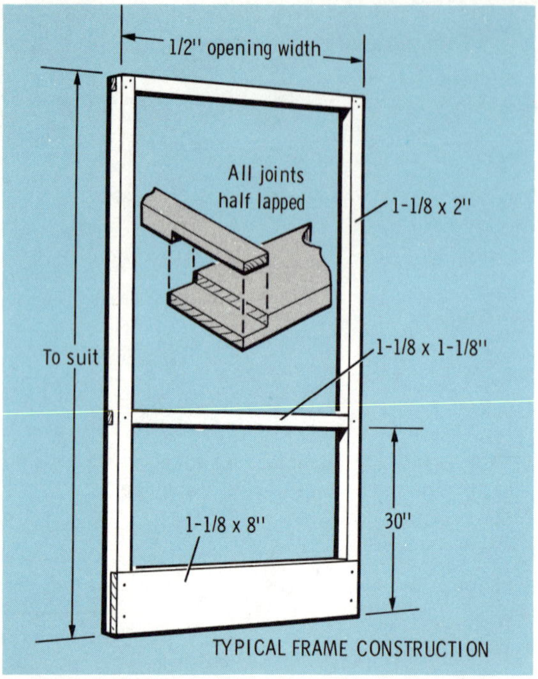

SCREEN FRAMES are built with half-lap joints for strength. Make two frames for each 8-ft. opening.

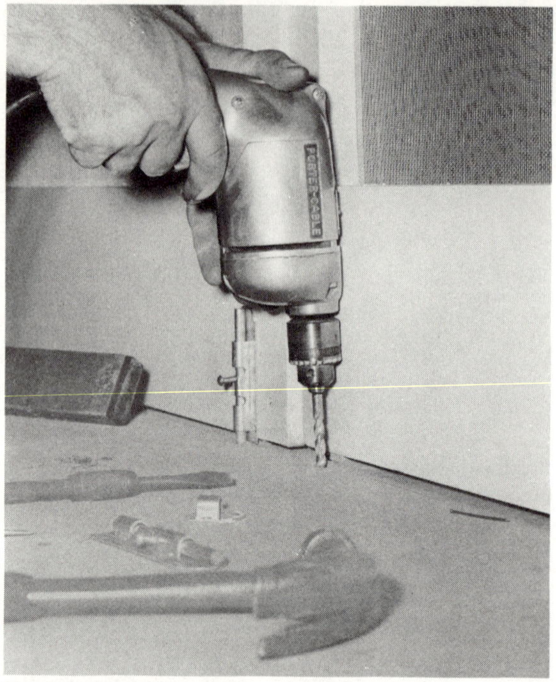

SLIDING-DOOR BOLTS lock screens to the slab. Use a masonry bit to drill holes in the slab.

latter case, door bolts are added to the bottom rails to engage holes drilled in the slab. Quarter-round molding nailed to the posts and lintel makes the screens fit bug-tight. Drain notches should be provided along the bottoms of the screens, and if screens are permanently installed, pick copper wire or aluminum, or one of the new plastic screening materials, to cover them.

The door opening in the end of the porch is framed with 2x4s which are anchored to the slab and the joist with angle brackets. You can buy a stock door as cheaply as you can make one. The area which surrounds the doorway is fitted with individual screens.

As the summer goes by you'll enjoy your porch more and more. You'll find it one of the best investments you can make for a small home.

QUARTER-ROUND MOLDING, tacked to posts and lintel, provides neat rabbets in which screens rest.

THE DOORWAY is framed in the end with 2x4s for a stock door. Openings around the door are screened.

Loose marble top

I've bought a nightstand with a marble top about 15 in. square. It is not attached. What adhesive or glue should I use to fasten it in place?—Roy Wilkins, Rochester, N.Y.

Although it may have been done, I've never seen a marble top of any size attached with adhesive. Usually it is held in place with some form of cleating that's made a part of the original construction and finished to match the wood. One marble top I've seen had shallow holes drilled near the four corners on the bottom face. Short locating dowels were fitted loosely in these holes to hold the top in place. I saw a small top recently that had a single cleat, or stop, cemented to the underside, but I suspect that this may not have been done originally.

As for your particular case, you might well find that a tape having adhesive on both sides will do an adequate job in holding the top in place.

Flooded asphalt-tile floor

The tiled floor (asphalt tile) in part of my basement was flooded recently. Water remained on the floor about three days and drained away slowly. Will the tile loosen?—Ruben Asp, Racine, Wis.

I don't know. But if tiles have not loosened at joints or corners by now, they are not likely to do so in the future, especially if they were properly installed originally. I wouldn't lose any sleep over this situation.

Crack patch

My patio floor is of natural stone laid in a concrete bed. Only 10x12 ft., it's cracked diagonally all the way across, right through the stones. The crack is a hairline part of the way and not more than ¼ in. at the widest. Do I fill it as is, chisel it wider or what?—C.E., N.J.

By "laid in a concrete bed," I assume you mean the stones were originally bedded in concrete over a gravel fill, and that the openings between the stones were concrete-mortared flush with the surface. Settling of whatever the builder used as fill has undoubtedly caused the crack. There's a possibility that the crack may open farther, but I'd try filling it "as is." Several types of concrete crack fillers are available, some of which come in a cartridge for use in a caulking gun. The main problem is to clean the crack thoroughly, removing all dirt and loose debris. Usually you can do this with a strong stream of water from a hose while using a small screwdriver or other pointed tool to loosen any embedded dirt. Thoroughness of the cleaning will determine the success of the repair patch.

A thin mix of concrete patcher will probably run deeper into the fine crack than most other patchers. Fill the crack a little over flush and then brush off lightly. Cover it with wet sacks or cloths and keep them damp for at least 36 hours.

Lumpy lawn

Why is my lawn so rough and bumpy under trees? I have a wide curb shaded by large trees and under these the lawn surface is so rough it is difficult to hang onto my power-mower handle. Is there any way it can be made smoother?—I.H., Ill

If you look closely during a heavy rain you will see water falling in streams from the tree limbs. This forces the soil into alternate depressions and hummocks and make mowing unpleasant, if not difficult. There isn't much you can do except to spread a thin dressing of black soil over the surface each season and then rake and roll it smooth. When spreading the dressing care must be taken not to cover the crowns of the grass plants. Also, be very careful when raking the dressing not to damage the plants or pull them loose. If the black soil is damp when spread and raked, let it dry sufficiently to prevent it from sticking to the roller. On sloping curbs or lawns it is often best to use a light top dressing of peat moss, cocoa-bean hulls or some similar lawn dressing rather than black soil which may wash away in a heavy rain.

Any of these dressings will help to "cushion" the bumps and depressions and make your mower more tractable. Of course, it may be possible to trim the trees in such a way as to break and disperse the streams that are causing the trouble, but this may be costly and difficult to carry out effectively.

Hide-a-fence planting

What plants can I use to conceal a chain-link fence? The fence is about 50 ft. long and, although quite new, I'd like to conceal it entirely.—J.L., Mich.

If the fence is located where the sun shines most of the day, a flowering vine such as clematis or climbing honeysuckle will do it in a season or two. However, you should consider that it also will contribute to the deterioration of the fence by opening the way to rust. Also, the weight of the vine eventually may cause the linkage to sag between posts.

THE BUG-FREE party room shown gives all the advantages of outdoor living plus protection from the weather. Whenever it rains, the garage doors still close.

Your garage can be a screened porch

By CRAIG WILSON

■ A QUICK, inexpensive way to gain a closed-in patio is simply to screen an existing garage. Though an attached garage is more desirable for this improvement, there's no reason why the idea can not be adapted to a detached one. Either way, you will gain by giving those noisy, sometimes clutter-prone, bored youngsters a place to play on a rainy day or creating a spot for Mom and Dad to get away from it all.

Since my garage has a 15-ft.- wide door opening, I laid out the screened wall in six panels, including the convenience door at one end. And, because my wife and I don't particularly care for airconditioning, I installed a 24-in. fan in the wall between the house and garage. Thus, the screened opening is ample for drawing cool, evening breezes into our home.

SEE ALSO
Garage doors . . . Garage remodeling . . . Garages, storage . . . Garden shelters . . . Gazebos . . . House additions . . . Patios . . . Screens

Before starting the project, make certain that the garage-door handle projects no farther than the garage-door stops. Then lay the sole plate along the garage-door opening and line it up with the stops on the *inside*. This is fastened with flat-head wood screws into lead anchors dropped into the concrete. When you disassemble the setup, the plugs can be filled with corks to prevent them from becoming clogged with dirt.

Divide your garage opening into panels 30 to 40 in. wide for best-looking results. The entrance door is optional but we have found that it was well worth the small amount of extra effort that building it required. For rigidity, I used a 2x2 as the door post (on the hinged side), fastening it at top and bottom with L-shaped brackets and screws.

For the usual reasons—weather and termite-resistant qualities—I used redwood throughout. The redwood can be stained natural or painted to suit your preference.

Caution: Since there's a more than even chance that your garage finished opening may be out of plumb or not level, trim and fit the individual screens to their exact position in sequence. Link each screen to its neighbor as shown in the drawings, and, to save yourself some frustration next spring when putting them back up, number the screens for easy identification and quick placement.

If you decide to paint your screens, the finished job will look a lot neater if you do all the carpentry first, including temporary assembly. Then, take them down, prime and paint the wood and fasten the wire screening.

For wrinkle-free screens, use the time-tested method of shimming both ends and clamping the middle before stapling the screening to the framework. To finish, cover the staples with conventional screen molding.

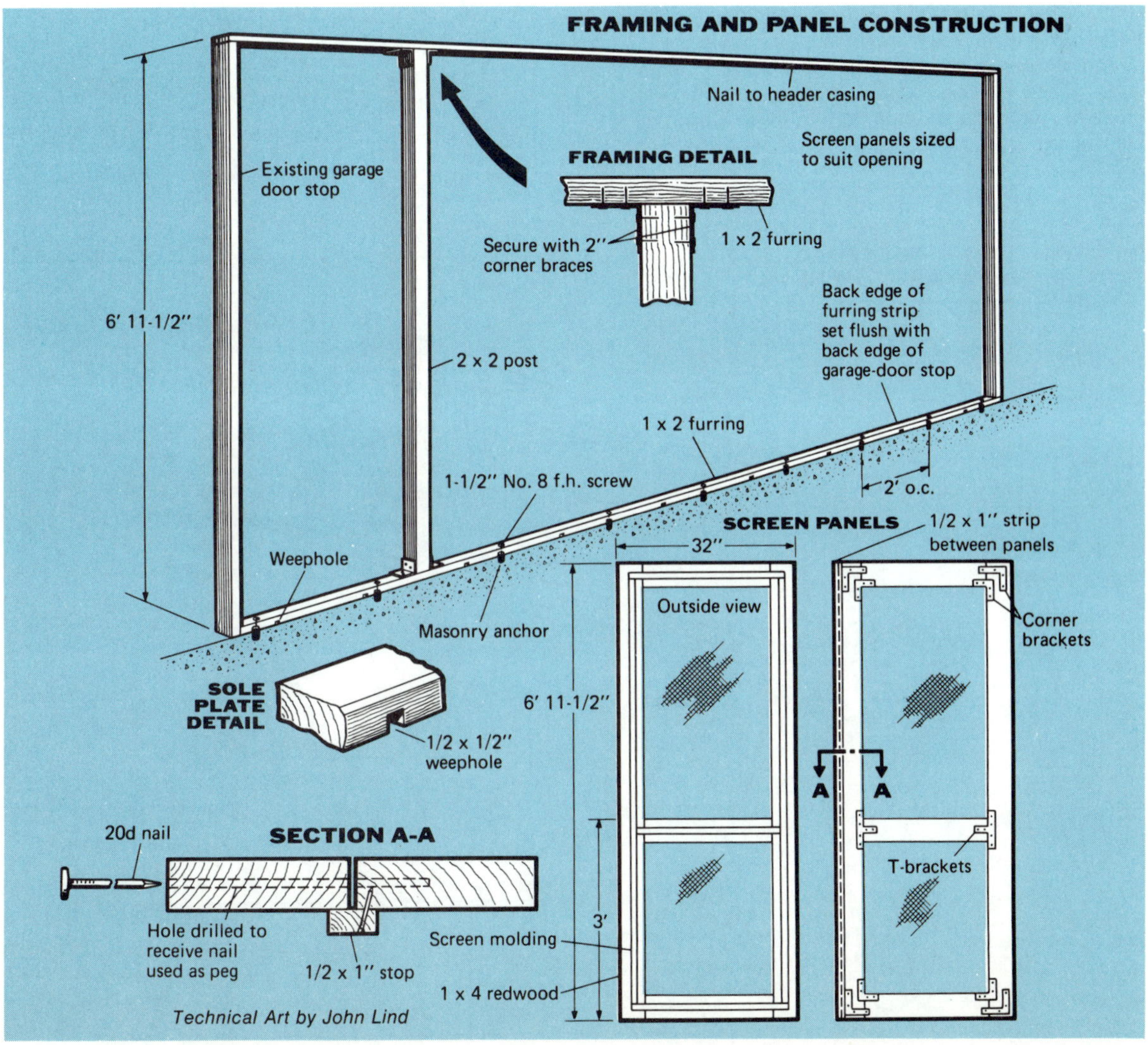

How to stretch screen wire

Play it smart; let frame do stretching

Ripping the old wire from wooden frames and stapling on the new is simple enough—it's the stretching that's the tricky part. Trying to get it smooth and taut by hand not only is hard on the fingers but invariably results in a belly in the wire, no matter how you tug and pull.

Actually, it's not that hard a job. If you play it smart, the frame itself can be used to do the stretching. Bowing the frame slightly is the most common method. This can be done with a couple of jack sticks, as at right, or with blocks and C-clamps, as shown below. After the wire is stapled to each end and the bow relieved, the frame will straighten out and stretch the wire as taut as a drumhead. The stapling is completed along each side while the frame is flat. This method works best on full-length frames, with the frame supported on a couple of sawhorses or wooden boxes. It doesn't take much of a bow; in fact, you should avoid bowing the frame too much as this could result in the wire pulling out the staples or tearing loose.

SEE ALSO
**Moldings . . . Remodeling ideas . . .
Storm doors and windows . . . Windows**

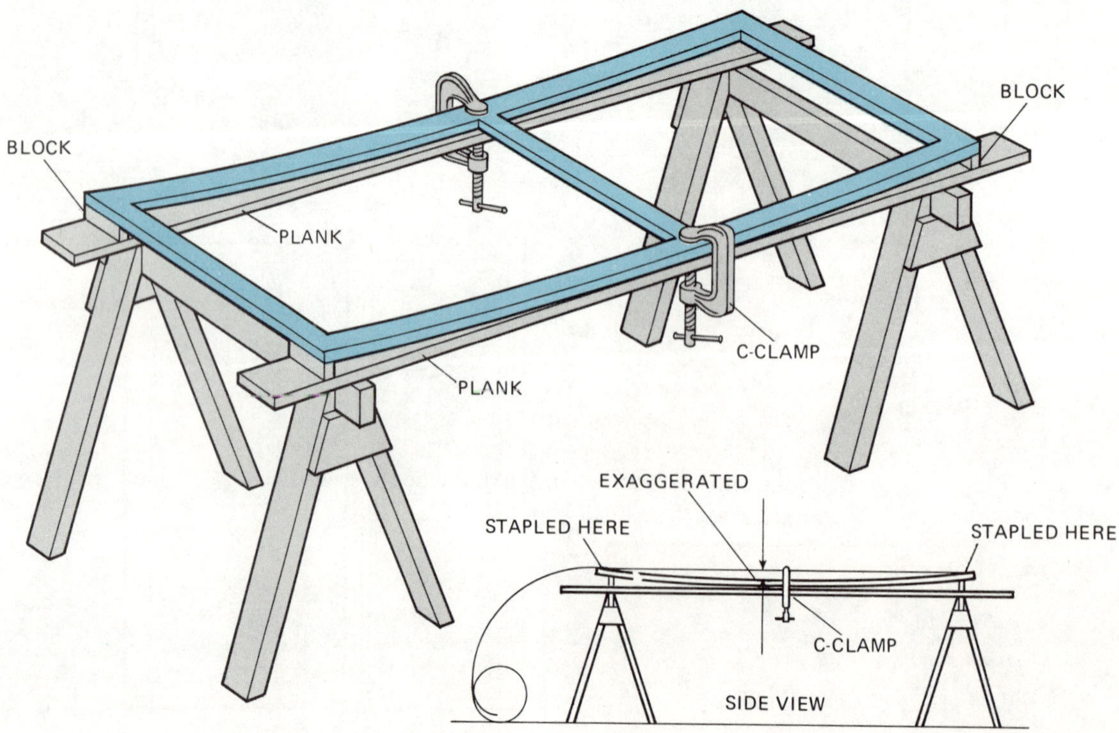

SCREEN WIRE is available in standard widths of 24, 26, 28, 30, 32, 36 and 42 inches. You have a choice of galvanized, aluminum, copper and fiberglass wire, and you may use either tacks or double-pointed screen staples to fasten it.

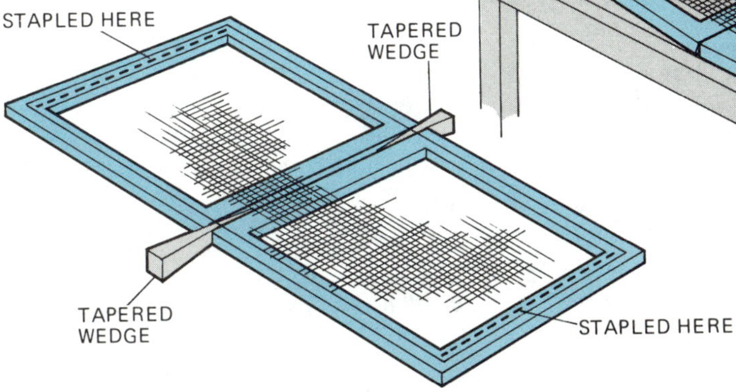

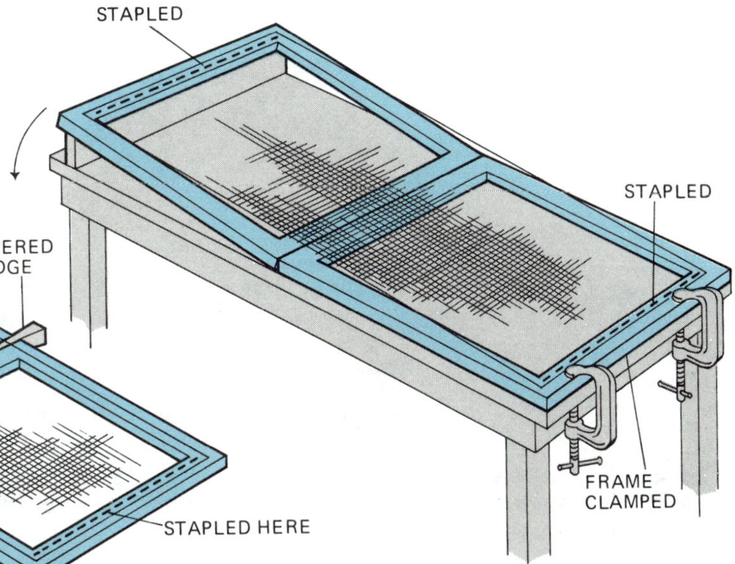

Small frames stretch each other

Small screens can be used to stretch the wire by covering two at a time (above). Frames are flat on a floor or table with one elevated a bit. In each case, they are butted and the wire stapled to the outer ends only. In method A, the wire is stretched by removing the block; in method B, it's done by forcing the frames apart with tapered wedges. Shown below is still another way for stretching wire on a full-length frame.

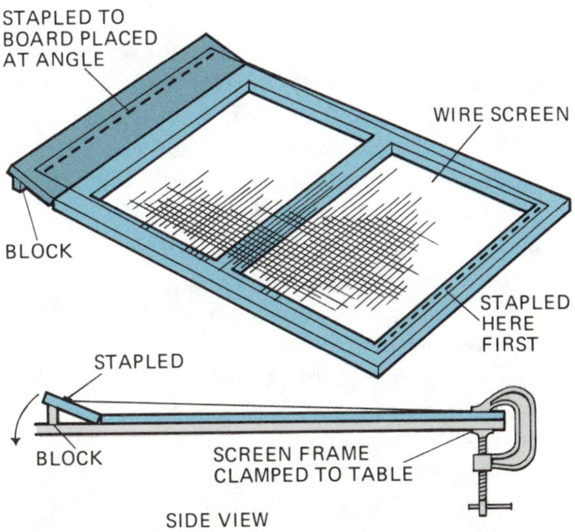

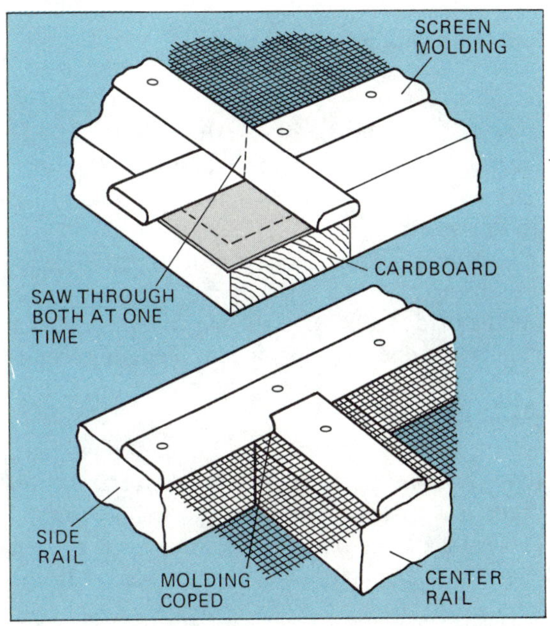

Slick molding trick

If you don't own a miterbox, you can do without one when mitering screen molding. Simply let one strip lap the other (above), then saw through both strips at a 45° angle at one time. Cardboard will protect frame from saw marks. Center-rail molding is coped to mate with side moldings.

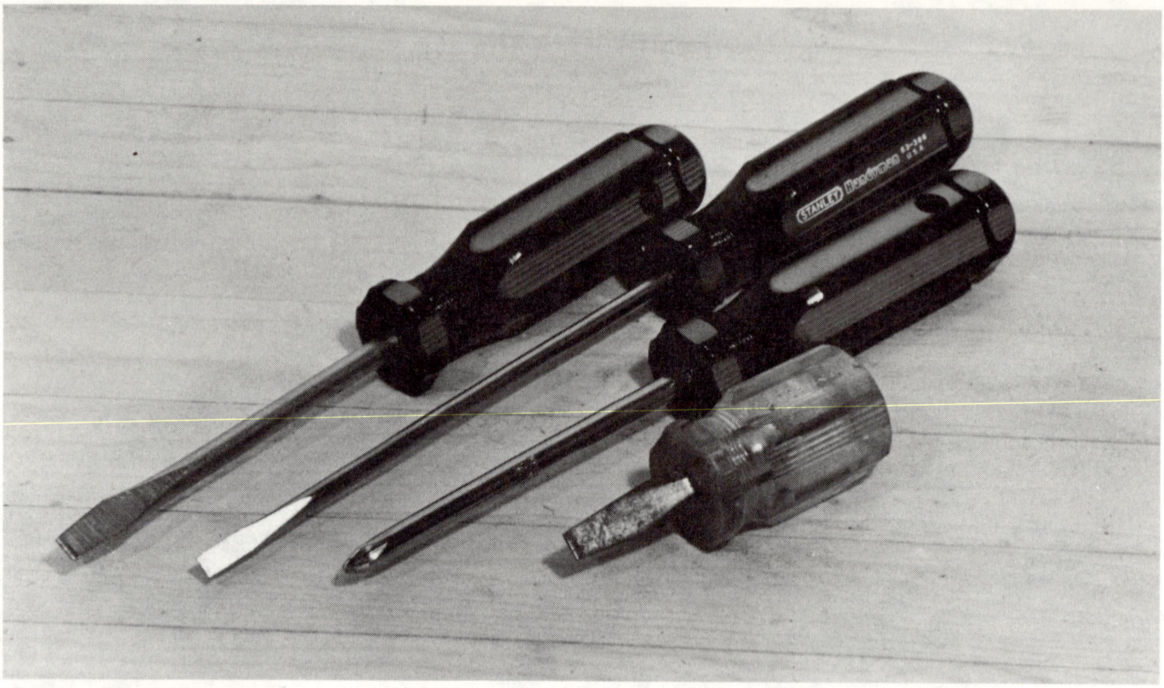

TYPICAL SCREWDRIVERS you should have in your home-repair toolbox: from left, driver with 6-in. shank for most tasks; cabinet screwdriver with thin shank for use in deep, counterbored holes; driver for Phillips screws; and a short stubby screwdriver for use in hard-to-work-in spots.

Screwdriver basics

By HARRY WICKS

■ SINCE IT IS USED as frequently—if not *more* often than—any other hand tool, the ordinary screwdriver probably takes more abuse than all the others.

Common abuses include use of the wrong-size driver to turn a screw home, grinding or filing the blade to the wrong shape, and prying with it, as when opening a paint can. Fledgling woodworkers have even been known to use the tool in place of a cold chisel!

The most common misuse of the screwdriver, though, is mismatching the screwdriver to the job that's to be done. If you use too small a screwdriver in a large screw's slot, you stand a good chance of damaging the driver's blade. If the blade is too large for the screw, you very likely will mar the wood surrounding the screwhead.

SEE ALSO

Caddies, tool . . . Screws . . . Sharpening, tool . . . Shop techniques . . . Shop tools . . . Toolboxes . . . Tools, hand

the right screwdriver

Take care in selecting the right screwdriver to match the screw. If you lack a Phillips screwdriver when one is needed, don't try to drive the screw with a narrow conventional screwdriver; in addition to burring the screwhead you will damage the tip of the screwdriver.

Using the wrong type screwdriver will almost always cause screwhead damage. And that can mean sheer frustration later when you have to remove that damaged screw.

The average home-repair toolbox should contain the four screwdrivers shown. With this assortment you can handle most household tasks. A good fifth screwdriver to have on hand is one that has a length of squared shank beneath its handle. This portion of the shank can be gripped with a wrench when you have to back out a stubborn screw.

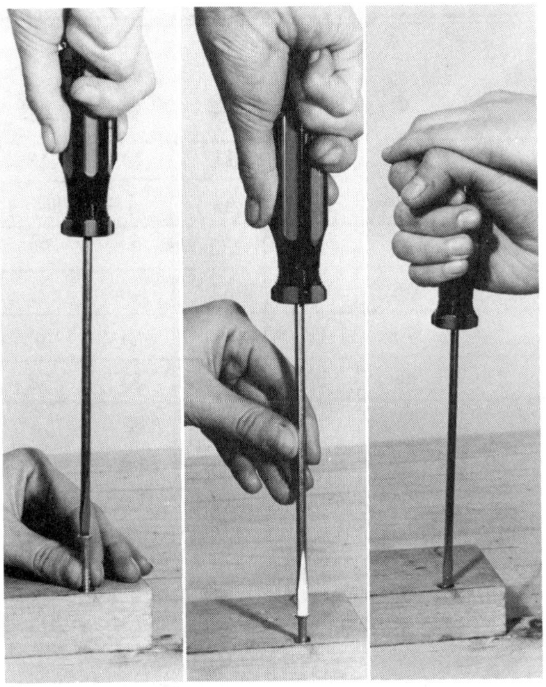

THE RIGHT WAY to drive a screw: Left, insert tip of screw into pilot hole, and the screwdriver tip in screw's slot. Hold the screw perpendicular with one hand, using the other hand to make certain screwdriver is in the same axis as the screw. Center, use one hand to keep the blade steady while the other turns the screwdriver handle. Finally, use both hands as shown to get good power for seating the screw securely.

always make a pilot hole

Get into the habit of making a pilot hole before driving *any* screw; this is a must, not a matter of preference.

When working with small screws and softwoods, the pilot hole can be made with an awl or ice pick. In hardwoods, and when the screw location is near the end of the board, always use a drill regardless of wood type. The bit should be sized so that the screw's thread will bite into the wood. For example, if you hold the screw and bit lined up with the bit between your eye and the screw, only the screw's threads, some shank, and head should show.

CLEARANCE hole for shank is a must when you are fastening two pieces of wood.

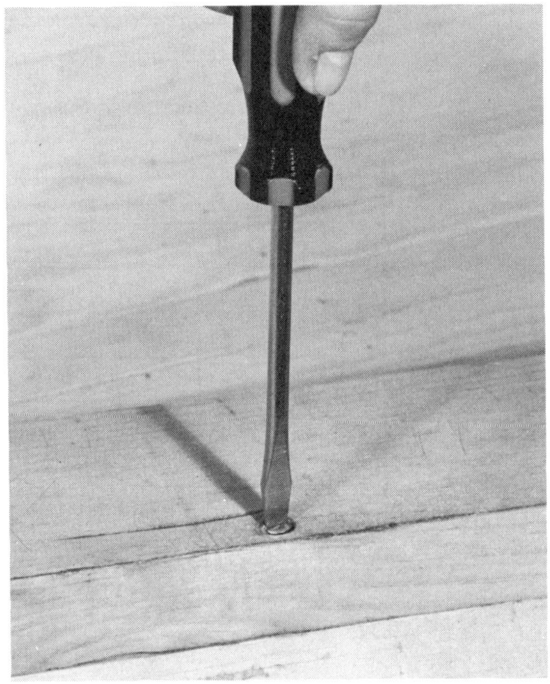

SCREWDRIVER BLADE should be sized to fit the screw. If it's too big the workpiece will be chewed; too small, both screw and screwdriver take beating.

When you are joining two pieces of material together, you must also drill a clearance hole for the shank. Here a hole equal in diameter to the body shank is bored in the *leading* (top) piece of wood. As the screw is turned home its head will draw the leading piece to the second piece of wood.

MOST COMMONLY USED screwheads from left to right: oval, round, pan and flat.

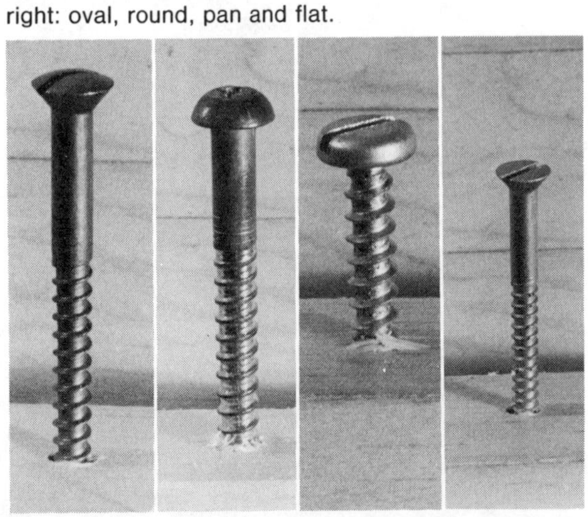

Gauge Numbers			0	1	2	3	4	5	6
Actual Cross Section of Screws			●	●	●	●	●	●	●
Basic Decimal Diameter			.060	.073	.086	.099	.112	.125	.138
Fractional Dia. Nearest 64th			1/16−	5/64−	5/64+	3/32+	7/64+	1/8−	9/64−
Drill Number			52	47	42	37	32	30	27
Pilot or Anchor-Hole Sizes	Hard-wood	Slotted Screws	70	66	56	54	52	49	47
		Phillips "			70	66	56	54	52
	Soft-wood	Slotted "	75	71	65	58	55	53	52
		Phillips "			75	71	65	58	55
Threads Per Inch			32	28	26	24	22	20	18
Maximum Head Diameter			.119	.146	.172	.199	.225	.252	.279

Drill sizes for body clearance holes are given in either numbered or lettered drill sizes. Dimensions are given in decimal or fractional parts of inches. In general, pilot holes should be about 90 per cent of screw-core sizes for hardwood, 70 per cent for softwood. In end grain and also in softwoods, such as

Choose the right screw for the job

By W. CLYDE LAMMEY

Joints made with screws resist pull, shear and shock very nearly as much as those joined with the best glues. Here are pointers on selecting the right screw

A WOOD SCREW HAS FAR greater holding power than a nail in either hard or softwood. A project joined with nails only can be racked out of shape or the joinery pried apart by judicious use of hammer claws or a pry-bar. But not so with screws; you have to back them out one by one with a screwdriver in order to disassemble the joints without damage.

A screw cuts its own threads in wood when turned into a counterbore of the proper size. As the screw is driven, the raised threads force the wood fibers apart, and the advance of the threads draws the parts being joined tightly together when the screwhead is finally seated. Once seated, a screw won't shake loose and it won't let go.

Most wood screws are made of steel, but screws also are available in brass, bronze and aluminum. Steel screws also come plated with brass, zinc, cadmium and chromium to resist rust and make them more attractive to the eye when used in exposed locations. Screws with flat heads are perhaps the most commonly used, but wood screws also are available in all ordinary sizes with oval, round, fillister and square heads, the latter supplied as lagscrews and as special screws for attaching ornamental hinges and latches. On some of these the heads are not only square, but they also are slotted so that they may be installed with a screwdriver. On lagscrews you have to use a wrench, as the head is square but not slotted.

Sizes (the shank diameters) are designated by

SEE ALSO
Bolts . . . Fasteners . . . Hinges . . . Nails

7	8	9	10	11	12	14	16	18	20	24
.151	.164	.177	.190	.203	.216	.242	.268	.294	.320	.372
5/32−	5/32+	11/64+	3/16+	13/64−	7/32−	15/64+	17/64+	19/64−	21/64−	3/8
22	18	14	10	4	2	D	I	N	P	V
44	40	37	33	31	30	25	18	13	4	1
49	47	44	40	37	33	31	30	25	18	13
51	48	45	43	40	38	32	29	26	19	15
53	52	51	48	45	43	40	38	32	29	26
16	15	14	13	12	11	10	9	8	8	7
.305	.332	.358	.385	.411	.438	.491	.544	.597	.650	.756

pine, it frequently is unnecessary to drill a pilot hole.

There are nearly 300 standard screws of various sizes, lengths and types. Regular screws have gimlet points; cone and diamond points are special. Length is measured from the threaded tip to the largest bearing surface of the head. Body diameters—gauge sizes—increase in steps of .013 in. Tolerance from specified sizes ranges from .004 in. plus to .007 in. minus. A 10-per-cent variation in threads per inch is permitted. Head dimensions of wood screws are identical to those of machine screws of the same size and type.

WOOD SCREWS

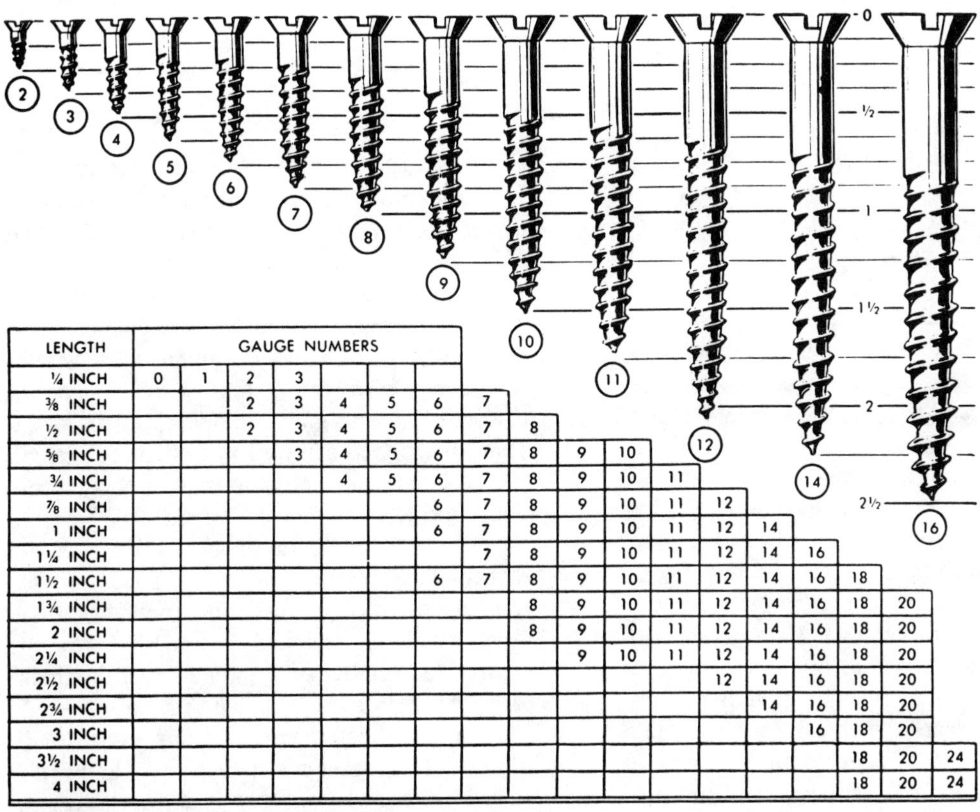

LENGTH	GAUGE NUMBERS																
¼ INCH	0	1	2	3													
⅜ INCH			2	3	4	5	6	7									
½ INCH			2	3	4	5	6	7	8								
⅝ INCH				3	4	5	6	7	8	9	10						
¾ INCH					4	5	6	7	8	9	10	11					
⅞ INCH							6	7	8	9	10	11	12				
1 INCH							6	7	8	9	10	11	12	14			
1¼ INCH								7	8	9	10	11	12	14	16		
1½ INCH							6	7	8	9	10	11	12	14	16	18	
1¾ INCH									8	9	10	11	12	14	16	18	20
2 INCH									8	9	10	11	12	14	16	18	20
2¼ INCH										9	10	11	12	14	16	18	20
2½ INCH													12	14	16	18	20
2¾ INCH														14	16	18	20
3 INCH															16	18	20
3½ INCH																18	20	24
4 INCH																18	20	24

WHEN YOU BUY SCREWS, SPECIFY (1) LENGTH, (2) GAUGE NUMBER, (3) TYPE OF HEAD-FLAT ROUND OR OVAL, (4) MATERIAL-STEEL, BRASS BRONZE, ETC., (5) FINISH-BRIGHT STEEL BLUED CADMIUM NICKEL OR CHROMIUM PLATED

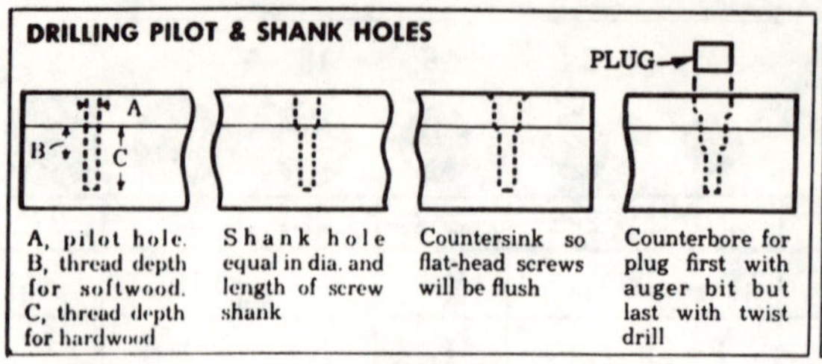

LAG SCREWS — LENGTHS AND DIAMETERS (in inches)

Lengths	Diameters			
	¼	⅜, 7/16, ½	⅝, ¾	⅞, 1
1	x	x		
1½	x	x	x	
2, 2½, etc., to 10	x	x	x	x
11 & 12		x	x	x
13 to 16			x	x

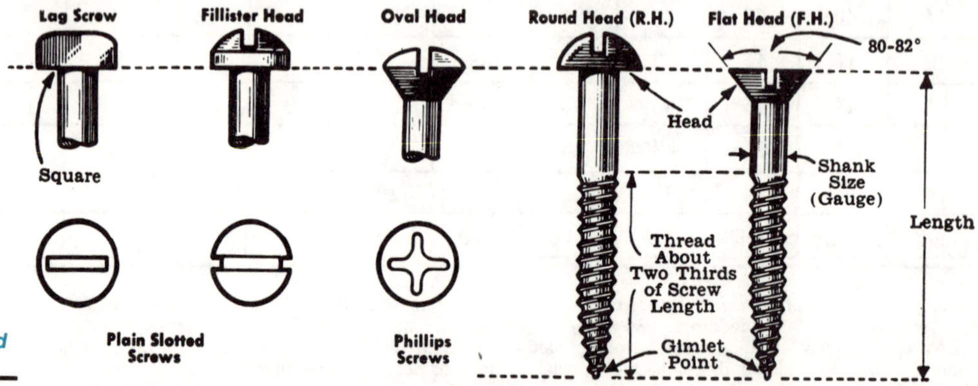

choosing screws, continued

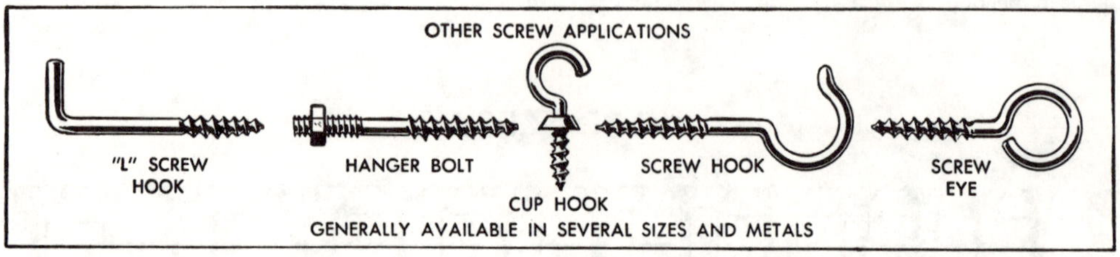

numbers. Only sizes (numbers) 2 through 16 are detailed. The sizes go up with the numbers and only the average sizes in common use are shown.

Slots in screwheads are of three common types: those slotted all the way across the head; another in which a stopped slot is milled into the head; and a third having the head recessed or cross-slotted to take the tip of the special Phillips screwdriver.

Lengths of common screws usually are in inches and even fractions of an inch as 1, 1¼, 1½ and so on. Those having a length of less than 1 in. also come in eighths as ⅜ in., ⅝ in. and so on.

When turning in screws it's important to use a screwdriver of the correct size. If the blade tip is too small it may twist out of the slot; if too large it may slip out of the slot or damage the wood when you seat a flathead screw. When seating a flathead screw, select a blade having a width slightly less than the full width of the slot in the screwhead. The blade should fit the slot snugly with a minimum of side play. Otherwise it may slip out when you apply torque, and damage the wood, the slot or both.

The size of the screw hole also is important. The wood must be counterbored and countersunk if you're using flathead screws. The first portion of the counterbore must be just large enough (see the tables) to take the shank, and the second portion should be of a diameter and depth to take the threaded section, the diameter being measured at the bottom of the threads. In softwoods and end grain, the depth of the counterbore is stopped a little short of the full length of the screw. In hardwoods the counterbore should normally be the full length.

Ideally, the length of the screw used should be such that the full thread is turned into the stationary piece of the assembly, with the shank in the piece being attached. Put another way, the length of the smaller hole should equal the thickness of the stationary piece, and the larger should equal the depth of the piece being joined to it. Of course this ratio isn't always possible, but the common rule is to approach it as nearly as possible in any joinery which is to be made with screws. This position of the screw in the parts being joined normally gives the maximum holding power.

WHEN NAILING STRIPS of tongue-and-groove flooring, protect them from denting hammer blows with this simple shield. It's just a 3 or 4-in.-long section of angle iron with one leg cut to the height of the tongue to the face. The center of this shortened leg then is notched for the nail. Even if you should miss the nailhead, the angle will absorb the force of the blow.

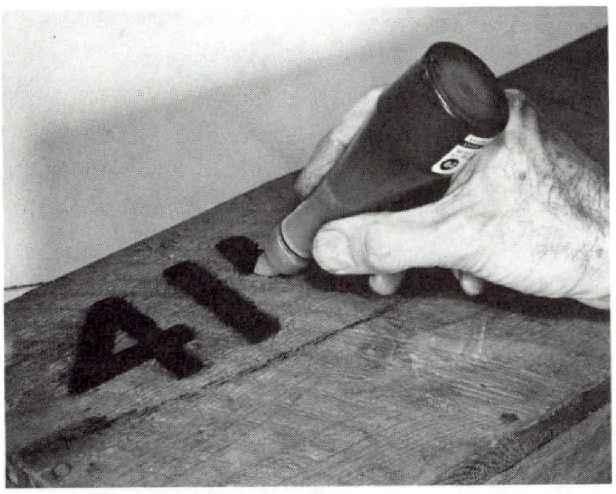

WHEN FILLED WITH INK or paint, a spreader-type glue bottle will make it easy to address shipping crates or cartons. Just press the rubber cap of the bottle down against the crate so ink begins to flow, then draw the cap through the ink to form the necessary letters or numerals. Just be sure to apply only light pressure to avoid covering the surface of the crate with unsightly and unreadable blobs of ink. Show this trick to your children—it will help them make school posters.

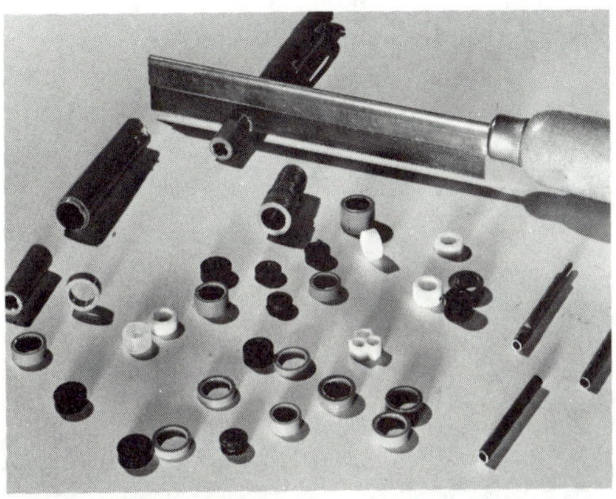

OLD BALLPOINT PENS can be made into useful items for your workshop supply. Remove the ink cartridge and all metal fittings, then slice the body, cap and even the ink cartridge into segments of assorted lengths. The result is a collection of plastic washers and spacers useful for building or repairing different projects. Some of the rings and spacers shown at the left were cut from the body or cap using the saw shown, while others were cut off on a lathe.

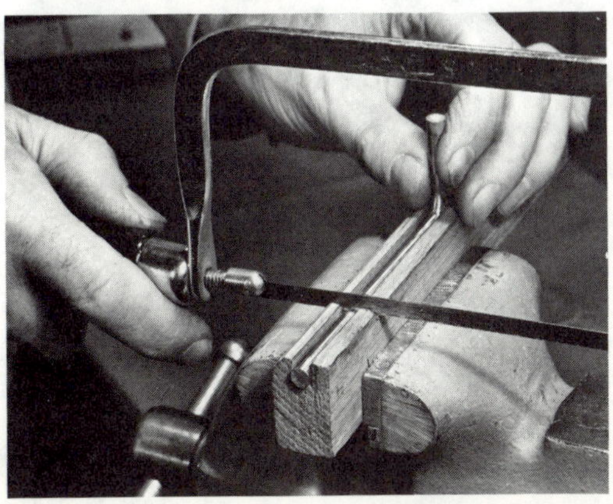

TO SQUARELY CUT sections of small-diameter tubes or thin, limber rods, clamp a suitable length of tongue-and-groove flooring in a bench vise so that the groove side faces upward. Cut a fine kerf across the lips of the groove, much like the slots in a miterbox. Then just position the tube or rod in the groove so the cutoff point is aligned with the fine kerf and saw through the work with a hacksaw. Supporting the work this way also prevents it from becoming marred in the vise jaws.

Fun with a doodling engraver

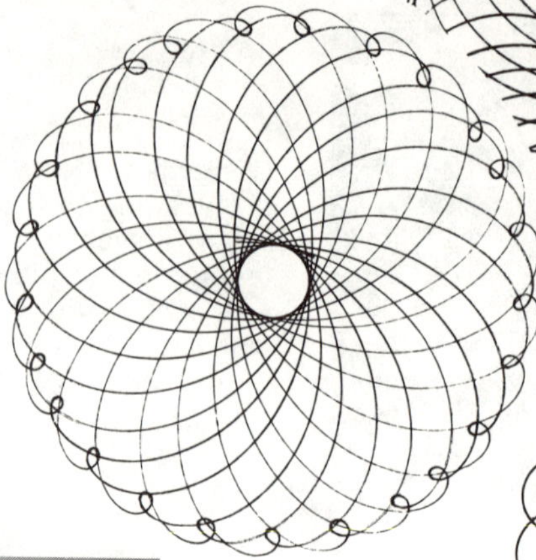

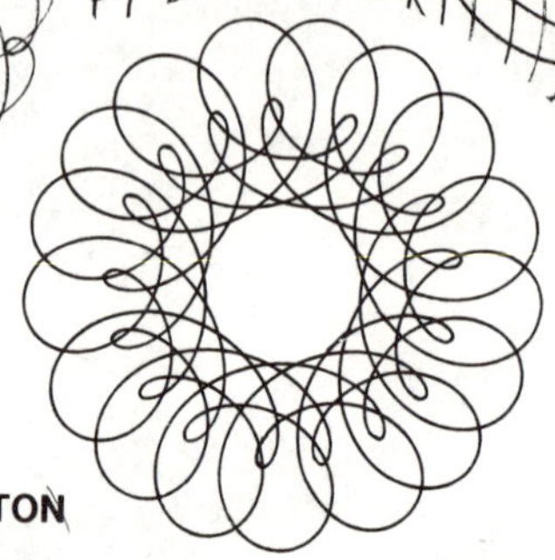

A FINE ballpoint pen is used to form a design on cardboard taped to a wood wheel. For scribing metal, use a diamond stylus

By WALTER E. BURTON

■ IF YOU LIKE TO DOODLE, you'll love the way you can do it with this updated version of an old-time polygraph machine. It uses a ballpoint pen for paper or a diamond-point, abrasive-wheel dresser for metal. All you do is turn a crank and watch the design appear like magic.

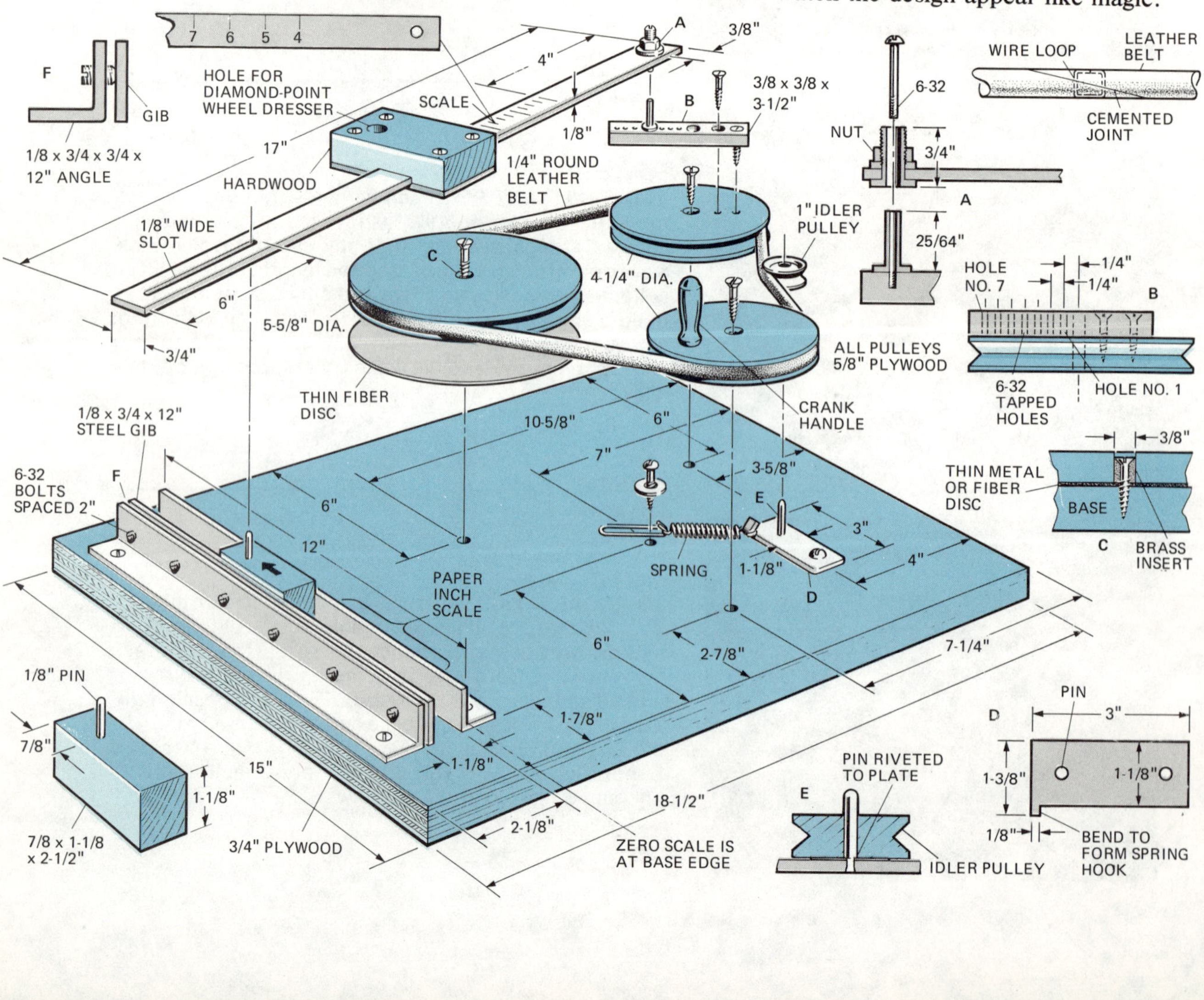

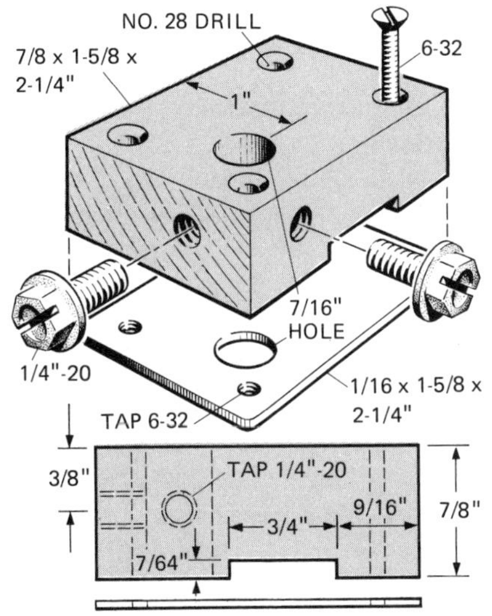

THIS HANDSOME clock dial, an example of the use of metal designs, was engraved in wire-brushed aluminum

THE CIRCULAR design on this trinket-box lid was given a ground finish with abrasive grains and then inset in the lid

Basically, the machine consists of three plywood wheels connected by a leather belt. Bits of masking tape attach the item to be decorated to the wheel, which acts as a rotating "drawing board." As this wheel turns, a block carrying the stylus (diamond tool or pen) moves over it, guided by the stylus arm.

The rotating wheel draws circles; the stylus arm draws oval figures. The combination of these two kinds of curves forms a decorative, usually symmetrical, pattern. Patterns are easily varied by changing the position of the pin that guides the stylus arm, the position of the stylus block along the arm, or the distance of the pivot point from the center of the wheel that operates the stylus arm.

The relative sizes of pivot wheel and pattern-holding wheel, as well as distance of stylus from centerline of arm and effective arm length, also determine the pattern.

The machine's base is a piece of ¾-in. plywood. (Locations of the various parts are given in relation to bottom and right-hand edges when the crank wheel faces the operator.)

I turned the wheels from ⅝-in. fir plywood and grooved the edges for ¼-in. round leather belts.

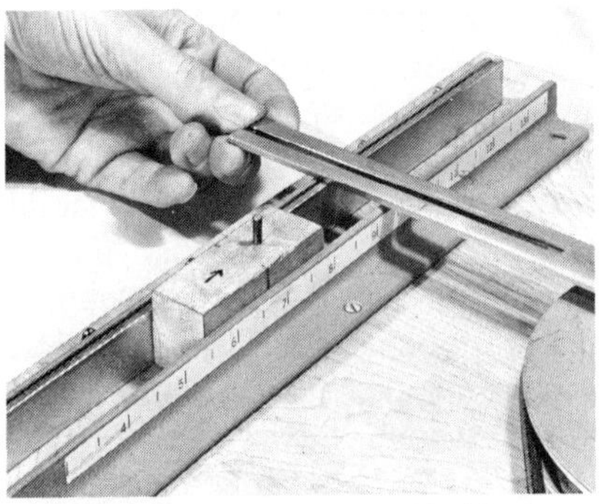
THE INDEX mark on the guide block is set by the inch scale

A SPRING-LOADED idler pulley keeps the belt taut and slip free

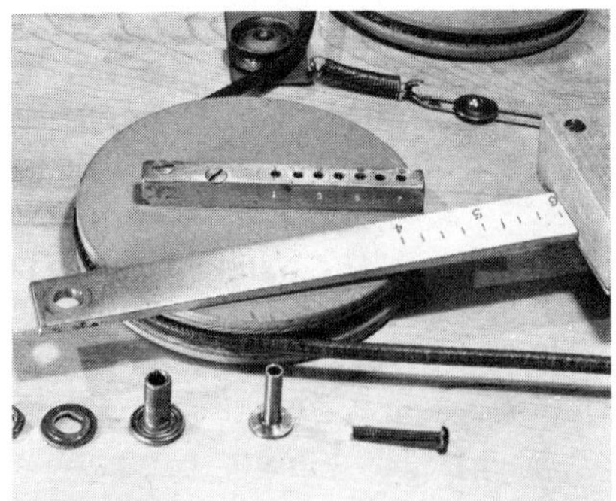
THESE are parts of the pivot assembly linking the stylus and the wood wheel

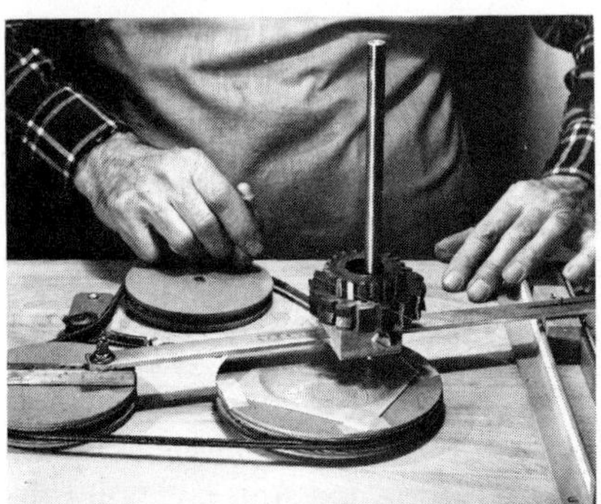
LIGHT oil applied to the metal surface beforehand reduces stylus friction

TABS OF masking tape at the corners hold the metal plate flat

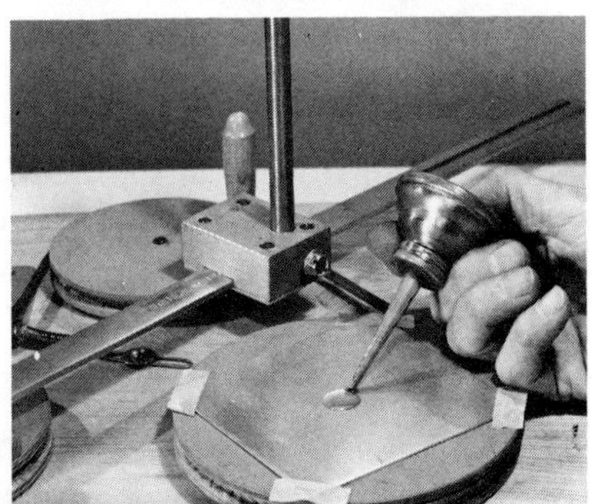
ADDED WEIGHT on the stylus arm lets the diamond cut the brass deeper

Each wheel bearing consists of a brass insert drilled to rotate snugly around a No. 6 wood screw. You can improve the wheel action by placing a thin washer of cardboard-like fiber between the wheel and the base.

I used a round leather sewing-machine belt, spliced the ends as shown and used Duco household cement and a wire-loop reinforcement to hold them in place. A coating of stick-type belt dressing will help to reduce the slipping.

A 1-in. idler pulley turns on a pin riveted to a thin steel plate, and a coil tension spring holds the pulley against the belt. An elongated wire loop clamped by a wood screw and washer anchors the spring.

The stylus has a ⅛ x 6-in. slot extending almost to one end. A ⅜-in. hole at the opposite end accepts the pivot assembly, which operates the stylus arm.

The steel crank bar has a series of 6-32 tapped holes on ¼-in. centers and is mounted so that hole No. 1 is ¼ in. from the wheel center. For small designs, an additional hole nearer the center is useful.

maple block holds stylus

A maple block grooved on the bottom holds the stylus. Depth of the groove is slightly less than arm thickness, so when the four 6-32 bolts are tightened, the block is locked securely on the arm.

Bore a 7/16-in. hole almost tangent to the groove to accept a diamond-tipped, abrasive-wheel dresser. The block can hold other tools, such as a ballpoint pen if built up with a piece of rubber tubing.

The weight of the stylus arm and block is sufficient for holding a ballpoint pen in contact with paper. For engraving metal, additional weight is required. Milling cutters (which weigh about 1½ lbs.) slipped over the diamond-tipped rod will do the trick although any similar weight may be used.

The maple arm-guide block rests in a channel formed by two pieces of metal angle. A gib positioned between the block and left-hand angle is used to lock the block in a fixed position. One bolt enters a hole drilled about halfway through the gib to prevent endwise slippage.

The block's pin engages the slot in the stylus arm and is positioned somewhat nearer one end of the block than the other. Reverse the block and a greater range of pin position can be obtained in one direction. At the block's midpoint, on each side, is an index mark for positioning the block relative to a scale. An arrow on top of the block points normally to the rear edge of the base.

Three scales enable setting for repeat drawing of a particular design.

- An inch scale 13-in. long is glued to the outer vertical surface of the right-hand metal angle 3 in. from the end for gauging the position of sliding block.
- An inch scale, with ¼-in. divisions, is stamped along the top of the stylus arm, with the "0" position coinciding with the center of the pivot hole over the pulley. Only the portion from 4 to 8 in. is needed. The right-hand edge of the block is used as an index line in setting the position of the stylus.
- A series of numbers—1, 3, 5 and 7—identify the tapped holes along the top of the steel bar. These numbers, with No. 1 hole near pulley center, indicate different positions of the stylus-arm pivot with respect to the axis of the pulley.

record design's 'formula'

Once a design has been worked out by trial, record its "formula" by writing down the three scale readings in left-to-right sequence. For example, 7, 5¾, 6 indicates that the guide block is at 7 in., the stylus-holding block is at 5¾ in. and the arm pivot is at hole No. 6. If desired, an arrow pointing upward for the "normal" position of the block, or downward for the reversed position, can be added to the formula.

Aluminum is easy to engrave; brass requires more pressure. Best pressure for various metals can be found by trial. Actually, when using a rounded diamond or other point, the "engraving" is more of a rubbing than a cutting action.

The metal blank should be flat. Its surface can be prepared in various ways, ranging from polishing to dulling by chemical etching or rubbing with a mixture of abrasive grit and water. For a ground-glass effect on aluminum, rub 180-grit aluminum-oxide grains mixed with water over the surface with a small metal block.

Fasten the blank with self-adhering tape and spread a thin layer of oil over the surface to reduce stylus friction. Bring the stylus against the blank with the arm elevated slightly above the guide block. Put additional weights in place, then turn the guide pulley slowly. Count the number of revolutions the wheel requires to create a pattern and record it along with the "formula." Best starting and stopping points for the stylus tip are on the smallest diameter of a pattern.

Protect your home from burglars

Why invite burglars when a small investment in locks, alarms, hardware and time can pay off in security and peace of mind? On these pages you will find many ideas to prevent thieves from getting into any room in your home

By IVAN BERGER

"BURGLARS LOOK FOR what we call 'targets of opportunity'—easy pickings," says Detective Jon Inzalaco of New York City's Police Crime Prevention Squad. "They're not out for hard work, or they'd be working. And despite their line of work, they're cowards, avoiding risk as much as they can. So the more trouble you can give a burglar, and the more obvious that trouble is, the more likely he is to go somewhere else."

Sending the burglar somewhere else isn't too hard, either. Locks, alarms and common sense are all you need—and all but the common sense are widely available and easy to install.

"Burglars hate noise, light or anything else that can call attention to them," says Detective Inzalaco. So an alarm can scare off a burglar when he's just started work—and knowing there's an alarm can do it even before he's started. If he's still not scared off, the alarm can summon help to stop him.

Yet even alarms, the most sophisticated defense in your home security arsenal, are easy to buy and install yourself—and comparatively inexpensive, too. (Systems that will protect eight doors and windows—and give fire warnings as well—are available for around $100 in ready-to-install form.)

There are three basic types of alarms: self-contained units that protect a single door or win-

THREE WAYS TO PROTECT YOUR HOME ELECTRONICALLY

COMBINATION SELF-CONTAINED alarm and patio latch made by 3M Corp. protects entrance that's often neglected by homeowners. Self-contained alarms are the cheapest type, not necessarily the best.

MOTION-DETECTOR triggers alarm if its wave field should be disturbed by a moving burglar—or a pet. This is easiest type alarm to install; most cover a room at a time; intruder usually must be in house before it will go off.

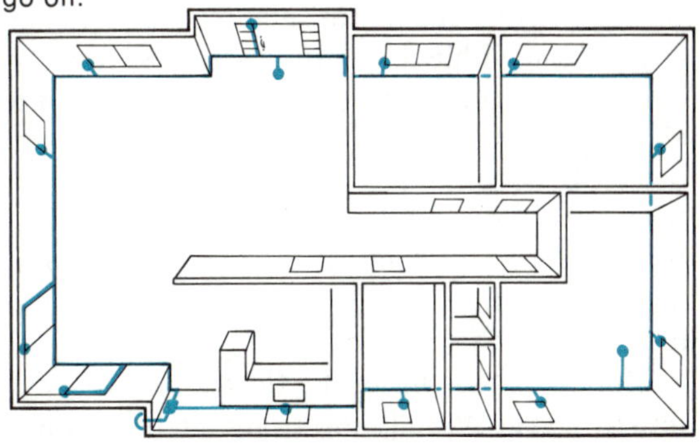

PERIMETER ALARMS give burglary warnings at as many parts or openings of the house as you like, can warn of other problems, too. "Wireless" types install easily.

SEE ALSO

Alarms, smoke . . . Burglar proofing . . . Closets . . . Doors . . . Hinges . . . Locks, door . . . Sliding glass doors . . . Storm doors and windows

dow, motion-sensing types that cover a single room or area, and perimeter types that can cover every critical point about your home.

The single-entry, self-contained type is a small box containing a battery, horn or siren, and some kind of triggering device; you fit one to each door or window that you want to protect. Some, in fact, are combined with door or window locks—a bargain only if *both* the lock and alarm are top quality.

Self-contained entry alarms are the least expensive alarms you can buy, and are easy to install: Alarm/lock combinations usually install in the same hole a normal rim-lock's cylinder would use, and door alarms usually require no keyhole (a delay lets you get in and turn them off).

small alarms may not do

But these small alarms aren't very loud—enough to warn anyone at home and possibly in the next apartment, but not enough to carry down a noisy block. And with everything right where the burglar is, they're vulnerable to any thief who can keep cool enough to silence them. (Obviously, solid construction is a must.) Cheap as they are, their cost mounts rapidly as the number of doors and windows covered increases; in a big house, it could quickly approach the cost of more sophisticated systems—and you'd still have to check and set each alarm individually every time you left the house.

Motion-sensing alarms can be even easier to install: Just set a self-contained motion-sensor in an inconspicuous corner of the room you want to protect, turn it on, and leave the room in the few seconds before the alarm sets itself. After that, any motion within the alarm's area first turns on a light (to frighten a thief, and to remind you to shut if off when you come in), then squawks its head off seconds later. Motion-sensors vary from about $70 to $500, some self-contained with built-in horns or sirens, others triggering remote indoor or outdoor warnings, with satellites monitoring other rooms.

Motion-sensor alarms fill the room with a pattern of waves (usually ultrasonic, in home models), and sense the frequency shifts when the waves are reflected back by moving objects (just as car horns shift pitch when traveling toward or away from you).

Older ultrasonics could be triggered by flapping drapes; more modern units are immune to this, but will be set off by pets within their coverage areas—or family members going for a mid-

DOUBLE-CYLINDER locks can't be opened by a burglar breaking through the glass panes of a door.

WINDOW GATES—strong but ugly—help keep tools and ladders locked in your garage where a burglar can't use them.

LIGHTS AT DOORS help you identify after-dark callers and expose night burglars working on your locks.

.ARM BELL under eaves is visible—but accessible—deterrent. Flashing light aws extra attention.

FIRE ALARMS belong in halls near bedrooms for maximum effect.

ALARM SENSOR above door triggers when door opens. Peephole reveals callers.

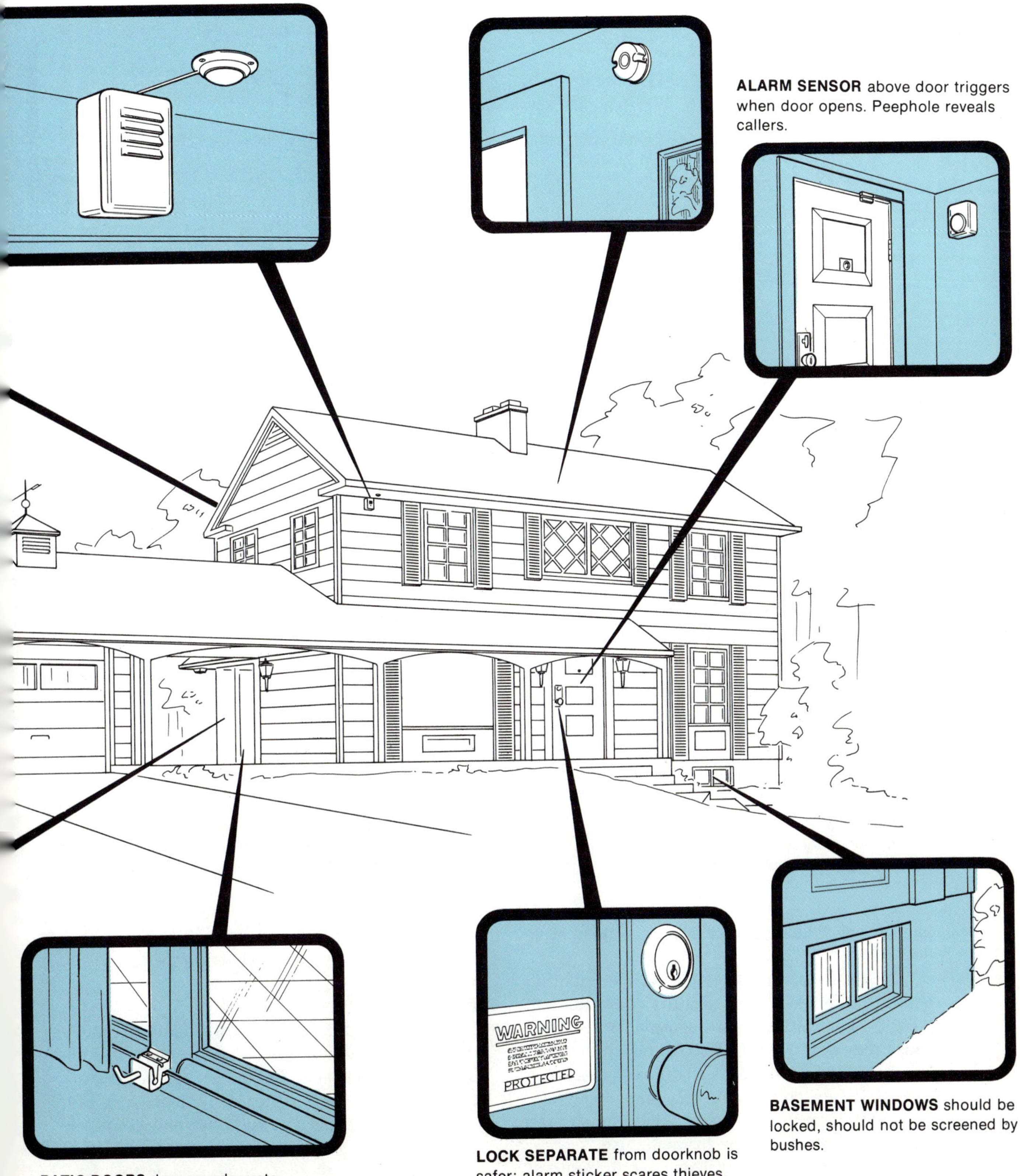

PATIO DOORS deserve adequate locks, too. This pin-type is good, but a key lock is even better.

LOCK SEPARATE from doorknob is safer; alarm sticker scares thieves.

BASEMENT WINDOWS should be locked, should not be screened by bushes.

ALARMS—A SOPHISTICATED DEFENSE

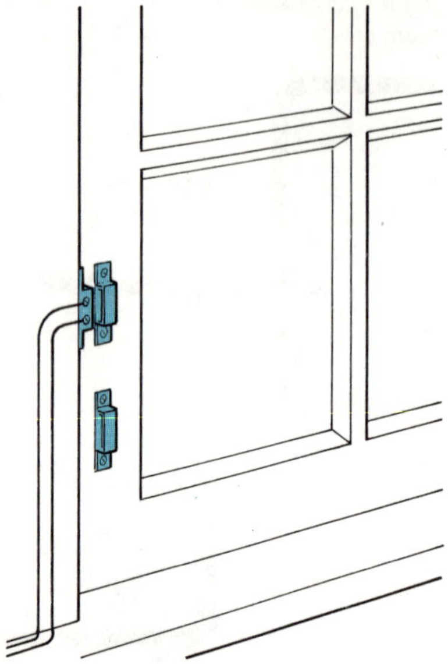

MAGNETIC SENSOR triggers when a window is opened. Extra magnet lets you open it a few inches for ventilation.

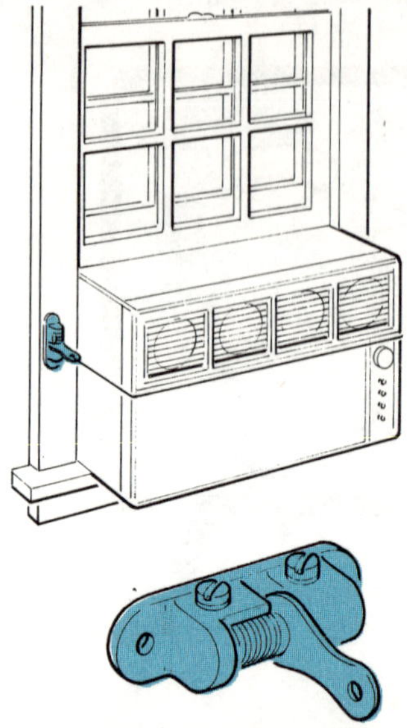

TRAP SWITCH—here guarding an airconditioning unit—triggers when the string pulls the tab out.

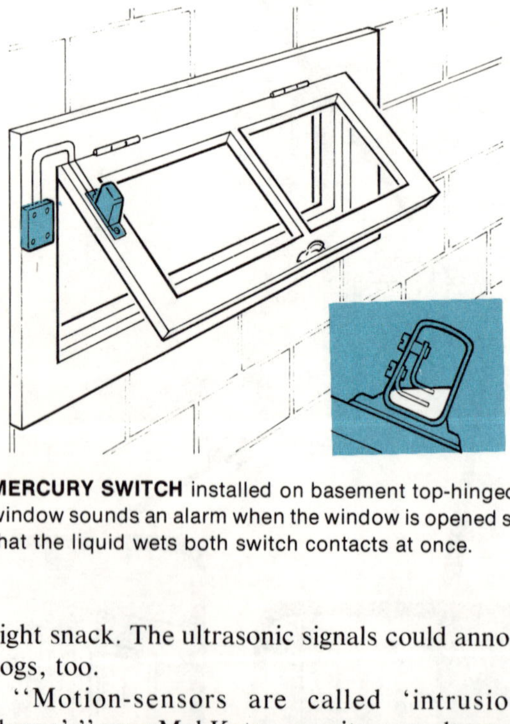

MERCURY SWITCH installed on basement top-hinged window sounds an alarm when the window is opened so that the liquid wets both switch contacts at once.

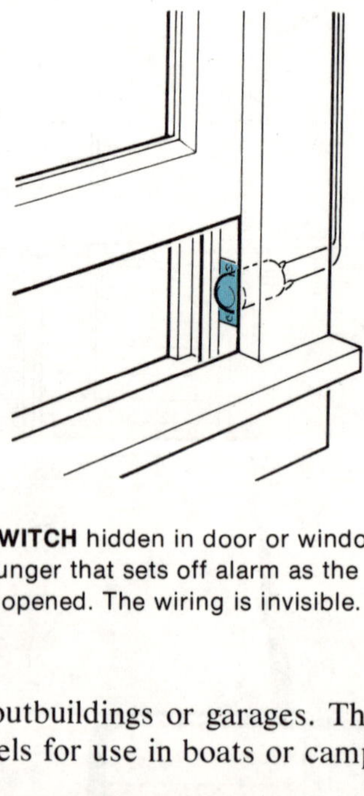

BULLET SWITCH hidden in door or window frame has tapered plunger that sets off alarm as the door or the window is opened. The wiring is invisible.

night snack. The ultrasonic signals could annoy dogs, too.

"Motion-sensors are called 'intrusion alarms'," says Mel Katz, security consultant of New York's Electro-Dyne Security Corp., "because they don't go off till someone's intruded. Perimeter and door alarms go off as soon as the openings they protect are breached. Not that intrusion alarms aren't useful—they're just not our first recommendation for home use."

But they are excellent if one room requires special protection (because of valuables stored there), and for relatively untrafficked rooms, such as outbuildings or garages. There are 12-volt models for use in boats or campers.

perimeter alarm recommended

Pros like Katz usually recommend the perimeter alarm—and not just because they make money installing them. Perimeter systems have a central control box triggered by a network of alarm sensors throughout a house and, in turn, setting off bells or other warnings where needed. (Some systems, though, combine control and bell in one box.)

Perimeter systems do the most complete

FOIL TAPE breaks if the window's broken, setting off an alarm. Plunger of tamper switch on the sill releases if the window is opened.

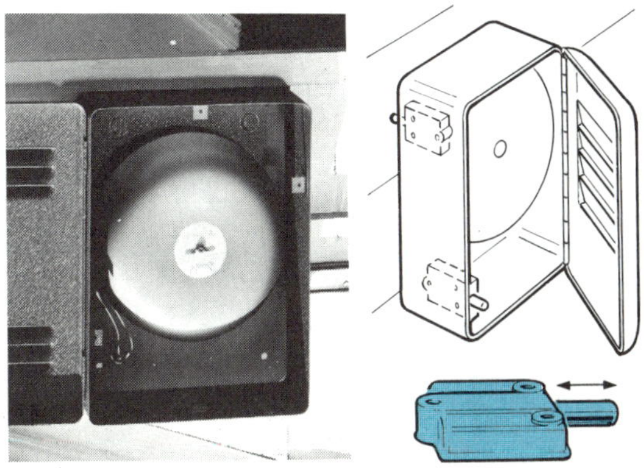

ALARM BELL or siren should be mounted where it's conspicuous, easy to hear, but inaccessible to burglars. Tamper switch in the box triggers the alarm if box lid is opened or the box is pried from the wall.

SEVERAL OUTFITS are sold for do-it-yourself installation. Eico system shown is about $150, gives separate fire and burglary warnings. Master Lock has a similar system and Heath makes build-it-yourself kits.

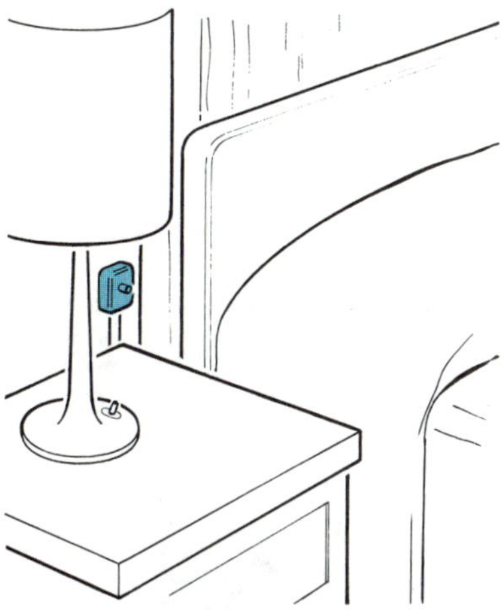

PANIC BUTTON can trip alarm from bed or front door. Some alarms have separate, always-on panic circuits.

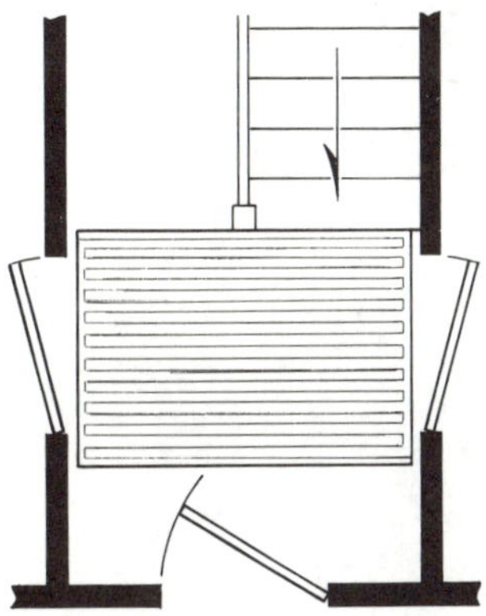

PRESSURE-SENSITIVE mat switch should go where burglars are almost sure to tread on them, as in this entrance hall.

FIRE WARNINGS

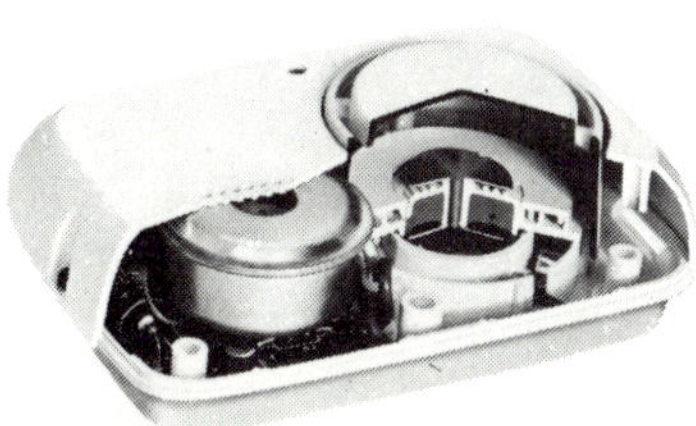

FIRE DETECTORS come in several types, for connection to perimeter systems as well as for self-contained use. This Pyr-A-Larm Guardion is a self-contained ionization detector type shown in the chart at right as being highly effective.

DETECTORS AND THE FOUR STAGES OF FIRE

DETECTORS AND THE FOUR STAGES OF FIRE

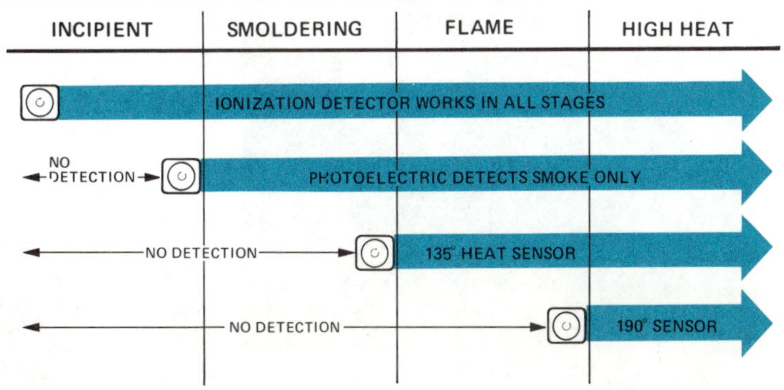

DOOR LOCKS WITH VARYING DEGREES OF SECURITY

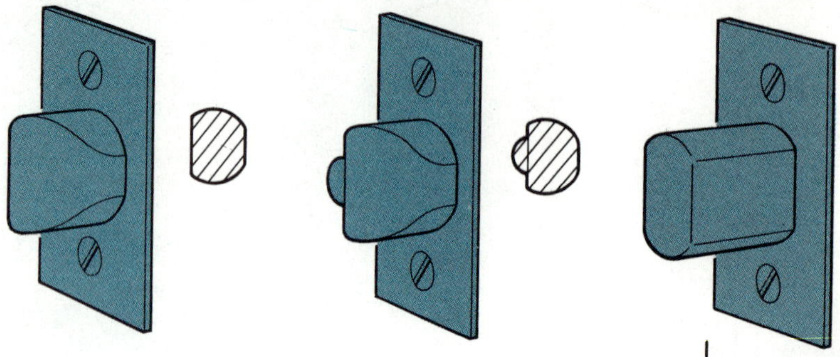

SOME LOCKS are more secure than others. Above, from left to right, are: Common, snap-locking night latch that a child can defeat; night latch with a dead-latch tab; dead bolt (this is stronger, but it must be locked deliberately), combination night latch and dead bolt (frequently found, but infrequently bolted). To the right is a vertical-bolt rimlock—tough, but obtrusive, here it is shown with inside cylinder.

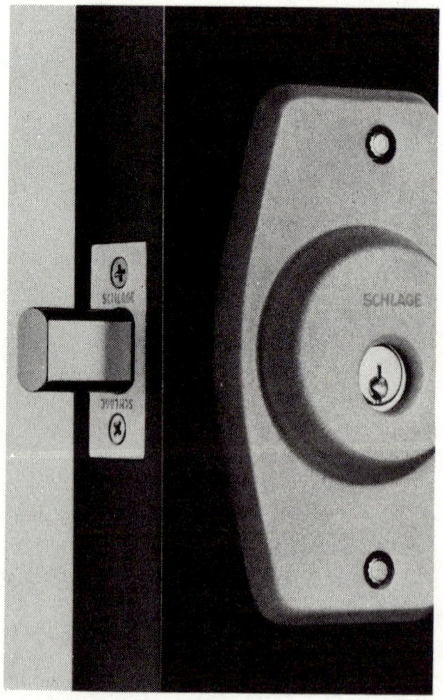

"POLICE LOCKS" are tough, but ugly to look at. Rack-and-pinion bolt type (directly below) is about \$60 - \$100; diagonal bolt types, which transfer stress to the floor (bottom and below right), sell for approximately \$20.

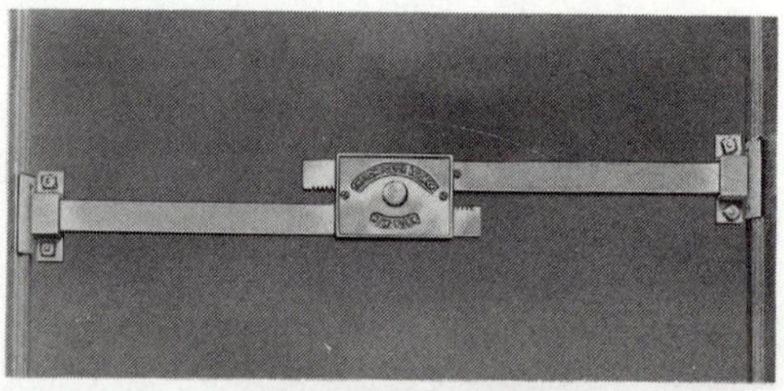

ENGRAVING NAMES or identifying numbers on any valuables such as cameras, tools and the like can help recover them and at the same time convict the thieves.

EASY-TO-FIND SECURITY AIDS

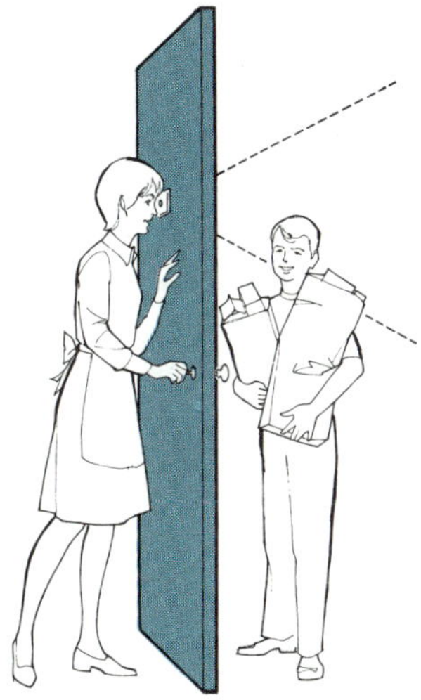

PEEPHOLES LET YOU see who's out there without opening your door. The best types are those with widest view angle (to 180°).

CHAIN LOCKS should be installed on a slant; allow only 2 or 3-in. opening. Peephole is best for identification, since chain lock can be broken.

WEDGE LOCK for windows and sliding doors (above) is inexpensive, easy to install, but vulnerable if burglar breaks glass. Key locks (like that shown at left as replacement for the common, swivel type of window lock) are a lot more secure and cost little. Keep keys handy in case of a fire or other emergency.

overall job—they can cover every door and window, check for intruders inside the house, warn you of fire, even call the police if no one's home. They can also warn if your freezer's melting or your pipes are freezing, and if anyone falls into your pool.

"Their versatility—and the fact that they're usually hooked to a good, loud, remote bell or siren—make perimeter systems more effective," says Katz. "But it's even more significant that they make it easier for you to use them more effectively."

That's because they're centrally controlled. You're more likely to set one alarm when you leave the house than to check and set one for every opening. And most perimeter systems are "supervised": They tell you if you've left a door or window open (though not whether you left it closed but unlocked). You're also more likely to check and replace one battery than several, and the better systems use a battery only for a back-up, otherwise running on a.c.

Most such systems are "hard-wired," with direct connections from sensors (which come in a wide variety—see pages 2550-2551 to the central control. But there are also "carrier" systems, whose sensors send signals to the control panel through your home's a.c. wiring, and RF wireless types, which send brief radio signals to the control box when breached.

pros and cons of RF, carriers

Both RF and carrier systems are easier to install than hard-wired types. But carrier systems won't work if your a.c. current goes off; and RF types, which cost more, aren't "supervised," because their sensors signal only when a door or window opens—so they can't tell you one's already open when you turn them on. However, RF systems can be set to go off in a nearby neighbor's house, if you're away. (So can "carrier" types, if you and your neighbor get power through the same transformer.)

Wired alarms also come in two types: open and closed circuit. Open-circuit systems, a trifle cheaper, trigger when their sensor switches close, completing the alarm circuit. Closed-circuit types trigger when a sensor switch opens—or when there's a break in the wires. That gives them an extra degree of self-checking, and insures against a burglar defeating them by clipping wires. (He can defeat a closed-circuit system with a jumper—but only if he knows it's a closed-circuit type, and if it's accessible.)

The more doors and windows your system covers, the better you're protected—but the more your system will cost. Install it yourself, and the additional cost is minor—about $5 per opening for the common magnetic switches, and about $2 per room for the additional wiring. Professional installation costs can run as high as around $40 per window or door.

So which openings should you protect? Your doors, of course, every ground-floor window, and every window within reach of (not just directly over) porches, garage and shed roofs, fire escapes—even trees.

It's up to you whether to protect all your second-story windows; some burglars do use ladders, either by bringing their own or taking them from nearby sheds or garages.

On a limited budget, that extra money might be better spent on an alarm system with more features: a rechargeable back-up battery with trickle-charger, for instance, or circuits (required by some local noise pollution laws) that shut the alarm off after about 15 minutes.

Fire alarms can be part of any perimeter alarm system, simply by adding sensors that detect heat, fast temperature increases or smoke. But to avoid confusion, systems that sound separate warnings for fire and intrusion are better—and self-contained fire alarms, which don't go dead if the fire takes your power out, are better still. For fire, the emphasis should be on *inside* sirens, to wake you and your family and get you out.

Once your door is set to trigger the alarm, how do you get back in the house? Some alarms have outside keylocks that disconnect the door's alarm so you can enter. Others have a delayed action; you can shut them off as soon as you come in (burglars, presumably, won't know where to find the switch before the delay time's up).

Delay systems require less wiring, and can't be picked from outside. But key switches do show the burglar that your alarm is real, not just a decal stuck on as a bluff. (Even the decals will make some burglars think twice before they try to break in.)

A light at the door to show the alarm's on can tell late-coming family members whether someone's come home and shut the system off. If you all come home together, it can tip you off that a burglar—who might still be inside—has come in and shut it off before you. (But if you're likely to forget to turn the alarm on, the light can tip off the burglar.)

Flashing lights added to your alarm's bell or siren can speed response, showing at a glance just which house the noise is coming from. Telephone dialers are another good (but expensive—$180 to $225 for professional-quality) supplement, dialing neighbors, friends or police with a recorded trouble message when the main alarm goes off. Most good ones have two tracks; one for burglary, one for fire. Dialers are especially worthwhile for summer or isolated homes.

"But check your local laws before setting up a dialer," Katz cautions. "False alarms are common in home alarm systems because people come in on irregular schedules. So, many towns prohibit programming dialers from calling police or fire department directly."

Even better than setting off an alarm when a burglar breaks in, though, is keeping him out altogether. Sometimes it's less expensive, too. All it takes are good locks and remembering to use them.

check locks after moving

The best time to look at your locks is right after you move; you never know who might have gotten keys from the old tenant or, if it's a new home, from the builder.

You don't have to replace the locks. Just take the cylinders to a locksmith for rekeying, or replace the cylinders with new ones. You can get pick-resistant cylinders (*no* key lock is pick-*proof*) for about $10 to $20 more than regular ones; the Medeco, Abloy, Sargent Kesco and Duo, among others, will make a burglar spend more time than he likes working on your door. But comparatively few burglars pick locks. "The pick man is highly skilled," says Detective Inzalaco, "and expects a return for his skill. Unless you've got a lot to steal, he probably won't bother you."

Combination locks are pickproof, but expensive, and fumbling with one can cost you precious time if you're trying to get in quickly to avoid a mugger or the rain.

But before rekeying your lock, consider whether the lock itself might not need replacement or protection. A simple "night-latch" type that locks whenever it springs shut (see page 2552) should definitely be replaced. Slipping a plastic credit card between the door and the frame can open it.

"Dead-latching" snap-locks are a slight improvement—a small tab keeps the spring latch from pushing back when the door's closed. Square-ended dead bolts that slide straight into the jamb are more secure, and the longer the bolt, the better it will hold against a burglar trying to burst or pry his way in.

Vertical dead bolts are even more secure, since they can't be pried open. They can be pried off, though, so be sure you've fastened yours with the longest, biggest screws that will fit. If possible, the strike plate that meshes with the lock should be the type that wraps around two sides of the doorframe. An Ideal Security model has a cylinder shield that bolts to the lock for added protection.

Vertical-bolt locks are "rim" types that fasten to the inside of the door and frame; this makes them easy to install, but less attractive than locks that fit within the door.

be sure door is strong

But the strongest, safest locks won't hold weak doors securely. Hollow-core, wood-veneer flush doors and cheap paneled doors are a breeze to break through; hardboard-faced flush doors and better paneled ones are stronger, but solid or metal-faced doors are safer still. Make sure the door fits snugly in the frame and that the lock's bolt protrudes as far as possible into the frame.

If your door has glass panes in or near it, consider double-cylinder locks, which are opened with a key from inside, too, so a thief can't break the glass, reach in and open the lock. And where a burglar is most likely to come in a window or through a smashed-in door panel, use of double cylinder locks will limit his haul to what he can take *out* that way, too.

But to be sure of safe escape in case of fire, you should leave your keys in the lock's inside cylinder whenever you're home—and don't use double cylinders if you have children or elderly relatives in the house. For fire safety, it's best, then, to install "panic-proof" locks that open if you twist the inside knob either way—a feature on better locks from Schlage and others.

And there is another way to protect glazed doors: substitute impact-resistant polycarbonate (such as Lexan or Plexiglas) for the glass, or cover the glass with polycarbonate held by extra moldings.

To protect your lock from outside attack, use one whose cylinder is in the door itself, not in the knob (which can be pried off), and cover it with a cylinder guard, bolted through the door.

Back doors and hidden entrances need even more protection than front doors, since concealment gives burglars more time to work on them.

But windows deserve protection, too. Stan-

DO-IT-YOURSELF 'LOCKS' ARE EASY TO MAKE, INEXPENSIVE

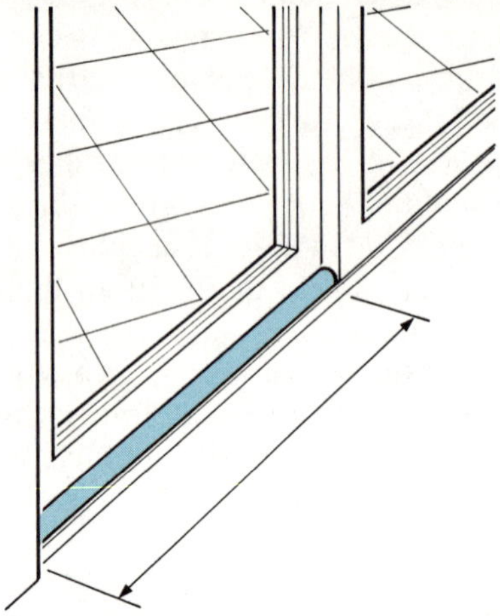

BROOMSTICK OR metal rod in patio door tracks keeps door from opening, even if lock is picked or broken.

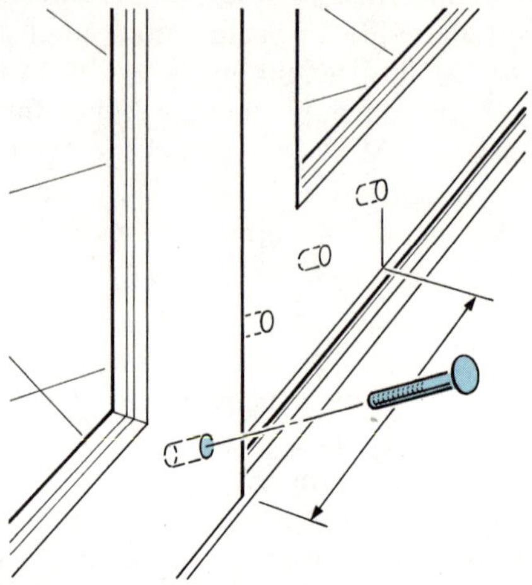

CARRIAGE BOLT or large nail in slanted holes locks patio doors. Extra holes allow up to 6-inch air opening.

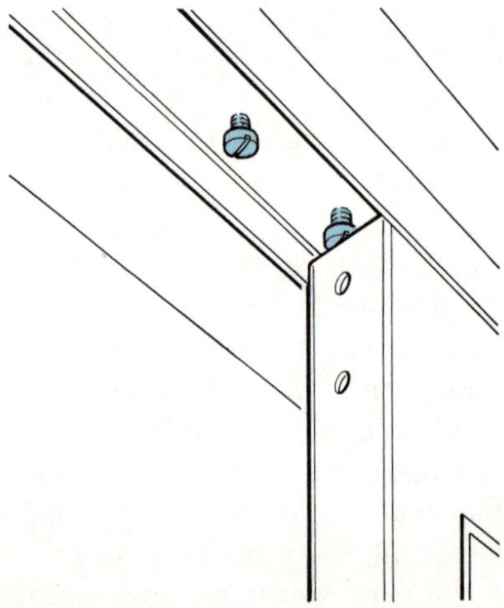

SCREWS IN PATIO door's upper track keep thieves from lifting door off; a good trick for sliding windows, too.

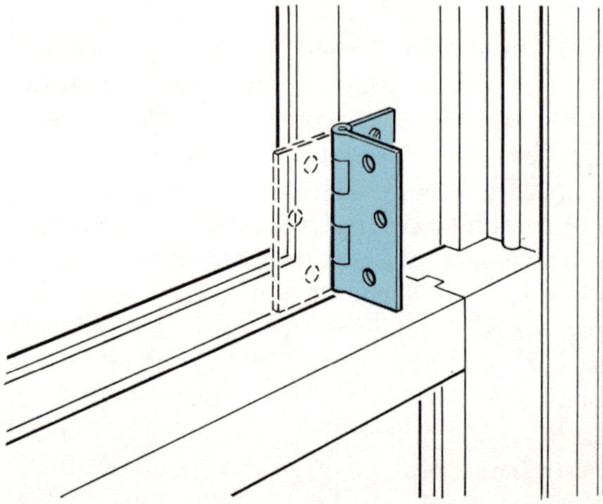

DOOR HINGE makes a good folding lock to hold sash window tightly shut. Improvisation costs just pennies.

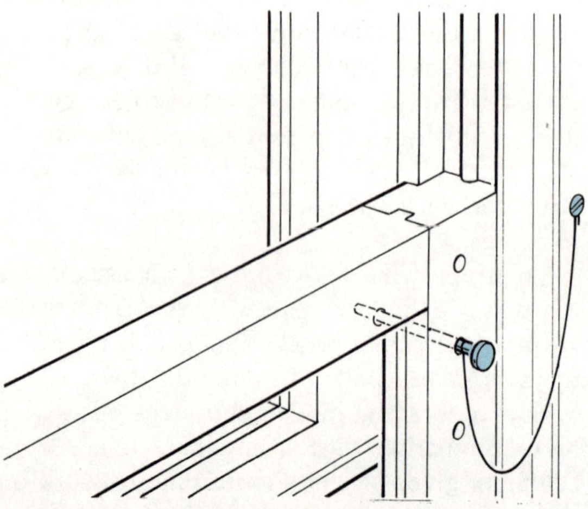

NAIL OR BOLT "latch" trick works well for windows, too; but here you allow only 2 to 3 inches for air.

dard, swiveling window latches can be opened from outside or through a broken or cut pane—key locks can't (and polycarbonate panes add extra protection). But if you lock your windows, leave the keys nearby and make sure everyone knows where to find them in case of fire—it's better to be burgled than to burn.

Commercial hardware isn't your only choice, either. Some standard do-it-yourself tricks are illustrated above; you may be able to come up with others.

But whatever locks, alarms or other tricks you may have up your sleeve, you must be sure to *use them*. More burglars than you might think slip in through unlocked doors and past unset alarms.

Siding on asbestos shingle

How do I re-side over asbestos shingles? My sheathing is the "soft" type and the fasteners are almost like a cotter pin, open or spread behind the sheathing. I can't nail into the shingles because they break. Even if I could, the sheathing wouldn't hold nails.—A. Taylor, Ambler, Pa.

Many homes built after World War II were sided in the manner you describe. This makes re-siding just a bit difficult. First, get used to the word "hanging," not nailing, when you're talking about aluminum or vinyl siding. It's not nailed tightly to the existing siding. That's why the slots on aluminum siding are provided. The pro will first locate and mark the studs under the sheathing. A 2-in. galvanized-steel nail is used to penetrate the asbestos shingle. Personally, I would put 15-lb. felt over the shingles before re-siding. Don't worry about shingles cracking underneath, as long as you're fastening them to a stud. The cracked shingle will act as a shim. From here on, follow installation instructions for the siding you choose, but don't drive the nails all the way home. The siding must expand and contract in the fastening slots.

Reglazing bathroom fixtures

How can I re-enamel sinks, bathtubs and wash basins so they can be cleaned and scrubbed properly? It is inconvenient, costly and sometimes impossible (because of odd sizes no longer available) to replace existing tubs and sinks.—E.C. Carson, San Rafael, Calif.

Many professionals won't repair a nick without reglazing the entire fixture, to be assured that water won't penetrate beneath the patch. Basically, the pro does the following: etches the tub with a mild acid to cut the existing glaze; patches and sands all nicks with an auto body-type filler and thoroughly washes and dries the fixture; and sprays on several coats of a special porcelain glaze. (This may be the time to change the color of your fixture.) After three days, you can use the tub, although the finish continues to set and harden for several months. The job will take five hours and cost less than $200 for a tub.

To find a professional, look in the Yellow Pages under "Bathtubs, Refinishing," or write: Kott Koatings, Paralta Drive, Suite K-12, Laguna Hills, Calif. 92653, for free brochure and name of refinisher in your area.

Another alternative is to use a kit to refinish the tub yourself. One manufacturer of these kits is: Spectrodyne Industries Inc., 2005 North Keystone Ave., Chicago, Ill. 60641. The price for a complete kit, including spray gun and compressor, is about $110.

When weighing the economics of refinishing or replacing, remember the hidden costs in replacement—plumber, tile setter and, of course, mess.

Humidity and insulation

I have blown-in cellulose insulation in my attic with no vapor barrier. I want to put a humidifier in my home. How will the moisture affect the insulation? Should I remove the cellulose and replace it with foil-backed fiberglass?—Peter Messina, Reston, Va.

Without a vapor barrier you shouldn't humidify. Moisture will penetrate insulation and condense, possibly rotting your framing. If money is no object, remove insulation and install a vapor barrier.

As a less costly step, I recommend using paint as a barrier. you should install new plasterboard on the ceiling (buy foil-backed type or prime the back of regular panels with aluminum paint). Even without the plasterboard, to keep moisture from penetrating your attic, paint all ceilings with at least two coats of vapor-resistant oil paint (water-base paint is generally not an effective barrier).

Flaking flagstones

Due to rain and freezing weather, my 40-year-old flagstone patio flakes apart in slivers. Is there a sealer that stops water from penetrating flagstone? I'd prefer a glossy sealer that's not slippery to walk on.—Dr. J.E. Terence Kavanagh, Warren, Ohio.

Flagstone is any hard rock that lends itself to cutting into layers. Some types are more impervious to water than others, but most have many-layered veins. You don't say whether your patio stones rest on earth or are embedded in mortar. Nor do you describe the type of joints.

Water generally penetrates flagstone layers and causes cracking when it freezes. Stone edges must be thoroughly cleaned before applying sealer. Since sealer won't "bridge" gaps between stone and mortar, if you have mortared joints, they should be pointed (refinished with fresh mortar) first. Toch Div., Carboline Co., 350 Hanley Ct., St. Louis, Mo. 63144, makes a good liquid sealer called Acri-Seal. It's nonflammable, nontoxic and covers 300 to 600 sq. ft. per gallon, depending on the porosity of the stone. Stones and bricks I tested with Acri-Seal darkened slightly and picked up a slight gloss. Toch claims it's a nonslip coating. I found that two thoroughly brushed-in coats were better looking than one thick coat.

Ten places to hide your valuables

By JOHN PEARSON and HARRY WICKS

WE'LL SPARE YOU the crime statistics. Suffice it to say that burglary remains a serious problem everywhere.

Security measures, including locks on doors and windows, may not stop the determined housebreaker. Dogs, too, have been known to prove less than effective in confrontation with intruders.

There is a third line of defense, however—and that's what the 10 hiding places shown on these pages are all about. The idea is to outwit the thief by secreting as many of your valuables as possible in unlikely places.

The 10 places shown by no means exhaust the possibilities for subterfuge. Your house or apartment may contain other ideal caches.

Remember, you're matching wits with a potential intruder who has a limited amount of time. You can find more ideas in *How to Hide Almost Anything* by David Krotz; William Morrow & Co.

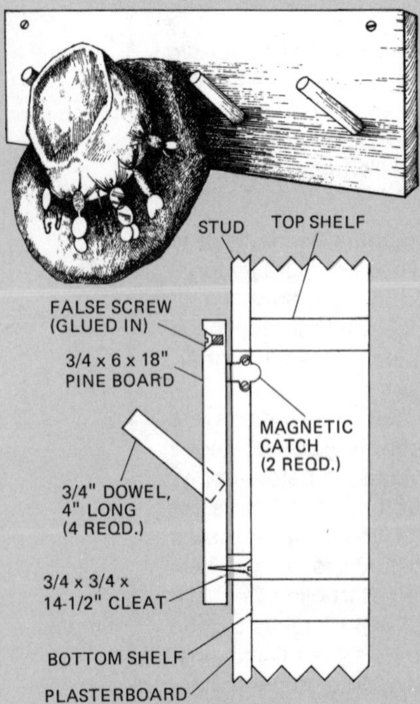

1 **FAKE HATRACK** hides a hole in the wall for jewelry and other small valuables. Cut between studs, then force-fit 2x4s between them to serve as the header and shelf. The rack rests on a cleat and is held by magnetic catches. A lightweight hat adds credibility to the set-up.

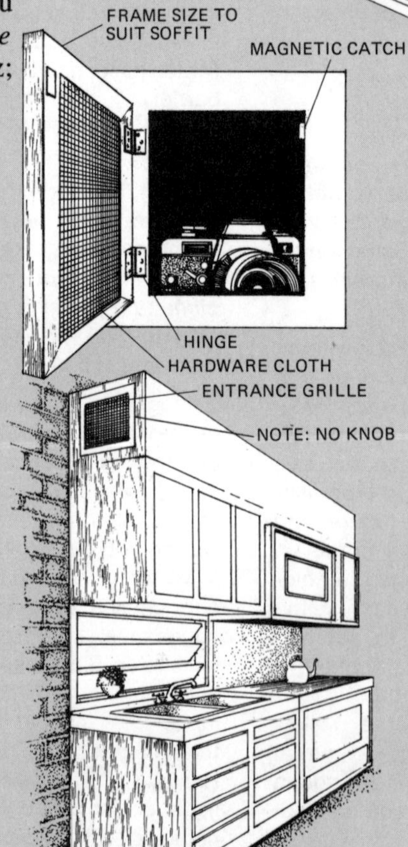

2 **A DOOR** that looks like a vent lets space over cabinets serve as a "safe." Use hinges that don't show. Hold the frame in with magnetic catches and don't use a knob.

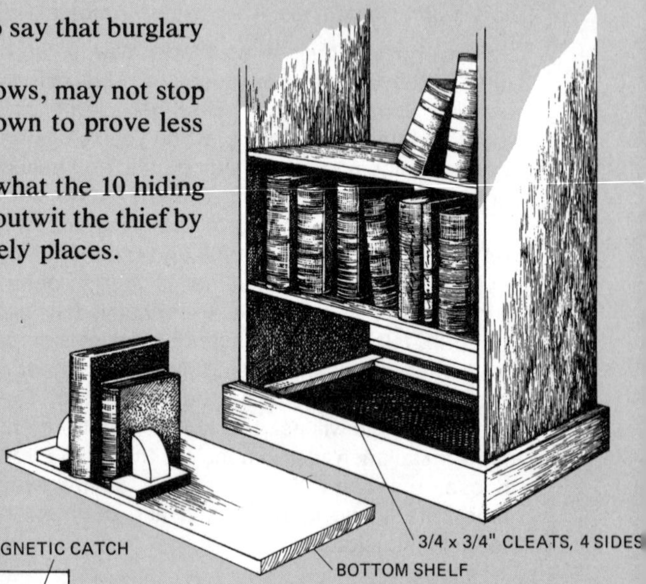

3 **SENSIBLE SPOT** for valuables is under the bottom bookcase shelf. Locate shelf cleats, held with 1¼-in. screws, so the shelf rides just above the unit's base for easy removal. Stock the shelf.

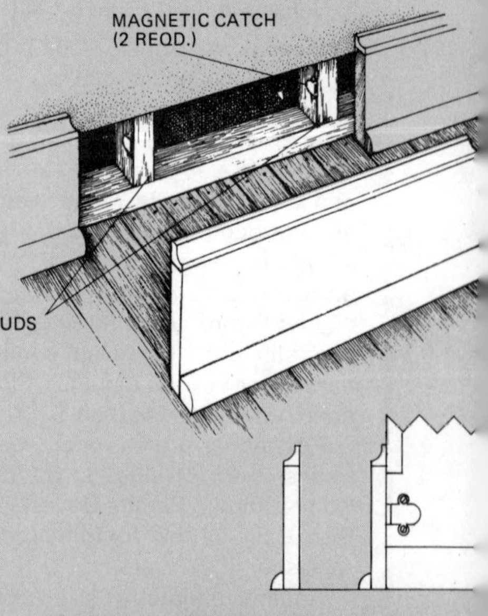

4 **SMALL KEEPSAKES** go handily behind baseboard section. Baseboard height limits available space, so older homes with 1x6 baseboards give the best opportunity here. Magnetic catches hold the "door" in place. Locate furniture to screen baseboard joints from easy view.

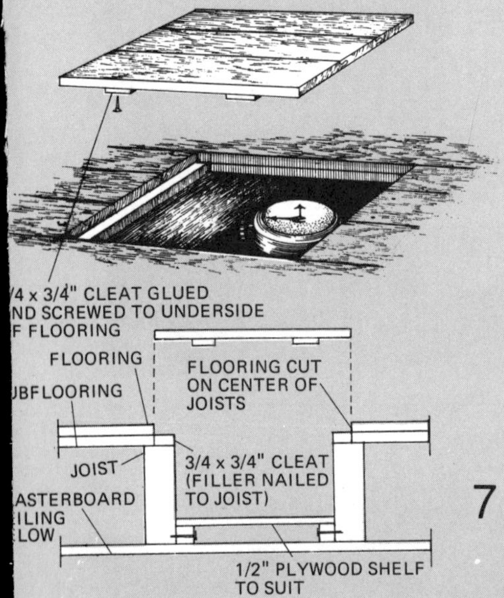

5 **AN IN-THE-FLOOR** "vault" is easy to make. It works best under a closet floor where the usual clutter will hide it. The false bottom keeps weight off the ceiling below.

HANDSOME wall shelf neatly hides a cutout area. Notice the screw-eyes' location; the bottom pair keeps the box parallel to the wall. Cut the hole first, then build the shelf to ample dimensions to ensure that you will cover the hole completely.

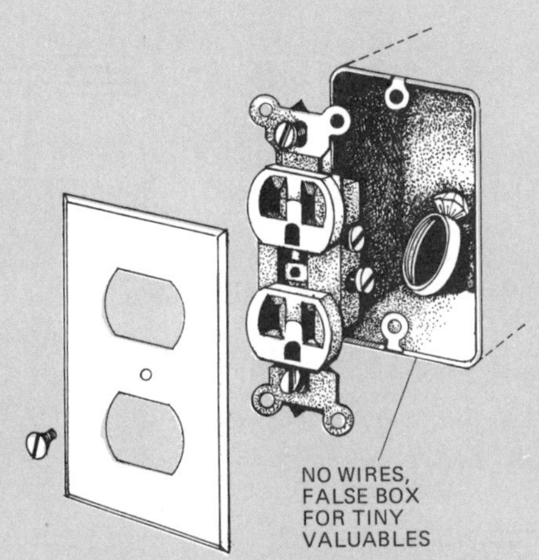

7 **DUMMY OUTLET** hides little items like rings and jewels. Put it behind furniture so it is unlikely to be tested and exposed as a fake.

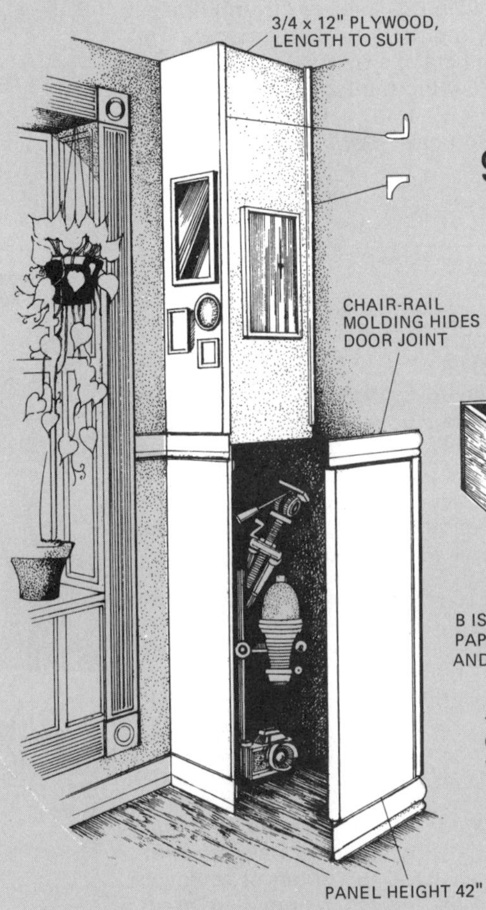

8 **SMALL APPLIANCES** are next to cash and jewels on thieves' hit parade. They'll fit handily in a false corner that looks like a boxed-in chimney. For an easier job, use ¾-in. plywood over 1x3 furring framework. Hide the joints with molding.

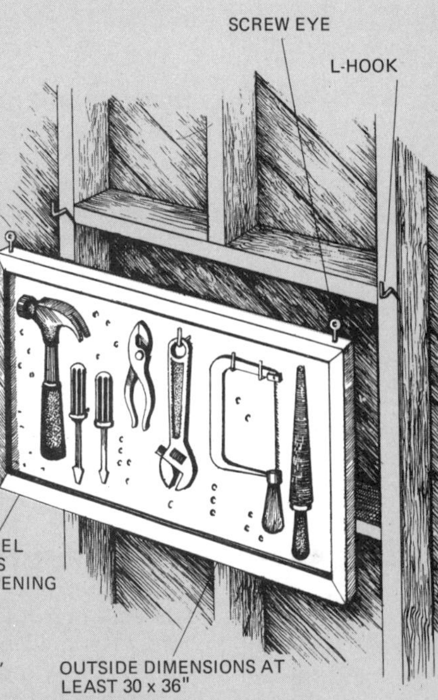

9 **WHO'D THINK** to go seeking valuables behind a tool board in the garage? The idea here is basically the same as at bottom left. Before mounting hardware, be sure the box covers the hole in the wall.

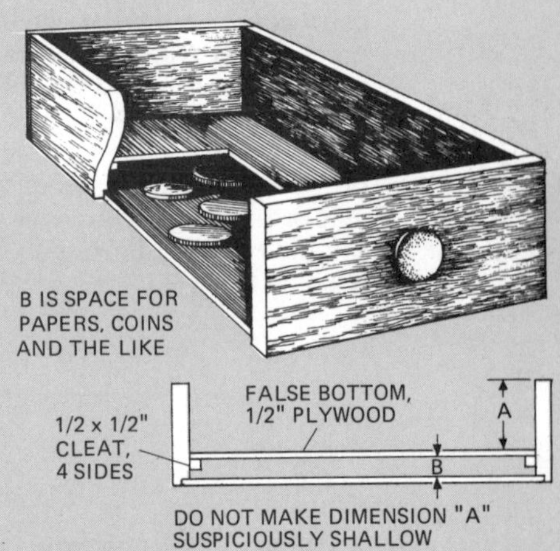

10 **FOR RARE** coins and the like, use space under drawer false bottom. But don't try for too much room, leaving Space A suspiciously shallow. Valuables that might "clink" should be wrapped in sound-deadening material. Solid construction helps, too.

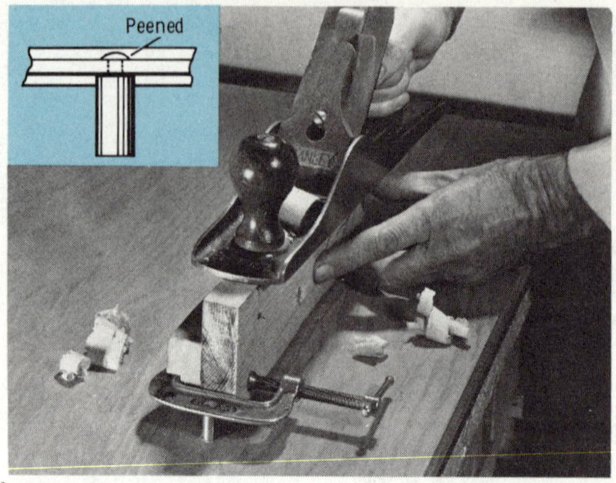

PEEN A LENGTH OF PIPE or heavy rod at right angles to a C-clamp frame and you have a handy workbench vise. Simply drop the stud projection in a hole drilled in the top of the bench, insert the work and tighten the clamp. You could also drill and tap a hole in the end of the rod, drill a hole through the clamp and attach the rod with a screw.—*Clarence Preitenfeldt.*

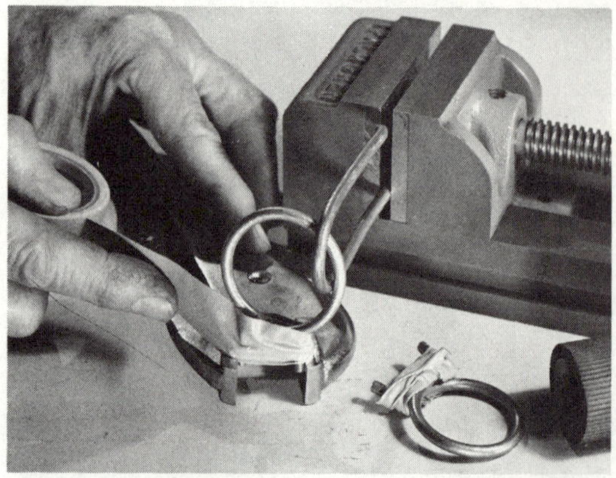

WITHOUT SPECIAL PLIERS, spring-steel hose clamps can be the hardest things to hold open when they're being installed. Invariably they'll twist and fly off the jaws of common pliers. After having this happen several times, I hit upon the idea of using tape to hold them open. This made it easy to place the clamps over the hose and to release them by simply cutting the tape. As a safety precaution, a wire yoke (see photo) will keep the clamp in tow while it's bound with tape.—*Daniel Boucha.*

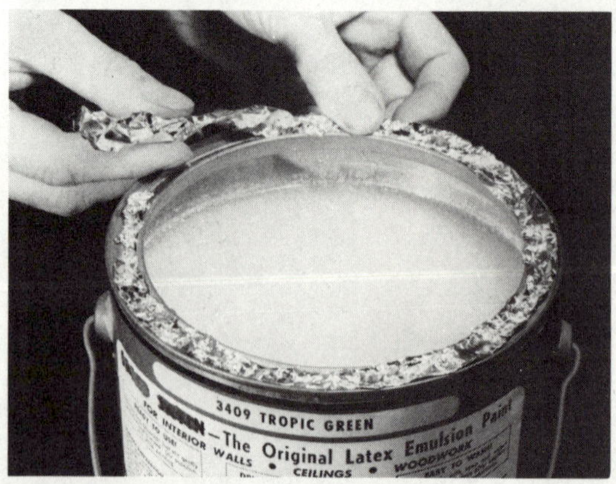

THERE ARE ANY NUMBER of ways to keep the rim of a paint can free of paint, including the stunt of making nail holes in it for the paint to drain back into the can. However, perhaps the simplest way of all is to crowd aluminum foil into the can rim as soon as the cover is removed. Then, no matter how much paint spills over the rim, you simply pull out the foil when you're ready to quit. The rim will be clean as a whistle and the cover will fit as tight as it did originally.—*Ken Patterson.*

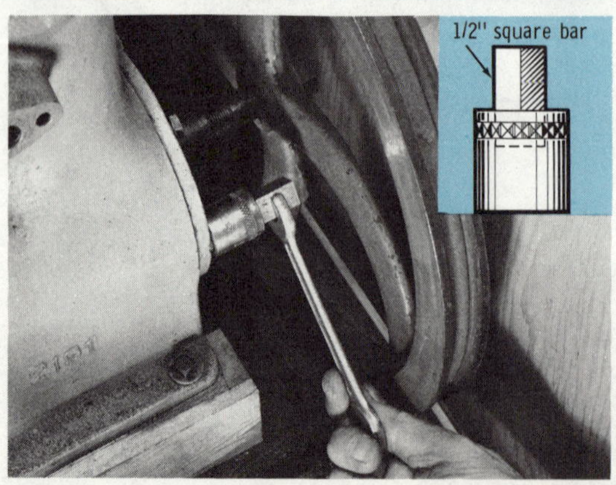

A USEFUL ACCESSORY for a ½-in. socket wrench is a ½-in.-square steel bar that's been cut into six or seven various lengths. When you need to tighten or remove a bolt in a cramped or awkward-to-reach area, just insert a suitable bar in the socket and use an open-end box wrench to turn the bar, socket and bolt. It's practically the only way to get into tight quarters where a ratchet, crossbar or universal-type extension won't fit (e.g., removing a VW fuel pump).—*H. G. Bennett.*

METRIC CONVERSION

Conversion factors can be carried so far they become impractical. In cases below where an entry is exact it is followed by an asterisk (*). Where considerable rounding off has taken place, the entry is followed by a + or a - sign.

CUSTOMARY TO METRIC

Linear Measure

inches	millimeters
1/16	1.5875*
1/8	3.2
3/16	4.8
1/4	6.35*
5/16	7.9
3/8	9.5
7/16	11.1
1/2	12.7*
9/16	14.3
5/8	15.9
11/16	17.5
3/4	19.05*
13/16	20.6
7/8	22.2
15/16	23.8
1	25.4*

inches	centimeters
1	2.54*
2	5.1
3	7.6
4	10.2
5	12.7*
6	15.2
7	17.8
8	20.3
9	22.9
10	25.4*
11	27.9
12	30.5

feet	centimeters	meters
1	30.48*	.3048*
2	61	.61
3	91	.91
4	122	1.22
5	152	1.52
6	183	1.83
7	213	2.13
8	244	2.44
9	274	2.74
10	305	3.05
50	1524*	15.24*
100	3048*	30.48*

1 yard =
.9144* meters
1 rod =
5.0292* meters
1 mile =
1.6 kilometers
1 nautical mile =
1.852* kilometers

Fluid Measure

(Milliliters [ml] and cubic centimeters [cc or cu cm] are equivalent, but it is customary to use milliliters for liquids.)

1 cu in = 16.39 ml
1 fl oz = 29.6 ml
1 cup = 237 ml
1 pint = 473 ml
1 quart = 946 ml
= .946 liters
1 gallon = 3785 ml
= 3.785 liters
Formula (exact):
fluid ounces × 29.573 529 562 5*
= milliliters

Weights

ounces	grams
1	28.3
2	56.7
3	85
4	113
5	142
6	170
7	198
8	227
9	255
10	283
11	312
12	340
13	369
14	397
15	425
16	454

Formula (exact):
ounces × 28.349 523 125* = grams

pounds	kilograms
1	.45
2	.9
3	1.4
4	1.8
5	2.3
6	2.7
7	3.2
8	3.6
9	4.1
10	4.5

1 short ton (2000 lbs) =
907 kilograms (kg)
Formula (exact):
pounds × .453 592 37* = kilograms

Volume

1 cu in = 16.39 cubic centimeters (cc)
1 cu ft = 28 316.7 cc
1 bushel = 35 239.1 cc
1 peck = 8 809.8 cc

Area

1 sq in = 6.45 sq cm
1 sq ft = 929 sq cm
= .093 sq meters
1 sq yd = .84 sq meters
1 acre = 4 046.9 sq meters
= .404 7 hectares
1 sq mile = 2 589 988 sq meters
= 259 hectares
= 2.589 9 sq kilometers

Kitchen Measure

1 teaspoon = 4.93 milliliters (ml)
1 Tablespoon = 14.79 milliliters (ml)

Miscellaneous

1 British thermal unit (Btu) (mean)
= 1 055.9 joules
1 calorie (mean) = 4.19 joules
1 horsepower = 745.7 watts
= .75 kilowatts
caliber (diameter of a firearm's bore in hundredths of an inch)
= .254 millimeters (mm)
1 atmosphere pressure = 101 325* pascals (newtons per sq meter)
1 pound per square inch (psi) = 6 895 pascals
1 pound per square foot = 47.9 pascals
1 knot = 1.85 kilometers per hour
25 miles per hour = 40.2 kilometers per hour
50 miles per hour = 80.5 kilometers per hour
75 miles per hour = 120.7 kilometers per hour